PUBLIC LIBRARY PROGRAMS AND SERVICES FOR MIDLIFE AND BEYOND

Expanding Opportunities for a Growing Population

Reneé K. Bennett-Kapusniak

LIBRARIES UNLIMITED™

An Imprint of ABC-CLIO, LLC

Santa Barbara, California • Denver, Colorado

Library of Congress Cataloging in Publication Control Number: 2018005116

ISBN: 978-1-4408-5778-2 (paperback)
     978-1-4408-5779-9 (e-book)

22 21 20 19 18   1 2 3 4 5

This book is also available as an e-book.

Libraries Unlimited
An Imprint of ABC-CLIO, LLC

ABC-CLIO, LLC
130 Cremona Drive, P.O. Box 1911
Santa Barbara, California 93116-1911
www.abc-clio.com

This book is printed on acid-free paper ∞

Manufactured in the United States of America

This book is for my family and for all those who dedicate their selfless gifts to serve others.

Contents

Preface

Midlife and older adults or adults 50+ are a large cohort that is steadily increasing in population. Different organizations define and categorize adults 50+. However, a uniform definition has been difficult because this age group has varying characteristics. Many adults are active and healthy, whereas others experience physical and cognitive changes as a natural process of aging. Some continue to work into their 70s and 80s, and others retire, travel, or volunteer in their communities. Technology usage among midlife and older adults is also increasing. However, there are still some adults 50+ who have had little or no training with computerized systems. These are just some of the diverse characteristics we need to consider when planning and implementing public library adult services and programs that will engage the aging community.

As public librarians, we are always striving for valuable resources and ideas to help us better serve all our community members. With this in mind, this book explores a random sample of American public libraries to see how they are serving, promoting, and engaging adults 50+ in their communities. Further contributions are gathered from our public library peers in the field, providing practical examples and views from librarians and directors to assist in the development and expansion of adult 50+ programs and services, allowing us to see how different ideas have worked within different types of communities.

Outreach and the importance of community collaborations are explored, detailing how utilizing partners within the community provides benefits and valuable resources. This includes peer examples to give ideas and suggestions in establishing our own partnerships. Marketing and funding strategies with peer examples are also included, providing resources and tips for working with adults 50+. Formal and informal lifelong learning opportunities are discussed, detailing the benefits and impact our peers have had with their library communities. Technology is part of our daily lives, with more information coming online every day. The importance of digital literacy and the role public libraries play for their community members, including overcoming barriers to access to assist in digital inclusion and to support all community members to participate fully in our technological society, are included with examples from the library field.

This book was developed to create more awareness and interest in the underserved adult 50+ populations within our public library system. The intent is to provide a manual about midlife and older adults to enrich understanding of the aging population. Plus, the book provides a valuable resource for adult 50+ public library programming and services, giving us the tools to create and expand our services and programs for adults 50+ in our own library communities.

Acknowledgments

First and foremost, I wish to thank Jessica Gribble and the editors of Libraries Unlimited for asking me to create this timely and valuable work on adults 50+. Your valuable advice and suggestions helped to improve the quality of my work.

In addition, I wish to thank all public librarians for your dedication to your professions and for always striving to find the perfect program or service for your community patrons. I also want to sincerely thank all the contributors to this text: Alexandra Annen, Adrienne Doman Calkins, Mariel Carter, Marian Christmon, Brianne Columbo, Richard Conroy, Marie Corbitt, Leslie DeLooze, Debra DeJonker-Berry, Elizabeth Eisen, Debbi Gallucci, Kathleen Goodson, Kristi Haman, Kathleen Handy, Lynn Harthorne, Dan Hubbs, Chris Jackson, Heather Johnson, Ryan Johnson, Buff Kahn, Lucine Kauffman, Tamar Kreke, Kelly Martin Laney, Meryle A. Leonard, Beth Neunaber, Lisa Picker, Lisa Prizio, Matthew Riley, Chad Robinson, Jenneffer Sixkiller, Kate Skinner, Terry Soave, Dorothy Stoltz, John J. Trause, Tracy Trotter, Christy Wagner, Melanie Wehrle, Leslie C. West, Melany Wilks, Jaci, Jeannine, Mary, Rebecca, and those who wished to remain anonymous, as well as Adriana McCleer; Dr. Jennifer Thiele; and other library directors, librarians, and staff. Without your willingness to share my project with others in our field and your creative ideas, suggestions, services, and programs that you have within your own library, I would not have had such wonderful insight into adult 50+ programming and services.

I am also grateful for my friends who provided unwavering support for creating this text. Finally, I wish to thank my family, who, without their love, help, and encouragement, I wouldn't be the person I am today. To my sister, Michele, who gave her time and much-needed support during the research process. I wish to thank my daughter, Amanda. She is a source of unbelievable joy in my life. I thank my husband Rich, for his encouragement and unwavering love. Most importantly, I wish to thank my son Nick, who passed away a few years ago. His love for his family, his exuberance for life, and his passion to serve others are a source of inspiration that I aspire to every day.

Introducing 50+ Adults and Their Library Services

When we examine our library services and programming and the populations we serve, we typically do not think about the community of adults 50+ as a separate area of focus for programming and services. Some library administrations believe that adults midlife and older blend in with their adult programming, whereas others believe adults 50+ are mostly part of their outreach or retired adults in their communities. Having a disparity in how we view adults 50+ can be due to preconceived perceptions and can affect how we determine our programing and services for our aging community.

BACKGROUND OF ADULTS 50+ OR ADULTS MIDLIFE AND OLDER

Aging is inevitable. It is a fact of life. As public librarians, we are noticing that the number of adults midlife and older is steadily increasing within our public library communities. Based on the Federal Interagency Forum on Aging-Related Statistics (2016), adults 65+ account for 15 percent of the total population in the United States. This is due to Baby Boomers getting older. Plus, individuals are living longer due to improved health and technological advances. Our public library's mission is to serve patrons of all ages (PLA, 2011). We need to consider and plan our programming and services to support our adult midlife and older community members.

Defining Age

Defining adults 50+ can be challenging. The Pew Research Center (Pew, 2009) divides adults midlife and older into four groups, noting differences from their research findings: Younger Boomers (born 1955–1964), Older

Boomers (born 1946–1954), the Silent Generation (born 1937–1945), and the GI Generation (born before and including 1936). In the library field, the Library of Congress Authorities 2015 records define older people as those between middle and advanced age. However, it is prudent for us to remember that chronological age does not clearly define adults midlife and older due to their varying characteristics.

In addition, many terms or labels are used to describe adults over 50 years of age: senior, aged, elderly, older adults, Boomers and beyond, the silver or greying generation, and many others. When we examine the public library community, it is also challenging to find a common age or label that we are using for this age group. Library Web sites and programs are using varying age ranges and terms (50+, 55+, 60+, 65+, seniors, mature adults, etc.). Not having a clear reference can cause challenges when we want to create and provide services for our adult midlife and older patrons. For the purpose of this book, "adults midlife and older" or "adults 50+" will be used to refer to adults who are 50 years of age and older.

Demographics

Comparison of the number of adults 50+ residing in the United States illustrates California, Florida, Texas, New York, Pennsylvania, Ohio, Illinois, Michigan, North Carolina, and New Jersey as the top 10 states with the most individuals 65+ years of age (Administration on Aging: Administration for Community Living, 2016) (see Table 1.1). However, this could change as the population grows older and individuals retire to different states or stay put in the state in which they currently reside. This is important when we determine services for our library communities. We should also keep in mind that a wide range of older immigrants from different countries have settled in the United States, generating more unique characteristics and challenges among this age group.

Health and Wellness

The following summarizes different aspects of the aging population and the factors that could affect adults as they age in society.

Life Expectancy

The Centers for Disease Control and Prevention (2016) reports that we are living to an average age of 79 years. A person's lifestyle, such as a healthier diet, activity level, and having close contact with family and friends, can be a contributing factor in living a longer life. Research has shown that if we have a positive outlook, it can lead to better life satisfaction. Currently, many adults 50+ have different opinions about life than did

TABLE 1.1. Adult 65+ Population by State

State	Population 65+	State	Population 65+	State	Population 65+
Alabama	764,162	Louisiana	653,094	Ohio	1,842,952
Alaska	72,837	Maine	250,536	Oklahoma	576,250
Arizona	1,120,054	Maryland	849,571	Oregon	660,876
Arkansas	477,149	Massachusetts	1,045,222	Pennsylvania	2,179,788
California	5,188,754	Michigan	1,570,671	Rhode Island	169,976
Colorado	711,625	Minnesota	805,643	South Carolina	794,795
Connecticut	566,806	Mississippi	439,701	South Dakota	134,420
Delaware	160,515	Missouri	954,922	Tennessee	1,016,552
Florida	3,942,468	Montana	178,011	Texas	3,225,168
Georgia	1,304,924	Nebraska	278,711	Utah	307,867
Hawaii	236,914	Nevada	422,118	Vermont	109,893
Idaho	243,494	New Hampshire	218,942	Virginia	1,188,393
Illinois	1,830,277	New Jersey	1,343,626	Washington	1,036,046
Indiana	966,127	New Mexico	330,405	West Virginia	336,288
Iowa	502,877	New York	2,964,315	Wisconsin	902,134
Kansas	426,410	North Carolina	1,516,824	Wyoming	84,699
Kentucky	672,765	North Dakota	107,281		

past generations (American Psychological Association, 2017). Many adults 50+ feel life does not end after retirement. Many are staying healthy and active in their communities for as long as possible, carrying out different types of activities. Some individuals are working longer instead of retiring early, and there are others who start second careers. Living longer creates diversity and changes in society, creating different family structures. Families today can have parents, grandparents, and even great-grandparents. There are grandparents taking care of grandchildren and also taking care of their own parents. Getting to know our adult 50+ community members will determine what library services and programs will best support these changing needs.

Physical and Cognitive Aspects

Along with adults 50+ who lead active, healthy lifestyles, there are some adults midlife and older who face challenges, such as physical and behavioral changes, as a natural process of aging (Hutchison, Eastman, & Tirrito, 1997). For instance, there could be age-related health issues, mobility problems with control and coordination difficulties, issues with sensation such as impaired vision and hearing, perception changes in their awareness of their environment, and cognitive changes dealing with reasoning and memory issues. These changes can cause difficulty understanding and using online computer systems or affect their ability to use standard Web site interface features (Fisk, Rogers, Charness, Czaja, & Sharit, 2009). Furthermore, adults 50+ sometimes experience a decline in motor control and coordination, as well as some disabling conditions such as arthritis. This can make it difficult to handle the functions of a computerized system. Visual acuity can also decline, creating challenges in viewing information due to the screen size or the font size on a Web site page (Mates, 2003). In addition, adults who experience a hearing loss or a hearing impairment can have difficulty accessing audio content on an online system. A noisy environment can cause difficulty in listening to voice prompts, which can cause errors in following directions or inputting and receiving the correct information (Harper, Yesilada, & Chen, 2011).

Besides the physical changes an adult can experience, behavioral changes can be encountered in adults 50+. For instance, three types of knowledge are used to perform an effective information search on a computerized system: information retrieval knowledge (search skills, strategies, and experience conducting a search); domain knowledge (understanding the current problem or want); and system knowledge (understanding the system's features and functions) (Xie, 2012). Changes in cognition and a lack of experience using online systems can cause anxiousness and decreased feelings of confidence in using technology and performing a successful online search. In addition, this can affect how motivated an individual is to learn and utilize new technologies. Adults midlife and older can have varied feelings of comfort and anxiety when using a technological device. This can cause more cognitive demand, leading to uncertainty, confusion, and frustration (Kuhlthau, 2005). An adult 50+ can have some or all of these varied characteristics. Therefore, it is important to keep these types of changes in mind when we are planning our programs, especially technology programs, as well as other types of information services.

Social Aspects

Social interactions are important for adults 50+. Individuals communicate with each other to seek out information, they search for information for other individuals, and they seek out others to verify information. A social environment can also be significant in learning technology (Ng, 2007). Peers can give support and comfort, leading to more confidence in learning and using an online system. This is important when we are planning the physical library environment and programs entailing technology.

Furthermore, keeping in contact with others by communicating through e-mail and social networking sites, such as Facebook, can help improve this population's quality of life (Decker, 2010). This is important when we are planning the types of technology programming for our adult 50+ library patrons. Noting the benefits of learning to use e-mail and other social networking sites successfully to communicate with others might encourage reluctant nontechnology users. Research has found adults midlife and older are steadily increasing their use of social networks to keep in touch with family and friends and to find out information (Anderson & Perrin, 2017). This is important to note with regard to marketing our programs and services for our adult 50+ tech-savvy patrons.

Additionally, creating spaces for social interactions for adults 50+ is beneficial. The National Institute on Aging (2017) mentions that there is a definite correlation between social interactions, an individual's health, and his or her overall well-being. Joseph (2009) discusses how important it is for adults 50+ to be provided with an area to socialize. This could significantly improve their quality of life, especially if individuals are retired and do not talk with or meet others on a daily basis. Creating formal and informal discussion groups at our libraries can provide enjoyable interactions, stimulate new and creative ideas, and increase overall life satisfaction.

Economics

Some adults midlife and older continue to work after retirement age, which can be because of economic reasons. However, some adults 50+ do not work and have few options for continuing their income, thus increasing their possibility of becoming economically disadvantaged. Disadvantaged groups are more likely to use the public library for access to online information. There are also rural communities that have difficulty with their broadband connectivity, making it difficult to download and stream information. Similarly, disadvantaged individuals can be found in economically depressed inner-city or rural neighborhoods that cannot afford Internet connections. Public libraries need to provide access to the Internet via a stable Wi-Fi connection or by offering public computers, which can play a role in equalizing access to all types of individuals, especially those who are economically disadvantaged. Additionally, libraries that are centered in areas or neighborhoods that are disadvantaged can help provide a safe, community-based environment and function as a place for learning and social opportunities. We can collaborate with nearby organizations and businesses to foster sharing of our resources. Offering free or low-cost classes and programs can provide opportunities for individuals to experience something that they may not have been able to afford or learn due to economic circumstances, especially with regard to new technologies. This can have a positive effect on the physical and mental health of adults 50+, including their quality of life (APA, 2017).

PUBLIC LIBRARIES

The American Library Association (2017) reports there are 16,536 public libraries in the United States, which includes central and branch libraries. We provide equal access to information, support intellectual freedom, and offer neutral spaces for everyone. We can accomplish our goals by helping our patrons develop new skills, provide expansive collections of materials and digital resources, and use a variety of methods to communicate to our patrons that we want to help make their communities a better place to live.

Community Benefits and Value

Most Americans (90 percent) believe public libraries are important and that closing them would have an impact on their community because public libraries play a role in literacy development and improve their quality of life (Zickuhr, Rainie, Purcell, & Duggan, 2013). Plus, most Americans look to public libraries to help them find reliable and trustworthy information and to help them learn new things in a variety of different ways (Geiger, 2017). We need to consistently examine the services and programs we offer and continually ask our community members about their wants and needs. We provide various opportunities to explore, imagine, and interact with a variety of materials, individuals, and experiences in a safe and welcoming environment. Edwards, Rauseo, and Unger (2013) discuss the value of libraries in five broad categories:

1. Libraries as community builders
2. Libraries as community centers for diverse populations
3. Libraries as centers for the arts
4. Libraries as universities
5. Libraries as champions of youth

With these in mind, we can enhance and provide valuable resources, programming, and services to our adult midlife and older community members.

American Library Association Guidelines

The American Library Association (ALA) has created new and updated guidelines to assist libraries in the development of services and programs for the adult 60+ population. The initial guidelines were developed in the 1980s, revised in 2008, and have currently been updated and revised in June 2017 by the Library Services to an Aging Population Committee and approved by the RUSA (Reference and User Services Association) Board in September 2017. The updated practices encourage diversity and variety in planning for collections, programs, and services for the 60+ population (RUSA, 2017). These guidelines need to be considered a reference to help guide our programming and services for our midlife and older adult community members. The following guidelines are used with permission from the American Library Association: Reference and User Services Division.

GUIDELINES FOR LIBRARY SERVICES WITH 60+ AUDIENCE: BEST PRACTICES

1.0 **Staff Training**
1.1 Develop the library's staff, cultivating an environment where the audience is welcomed and engaged.
1.2 Provide learning opportunities to build awareness about the aspects of aging.
1.3 Encourage staff to recognize and understand the multidimensional aspects of aging.
1.4 Ensure that all staff is aware of programs and services the library offers that may be of interest to the audience, such as deposit collections at facilities, lobby service, reader services, home delivery services, talking book collections, volunteer opportunities, reading aids, or waiving of fines or fees.
1.5 Partner with local organizations to design training opportunities for library staff.

2.0 Information Services and Collections

2.1 Appoint a librarian to act as a coordinator of services to the audience, ensuring that there is at least one designated staff member monitoring and developing the library's collections and services with the audience in mind.

2.2 Establish an advisory group that reflects the audience and the diversity of the community.

2.3 Identify interests through focus groups or surveys.

2.4 Cooperate with local area Agencies on Aging, senior nutrition programs, senior volunteer programs, and others in the aging service provider network by advertising their services and making their publications and other information more readily accessible either online or in paper format.

2.5 Organize and consolidate information about government and community programs and services available for the audience.

2.6 Ensure that the library's collection includes materials that are pertinent for the audience, caregivers, and family members, and for professional caregivers in the community.

3.0 Programming

3.1 Identify program and service opportunities based on interest and community need.

3.2 Select themes for programs that deal with specific interests of the audience identified through strategic planning, community asset mapping, user surveys, focus groups, and/or circulation statistics reflecting borrowing patterns.

3.3 Create engaging programs that promote lifelong learning, being aware that interests and information needs greatly vary.

3.4 Plan programs for specific age groups or generations within the audience enhancing capacity to remain independent.

3.5 Offer intergenerational programs and participate in intergenerational projects that are sponsored by others in the community. Consider partnerships with local schools, daycare facilities, or community organizations.

3.6 Pursue other opportunities for cooperative programming with partners, such as community and senior centers, area Agencies on Aging, senior employment organizations, and other community agencies, as well as educational institutions offering community-based educational programs for the audience. Cooperative efforts might involve active participation in planning and delivering programs; assistance in publicizing and marketing programs; or providing displays, exhibits, and booklists in conjunction with the library's programs.

3.7 Develop technology programs specifically of interest to the audience considering potential visual, physical, or hearing disabilities. Provide instruction for the use of electronic devices and social media.

3.8 Explore outreach and partnership opportunities to provide library services and programming to the audience outside the library, such as senior or community centers, nursing homes, and senior housing units. Consider offering technology training in these locations.

3.9 Promote active aging through library displays and exhibits.

3.10 Consider opportunities for the audience to volunteer in the library.

3.11 Develop and implement outcome measures for programs and services for effective evaluation.

4.0 Technology

4.1 Use electronic newsletters, the library home page, and social media sites for the audience.

4.2 Update software on the library website to minimize accessibility issues, including the ability to increase font sizes.

4.3 Provide devices preloaded with e-books.

4.4 Provide a mobile community technology lab (similar to a bookmobile) equipped with Wi-Fi, iPads, e-readers, etc., as well as assistive technology and adaptive hardware.

4.5 Engage audience with current digital collections offering assistive technology and adaptive hardware.

4.6 Offer computer and Internet training in assisted living, alternative housing, senior daycare, congregate meal sites, senior community centers, nursing homes, and senior residential or care homes in the community.

5.0 Outreach and Partnerships

5.1 Provide library information to those who serve the audience on a regular basis.

5.2 Participate in community activities to increase library awareness, such as community fairs and festivals.

5.3 Recruit volunteers who are 60+ to become advocates for the library community.

5.4 Establish an ongoing liaison partnership with local area Agencies on Aging, as well as other agencies that serve the audience, especially senior centers that employ activity coordinators.

5.5 Seek partnerships with health clubs, colleges, museums, cultural organizations, zoos, and schools/recreational centers to offer intergenerational programming.

5.6 Provide library materials to assisted living, retirement, and nursing facilities, as well as adult care homes and day centers, in whatever form fits their space and program.

5.7 Connect with diverse groups to strengthen collective impact.

5.8 Identify outreach and partnership opportunities to provide programming to the audience outside the library.

5.9 Advertise the library's services through local media, public health agencies, and other agencies that work with the audience.

6.0 Services to the Homebound and Special Populations

6.1 Survey community needs of homebound and other special populations, such as those with cognitive impairments. Analyze community demographics, population forecasts, and housing trends to plan to meet this need effectively.

6.2 Offer the library's services to assisted living, alternative housing, senior daycare, congregate meal sites, senior community centers, nursing homes, and senior residential or care homes in the community. Also offer assistance to those confined to private residences or who are unable to carry library materials home.

6.3 Establish partnerships with community agencies and organizations that work with the audience to develop and present library programs and services, and facilitate access to programs and services.

6.4 Tailor library services to the individual, using various delivery methods, including mail, volunteer delivery, and staff resources, depending on the reading needs and living situation of the patron. Use volunteers strategically to increase the capacity of outreach staff.

6.5 Partner with Regional Libraries for the Blind and Physically Handicapped to expand available services.

6.6 Evaluate your library's accessibility by the audience with physical, visual, aural, reading, and other disabilities according to the Accessibility Guidelines for Buildings and Facilities of the Americans with Disabilities Act.

6.7 Acquire and make available books and periodicals in large print.

7.0 Facilities

7.1 Create an area to socialize, offering an experience some of the audience might not currently have in their lives.

7.2 Accommodate users for whom prolonged standing is difficult by placing chairs or stools near stacks, information desks, checkout areas, computer terminals, and other areas. If possible, create a designated space using comfortable chairs gathered in an area adjacent to books and magazines of interest to the audience.

7.3 Consider placing materials frequently used by the audience on easily accessible shelves.

7.4 Ensure that spacing between shelving accommodates users in wheelchairs.

7.5 Ensure that signage is clear, Braille (where appropriate), and readily visible to all, including users in wheelchairs. Library brochures should be in at least 14 pt font type.

8.0 Funding and Budgeting

8.1 Assess funding needs.

8.2 Consider library budget planning to accommodate possible increases in demand for outreach services, such as delivery of library materials by mail and mobile library services.

8.3 Incorporate adequate funding for programs, materials, and services for the audience in the library's operating budget.

8.4 Seek supplemental funding through partnerships with other agencies, organizations, and foundations.

Programming and Services

Traditional Roles

Our role as public librarians is to provide quality services and information to our community members. A number of public libraries have many programs and services delivered to children, youth, and the adult populations. Yet when we examine our public library services offered for adults midlife and older, they have not been typically considered when decisions are made about library programming, collection development, or the physical library environment. This is interesting because our adult patrons comprise individuals over 18 years of age who have diverse characteristics and a variety of age groups. Traditionally, serving adults 50+ in the library is to provide large-print materials in the existing collection, as well as outreach services to nursing homes, assisted living facilities, or homebound individuals. These services are valuable and needed in our library communities. However, other ideas need to be explored, examined, and implemented to suit the needs of the adult 50+ populations.

Public libraries have changed over the years for adults 50+, especially with regard to looking for and finding materials. Traditional card catalogs have been replaced by OPACs (online public access catalogs). Most public library catalogs today use a computerized system, and the only way to access information is through the use of a computer keyboard or mouse. However, OPACs can be hard to use (Borgman, 1986), especially for some adults 50+. Depending on the technological device being used, the screen and keyboard size, as well as the system software, can limit the resources found and their capabilities. Inputting information into the system can also be difficult to retrieve good results due to the varying devices. These can pose challenges for adults 50+ who have physical or cognitive limitations or for the tech-wary individual.

Furthermore, very few libraries have a dedicated staff member for adult 50+ library services (Mates, 2003). Most positions are in adult reference services that encompass adult 18+ patrons and an outreach librarian, who typically provides services outside of the physical public library environment. Again, these services are important to have for our adult 50+ communities. However, as society grows and changes, we need to consider changing our services to suit our community's needs.

ADA-Compliant and Assistive Technologies

As stated previously, physical and psychological changes that can affect everyday life can occur as individuals age. We need to be aware of these changes and offer services and programs that help with potential barriers of access to information, as well as being aware that not everyone will be experiencing these changes. Adults midlife and older make up a significant number of library users (Abram, 2010), and as we age, changes occur that can affect how we search for information. Assistive technologies and meeting the ADA Standards for Accessible Design (2010) are necessary in meeting all of our library patrons' needs. ALA provides 15 tip sheets to assist public libraries in understanding and managing access to information. These are located on the Association of Specialized and Cooperative Library Agencies Web site. Many resources are available in print and online that can help public libraries understand the different types of disabilities and what can be done to make our libraries more accessible. Due to space limitations, they are not listed here in this text. Please see Appendix B for a list of possible resources and corresponding Web site links.

U.S. PUBLIC LIBRARY REPRESENTATIVE SAMPLES

With the adult 50+ population increasing, there is a need to examine American public libraries to determine how they are addressing the needs of the midlife and older adult community and to create a resource of ideas and suggestions to enhance and create adult 50+ library programs and services in our own library systems. The information and statistics in this book are an expansion of an initial study conducted and published in *Public Library Quarterly* titled "Older Adults and the Public Library: The Impact of the Boomer Generation," which examined 50 public libraries, one from each state, and their adult 50+ services and programs (Bennett-Kapusniak, 2013). This text includes a broader sampling of public libraries to show how different types of libraries are serving their aging communities.

Selection Process

A random selection of public libraries in the United States was generated to examine programming and services for adults 50+. This included events, outreach, assistive technologies, Web sites, appointed staff, and collaborations with other organizations. The sample size was 1,317 U.S. public libraries. This figure allows for a 95 percent confidence level with a 2.5 percent margin of error, giving a representative sampling of American public libraries. As of July 3, 2016, there were 9,147 main public libraries in the United States, not including individual branches. However, the state of Hawaii has only one main public library. Therefore, to generate a representative sample from Hawaii, the branch libraries were counted only for that individual state. The libraries were selected randomly from Information Today's American Library Directory Online (2016). Public libraries were chosen using the following criteria: each main public library within each state was given a consecutive number (1, 2, 3 . . .); a percentage was generated to determine how many libraries would be represented from each state from the total number of the representative sample (see Table 1.2); and the Microsoft Excel random number generator was used to generate random numbers between one and the state representative number. These random numbers were then used

TABLE 1.2. State Sample Number

State	Main Libraries	Sample Number	State	Main Libraries	Sample Number
Alabama	172	25	Montana	82	12
Alaska	63	9	Nebraska	255	37
Arizona	88	13	Nevada	23	3
Arkansas	66	10	New Hampshire	231	33
California	182	26	New Jersey	291	42
Colorado	118	17	New Mexico	80	11
Connecticut	190	27	New York	751	108
Delaware	29	4	North Carolina	125	18
Florida	140	20	North Dakota	73	10
Georgia	34	5	Ohio	251	36
Hawaii	1 (49 branches)	7	Oklahoma	140	20
			Oregon	130	19
Idaho	108	15	Pennsylvania	497	71
Illinois	621	89	Rhode Island	49	7
Indiana	233	33	South Carolina	38	5
Iowa	532	76	South Dakota	68	10
Kansas	326	47	Tennessee	183	26
Kentucky	119	17	Texas	562	81
Louisiana	65	9	Utah	56	8
Maine	251	36	Vermont	181	26
Maryland	23	3	Virginia	85	12
Massachusetts	365	52	Washington	53	8
Michigan	374	54	West Virginia	93	13
Minnesota	174	25	Wisconsin	379	54
Mississippi	42	6	Wyoming	21	3
Missouri	133	19			

to find the public library allotted that particular number in the state. See Appendix A for the names of the public libraries examined in this text.

Library Data Usage Explanation

The data gathered from the representative libraries in this book comprised information examined on the public library's Web site. This includes their Web site pages, calendars, events, and, if available, their social network site on Facebook. Some libraries did not have a library Web site, and information was gathered from their available Facebook page. If the library did not have a library Web site or Facebook page, a letter was sent via e-mail, if available, to the library or via the U.S. Postal Service to ask if they would like to contribute information. Of the 1,317 libraries examined, 78 (6 percent) letters were sent by U.S. mail to directors and librarians who did not have an e-mail address.

Contributions

All 1,317 public libraries were contacted via e-mail or by the U.S. Postal Service to ask if they would like to include more extensive information by answering interview questions about their adult 50+ programs and services because some programs are marketed through print or other forms of media and might not have been found online. Public library directors, adult reference librarians, outreach librarians, digital inclusion managers, adult programming librarians, special audiences strategists, computer instructors, adult and technical services coordinators, and many other librarians contributed their opinions, programs, services, and ideas to assist us in adult 50+ library services. Contributors to this text represent 55 public libraries in 25 states (see Table 1.3). They are in rural, suburban, and urban communities and have small to extensive library collections (see Table 1.4). Contributing public library addresses can be found in Appendix D. Information on the public

TABLE 1.3. **Number of Contributing Public Libraries by State**

State	Number of Contributors
Alabama	2
California	2
Colorado	1
Connecticut	3
Idaho	2
Illinois	4
Indiana	3
Kansas	1
Maryland	1
Massachusetts	3
Michigan	3
Minnesota	1
New Hampshire	2
New Jersey	3
New Mexico	1
New York	5
North Carolina	2
Ohio	3
Oklahoma	1
Oregon	1
Pennsylvania	2
South Carolina	1
Tennessee	1
Texas	2
Wisconsin	5
TOTAL	**55**

TABLE 1.4. Public Library Population Served and Collections

Library Name and State	Population	Library Collection
New Durham Public Library, NH	2,638	11,201
Fife Lake Public Library, MI	2,791	21,467
Eastham Public Library, MA	4,956	46,204
Pioneer Memorial Library, KS	5,438	35,915
Essex Library Association, CT	6,683	35,485
Fairfield Free Public Library, NJ	7,466	60,755
Oradell Public Library, NJ	7,978	53,891
Guthrie Public Library, OK	10,345	26,445
Athol Public Library, MA	11,299	37,939
Wilbraham Public Library, MA	14,219	49,661
Wimberley Village Library, TX	18,389	38,369
Richmond Memorial Library, NY	19,703	94,602
Sherwood Public Library, OR	21,151	33,887
Matheson Memorial Library, WI	22,894	59,369
River Falls Public Library, WI	22,918	81,880
Simsbury Public Library, CT	23,511	134,988
O'Fallon Public Library, IL	28,281	66,904
Homewood Public Library, AL	30,662	69,624
Cranberry Public Library, PA	30,985	78,604
ELA Area Public Library, IL	34,462	169,738
Westerville Public Library, OH	38,985	409,221
Friendswood Public Library, TX	40,378	87,157
Quincy Public Library, IL	40,633	146,219
Marinette County Consolidated Public Library Services, WI	41,718	77,645
Webster Public Library, NY	42,641	112,935
Wallingford Public Library, CT	45,135	215,288
Saratoga Springs Public Library, NY	49,070	192,482
Adams Memorial Library, PA	51,544	90,223
Greenwood County Library System, SC	69,661	93,370
Findlay-Hancock County Public Library, OH	70,889	192,570
Muncie Public Library, IN	72,100	173,126
Appleton Public Library, WI	115,455	260,637
Yolo County Library, CA	146,487	334,644
Greene County Public Library, OH	161,573	484,948
Ann Arbor Library, MI	163,590	430,963
Carroll County (MD) Public Library, MD	170,089	405,362
Birmingham Public Library, AL	212,157	900,000
Santa Barbara Public Library, CA	218,613	297,489
Anoka County Library, MN	334,035	496,792
Ocean County Library, NJ	575, 397	1,054,680
Pikes Peak Library District, CO	616,089	714,424
Nashville Public Library, TN	668,347	2,546,825
Charlotte Mecklenburg Library, NC	940,697	946,694

libraries, including addresses, and the contributor who wished to remain anonymous are not included within the text, the public library index in Appendix D, or in any accompanying tables. Therefore, the tables do not have the full representation of all the libraries that contributed, but instead present a representation of the variety of libraries in the text. The contributions throughout the text are represented in italics.

CHAPTER SUMMARY

This chapter gives a summary of adults 50+ and the role public libraries serve for our aging community members. In the subsequent chapters, you will be able to see how different guidelines for library services for our aging population have been incorporated into different programs and services by the libraries that contributed to this text. Even though the guidelines are for adults 60+, there are adults 50+ who also could have the same characteristics and are therefore the focus audience for this text. The public libraries examined in this text were randomly selected to show how different types of public libraries are serving their adult 50+ communities. As stated earlier, this is a group of individuals that is difficult to find a definitive definition of, and the information in this chapter was given for consideration for adult 50+ library services and programming. It is up to each individual library to determine the best practices needed that suit their library community.

2

Not Just Your Average Retiree

SECOND CAREERS

It is not surprising in today's society for individuals to examine a second career choice. There have been instances where an adult 50+ is suddenly let go from their current employer after a long-standing career, for a variety of reasons, and left with figuring out how to make ends meet and pay the bills. Other individuals have decided they do not want the stress of their current profession and decide to pursue another occupation that might be more enjoyable, create less anxiety, or be less demanding than their previous employment. Still others decide to pursue a career change due to health reasons, whereas others just want to try something new. However, starting a second career can have rewards and challenges for adults 50+. Depending on the profession, the individual might need to further their education in the respective field, which also can have benefits and issues. Building a resume, preparing for interviews, and searching for positions can potentially overwhelm some adults 50+, especially if they have been in the same career for an extended period. Also, depending on their previous profession, they might not have been exposed to computer technology and now need to learn how to navigate an online system. The public library can be a valuable resource for adults 50+ starting a second career, especially if they need assistance in finding a job, utilizing computers to fill out applications or viewing online classes, taking exams, or exploring information on various professional fields.

EXTENDED WORK

Many adults midlife and older continue to work after retirement age, which is currently age 67 (Saad, 2016). This is the current minimum age for receiving Social Security benefits. Most adults 50+ continue to work due to economic reasons. This can include needing an employer's health insurance benefits or they need the extra income because of financial difficulties. Still others continue to work just for the joy of working and want to continue being active members in their community. Some love their careers and want to work as long as they can physically and mentally handle the workload (Koppen & Anderson, 2008). We need to consider our adults 50+ who continue to work when we plan our services and programs. Having a variety of times such as day and evening sessions will afford adults who continue to work the opportunity to attend a valuable program.

RETIREES

If you ask a library staff member to describe typical adults midlife and older, a number of them would reply that they are their retired members of their community. A number of adults 50+ are retired. However, our definition of retirement is changing from what it used to be years ago (Bateson, 2010). People are living longer and staying active; some want to start a new career, and others want to venture out and travel the world. Some adults 50+ have become caregivers of grandchildren or they are helping their parents age at home. Retirees are also contemplating how they will be spending their free time exploring different opportunities for leisure and recreational activities, travel, volunteering, and lifelong learning (Manheimer & Kidahashi, 2010). We librarians are in a position to offer many types of programs and services that will appeal to the retired members of our communities.

Keep in mind that as some individuals retire from the workforce, they are experiencing certain lifestyle changes. They are not leaving the house on a regular basis to go to work, and there is a possibility they are not interacting as much with other individuals. This may cause social disconnectedness and perceived isolation, which can result in feelings of loneliness and less life satisfaction (Cornwell & Waite, 2009). We need to consider creating opportunities to socialize before or after programming, providing weekly discussion groups, or having an informal meeting space to give adults 50+ multiple occasions to interact with other individuals.

To assist us in providing for our retired 50+ community members, we can collaborate with outside organizations, which can bring in experts on certain subject areas. Consider developing programs on planning for retirement, financial planners, Social Security, and realtors to discuss housing options. Furthermore, there are retirees who might want to start traveling or who may be interested in educational pursuits. We can bring in travel agencies or consider having patrons share their travel tips to various places. Contacting nearby universities or colleges can bring in more information on learning a new subject or language. In addition, there are adults who have had successful careers, and even though they are retired, they want to share their skills. This is important to note if the library needs volunteers for certain programs or services such as computer help, a craft class, or teaching a musical instrument. Marketing to adults 50+ different volunteer opportunities can give them a chance to stay active and involved within their community.

COMMUNITY SERVICE

Drawing from scholarly research, we learn that Baby Boomers and other adults 50+ are very civic minded. They are looking to make a difference in their communities and have a strong desire to volunteer (Williamson, Bannister, & Sullivan, 2010). This can be beneficial to public libraries. We can create different types of service opportunities for adults 50+ that can be either within or outside the library environment. This can also be a good opportunity for outside collaborations within the community. Adults 50+ have different knowledge and skills to assist in many types of programs and services. They may also have community connections that can be helpful in creating partnerships and community collaborations. The types of community service will vary depending on the adults 50+ within our communities and how involved they want to be with the library and their community.

AGEISM

Librarians are familiar with the term ageism, which is a type of bigotry or discrimination of an individual because of their chronological age (Butler, 2005). Ageism is perpetuated by society. If we examine the images that are depicted in films, television, magazines, and our advertisements, many are of young individuals. Adults midlife and older are not typically depicted in advertising. Even when individuals talk about adults 50+ or when adults 50+ express an opinion about themselves, some of the terms used are geezer, old fogy, dinosaur, or having a "senior moment" (Mates, 2003). However, Balazs (2014) finds that portrayals of adults midlife and older are slowly shifting to more positive depictions (successful, energetic, youthful, sexually attractive) in the media.

Many adults 50+ are still active, healthy, and well-educated individuals. Public libraries are a neutral space where we can offer services and programs that avoid stereotypes by providing open and equal access to information and services for everyone. We can assist in changing these stereotypical concepts of aging through our presentation of various programs and promoting awareness about the cultural attitude on aging (Schull & Thomas, 2010). Offering many types of programs that appeal to a variety of individuals, not just the typical Medicare and Social Security programs, will help in changing the depiction of adults 50+ as being "old."

When examining the 1,317 public libraries in this text, 1,079 libraries had an online presence. Of these libraries, many (79 percent) currently offer adult programs, though few (12 percent) offered programs specifically for adults 50+. Most of the libraries offered many types of programming and services, with a few presenting Medicare and Social Security programs as their only offerings for their adult library patrons. Please take note that this percentage depicts information that was found online, and a small percentage (5.5 percent) of the libraries examined did not have a Web site, a Facebook page, or information about their library that could be found on the Internet. Some programs are offered through other forms of media, print, or word of mouth, which are not depicted in this text. With regard to Medicare and Social Security programming, it is important to note that these programs are beneficial and are needed as part of our program offerings. However, offering other program possibilities can promote a different view of our adults 50+ and perhaps gather new library patrons in the process. Offering many types of programs will broaden the interests of the adults 50+ in the community and encourage many types of adults 50+ to attend program offerings. The following are a couple of examples from the contributors in this text depicting a variety of program offerings for adults 50+.

Lisa C. West at Homewood Public Library in Alabama: "I have found that my senior patrons are very interested in programs dealing with history, travel, financial, and health . . . examples of some of these types of programs . . . which I think hold special interest for seniors . . . yoga . . . iPad and iPhone . . . programs on dementia . . . and other diseases . . . garden planning . . . mystery dinners . . . storyteller and musician . . . book clubs and discussion groups . . . financial programs . . . genealogy . . . resources expo."

Brianne Columbo at Fairfield Free Public Library in New Jersey: "The Fairfield Free Public Library also coordinates . . . adult programs with seniors 50+ in mind. Our adult events coordinator routinely schedules lectures and talks with local physical therapists, doctors, dieticians, advisors, and the township departments. Topics include Social Security, slips and falls prevention, total joint replacement, diet and exercise, strengthening and training, and various other topics that appeal to seniors 50+. Arts and craft classes, which include monthly DIY projects, watercolor and other paint classes with instructors, a knitting club, a crochet club, and various others. Musical concerts . . . both in the afternoon and in the evening. Film Fridays. New release movies in the afternoon every other week, which includes refreshments and snacks. Bring Your Own Device (BYOD) each week for individual assistance with personal devices."

SELF-EFFICACY

Self-efficacy is an individual's confidence or belief in performing and succeeding in accomplishing a task (Bandura, 1994). Reports of research find individuals who have low self-efficacy have higher anxiety and less motivation in learning new things. This has been found in adults midlife and older when they are using computers and other technological systems (Czaja et al., 2006). Low self-efficacy in adults 50+ can be due to a lack of digital literacy skills. This can be due to some adults midlife and older not being exposed as much as others to computerized systems. Having an encouraging atmosphere for adults 50+ can decrease anxiety and foster a better learning environment. Based on past research studies, adults 50+ underestimate their computer knowledge due to feeling less confident about their computer usage (Piper, Palmer, & Xie, 2009). This might affect how motivated they are in learning about technology, especially newer devices. We need to encourage adults 50+ to overcome their fear of technology and help alleviate their anxiety. Offering a variety of technology programs, including one-on-one training, peer training, and having time to practice their skills, will foster a better learning environment, improving their skills and increasing their confidence using technology. The following are a few examples from contributors to this text that showcase computer programs that can help adults 50+ be more comfortable using technology.

Peer instructors. *Richard Conroy at Essex Library Association in Connecticut:* "We have a 'Book a Librarian' program that allows patrons to make an appointment for one-on-one training using a computer, tablet device, smartphone, etc. The person who runs that program is over age 50 and, though we don't specifically market it to them, the participants are invariably senior citizens. Over the years we have found that technology training for any age group works best when conducted in this manner. Group sessions can be very challenging since the level of proficiency of the attendees usually varies widely."

Self-efficacy sensitivity. *Kathleen Handy, computer instructor at Saratoga Springs Public Library in New York:* "We haven't done this (intergenerational programming) for Computer Courses because many of the adults (50+) are sensitive about their need to learn skills that they rightfully or wrongfully assume many young people have a high level of."

Specific age classes. *Christy Wagner at ELA Area Public Library in Illinois:* "We offer a series of Senior Computer Classes which range from On-line Senior Travel Resources, Health Resources to keyboarding, e-mail, Introduction to the Internet, Cyber Safety, etc. These are offered throughout the year and involve our Reference staff who serve as instructors. . . . Outreach staff acts as one-on-one help as needed."

PEER EXCHANGE AND SOCIAL DIALOGUES

As mentioned earlier, social interaction is important for adults 50+. Social experiences can have positive health benefits, both physically and mentally, leading to better life satisfaction (Schull, 2013). Providing different types of experiences that can inspire and foster social relationships with adults 50+ reduces stress and boosts immunological pathways (Cohen, 2009). Social experiences can be a face-to-face conversation and also done virtually through social media communication. Public libraries are a neutral space where individuals are welcome to interact with others on a variety of issues and topics. These interactions can be formal and informal, such as having refreshments before or after a program, poetry groups, and painting and writing classes, to a specific time for a program that involves a lively discussion on the civic issues in the community.

Another avenue to foster social dialogs is through the Internet. Utilizing social media Web sites can be beneficial in increasing social relationships and improve general well-being in adults midlife and older. Prior research has shown communicating on the Internet using e-mail, instant messaging, Facebook, blogs, and other social networking sites can provide mental stimulation and increase cognitive function (Slegers & van Boxtel, 2013). We need to consider utilizing social networking sites for our libraries, and we need to encourage adults 50+ to communicate with the library through posts and comments about pictures and events.

Furthermore, programs given by peers allows for social support by others who might understand how they are feeling. This can be due to sharing the same experiences because they are around the same age (Ng, 2007). For instance, many adults 50+ have difficulty reading a computerized screen because of the smaller print. If an adult 50+ is teaching the class, an attendee who is also 50+ might feel more comfortable asking how to enlarge the type on the screen for easier reading rather than asking a younger instructor. This can be because the younger adult does not have the same difficulty reading the smaller type as an adult who is older, and the adult 50+ might feel more anxious asking a younger person how to change the screen size. We need to consider creating different opportunities for social exchanges with peers and other individuals inside and outside the library environment. The following are a few examples from contributors to this text of some social opportunities provided in their libraries.

Elizabeth Eisen, adult programming librarian at Appleton Public Library in Wisconsin: "We offer Cocoa & Coloring Nights which attract patrons and families from ages 4 to 94. Adult coloring is very popular now. We offer coloring sheets, markers, and colored pencils for participants plus cocoa for refreshments."

Heather Johnson at River Falls Public Library in Wisconsin: "Spring Break Spelling Bee for Adults: Adults are encouraged to brush off their dictionary and join fellow community members for a fun and challenging spelling bee."

Kathleen Goodson at Wimberley Village Library in Texas: "Coloring for Grownup Girls & Boys. Men and women come to this monthly gathering to color for relaxation and to quietly socialize with friends. We provide light snacks and invite the group to bring their own wine if they so desire. It is a pleasant way to unwind for adults of all ages."

Ryan Johnson at O'Fallon Public Library in Illinois: "Our Book Bingo events have been popular . . . The Outreach Coordinator at one of our local assisted living communities donates her time to run the event. Her organization gets some free PR out of it, and we get a free presenter and the opportunity to provide the event. . . . When someone wins a game, they get to pick any book from our book sale area as a prize. I'm always surprised at how competitive the group is. Many of them pick out children's books for their grandkids. The library provides light snacks (cookies, crackers) and bottled juice and water. Occasionally we'll put on a pot of coffee, especially if it's cold out. There isn't much prep. We just set up tables and chairs in our community room. We did invest in a bingo set that we found on Amazon. It came with all the cards to call bingo, as well as plenty of grids and chips for the players. . . . The cost is very minimal. We purchase snacks and drinks in bulk to use for our various events. . . . We also had the one-time cost of the bingo set. I believe it was $10 or so."

Melanie Wehrle at Pikes Peak Library District in Colorado: "Half of our branches offer monthly movie showings of new release movies during the day. . . . Drop-in crafters groups as well as discussion or chat groups are also popular at many of our branches during the day as well as on evenings and weekends. Some of our branches also find that Saturday afternoon is a great time to get older adults into the library for programs. We also offer book discussion groups both in our branches, at the local Senior Center, and at one of the neighborhood community centers at various times during the day as well as in the evening. These programs cost very little. The main cost is staff time to reserve the room, plan book or movie selection, set up and run the program. Some of them have snacks such as donuts and coffee or popcorn and lemonade."

Fife Lake Public Library in Michigan: "We partner with the Grand Traverse Senior Center and Grand Traverse Parks and Recreation for many of our Senior Programs. . . . We share resources and funds to provide services in our community. In return, both the library and the Senior Center are able to reach a very rural, underserved community. Here are some of the programs provided through this partnership: Senior Luncheon . . . then following the luncheon we have a variety of programs, activities, and presenters . . . Grand Traverse Meals on Wheels usually provides the meal and has volunteers deliver it to the library. . . . We have special programs following most lunches. The majority of the programs are directed specifically to the aging community. Much of the information relates to concerns they might have but don't always know who to or how to ask (i.e., Medicare Updates, Hospice 101, Sleep & Insomnia, Commission on Aging, Funeral Plans, Grief to Gratitude, and Proper Drug Disposal). . . . The focus of our luncheon is not the meal itself, but the conversations it creates. Through conversation we can find out the needs of the community and focus on what support we can give. They are a lot of fun."

CHAPTER SUMMARY

This chapter explored the different views society has about adults 50+ and the variety of adults 50+ we can have in our communities. Some adults continue to work after retirement age due to different life circumstances or because of individual choice. Other adults 50+ decide to retire and get involved in volunteer work within their communities. Our understanding about adults 50+ will determine our planning and services for this age group. Views of adults 50+ are affected by society and can in turn affect how adults midlife and older view themselves. This can affect their confidence and anxiety in trying new things or the types of programs they attend. Offering social experiences and programs that avoid stereotypes creates a welcome environment for everyone and can improve a 50+ adult's confidence and well-being.

3

Landscaping and Curb Appeal:
The Physical Library

LIBRARY AS PLACE

As people are living longer and are generally maintaining a healthy and active lifestyle, there is a trend for adults to stay and grow older in their own homes and communities. We need to look at our communities and determine how our library services best suit the needs of our adult 50+ community members. The location of the public library can be a key factor for adults midlife and older accessing the physical library building. Chapter 1 discusses how adults 50+ experience physical and psychological changes such as reduced vision, hearing loss, and changes in mobility and dexterity, as well as cognitive changes, which can make accessing and retrieving information challenging, especially from an online system. We, as librarians, need to be aware of these changes to help everyone have safe access to materials within our physical library environment.

Building Layout

The Information and Technical Assistance of the Americans with Disabilities Act *ADA Standards for Accessible Design* (2010) has accessibility standards for construction and alterations of buildings (see Appendix B). Our public libraries welcome everyone, and we need to be mindful of all types of individuals who will have access to our physical environment. We need to consider including adults 50+ on committees when planning and reconfiguring the design and layout of the library to give us valuable insight into the wants and needs of their age group. Furthermore, when examining our physical library building, we need to consider the inside and outside areas that can assist all types of patrons. For instance, we need to provide accessible parking, handrails, and ramps to provide easier access to our library facilities. We also need to look at our public service desks and other tables throughout the library to determine if they are easily accessible and at a height convenient for wheelchairs. If we have a building with more than one story, we need to have elevators for adults 50+ who have physical limitations and cannot use the stairs so they will have access to all materials throughout the building. In addition, we need to provide adequate seating throughout the library, which can assist adults 50+ who may get tired while walking around the library and need a place to rest. The International Federation of Library Associations and Institutions report by Irvall and Nielsen (2005) has an excellent checklist to help in creating an accessibility-friendly library environment. Table 3.1 has some highlights to make our libraries more user friendly. Creating an environment that permits access to all areas of the library generates inclusion and breaks down barriers among all members of society.

Social Areas

As people age, social networks can shrink due to life-changing events. Chapter 2 mentions the importance of social interactions for adults 50+. Libraries can help in providing different opportunities to socialize with other individuals in their community. These social opportunities can be within the physical library environment, occur at another place within the community, or be social exchanges online.

Some of our library patrons want a multifunctional space where they can go to be quiet and also have a place to gather with others for events, socialization, and learning experiences. Libraries today typically are not the quiet places that adults 50+ experienced when they were younger. We now have areas where there can be social interactions among community members. We need to consider a possible quiet space where adults 50+ can go if they want to focus, read, or study, as well as have a space for social interactions. Some libraries have a café or eatery within the library where patrons can eat and socialize. Or we can consider designating a small space or a meeting room for certain times of the day or evening where adults 50+ can gather. Surveying the interests of our adults midlife and older for a formal or informal space will help gauge the community needs.

Besides the physical spaces within our libraries for social interactions, online social networking sites can be another opportunity for adults 50+ to engage in communicating with the library and with others in the community. Most adults midlife and older are using e-mail to communicate with others online. However, we need to be teaching the benefits of social networking with friends and family, as well as creating training programs on how to use certain networking sites (Facebook, instant messaging, Twitter, etc.) (Abram, 2010). What better way to encourage social

TABLE 3.1. Adults 50+ User-Friendly Checklist

Accessibility	Assistive Devices	Furniture	Indoor Environment
Drinking fountains wheelchair accessible	CCTV displays	Baskets or carts with wheels	Handrails on both sides of a stairway
Switches, doorknobs, and faucets are easy to operate and wheelchair accessible	Electronic and handheld magnifiers	Bookstands to hold reading material	Mark changes in floor surface
	FM listening system in meeting rooms	Low bookcases	Secure doormats
	Listening devices	Nontipping, sturdy armchairs	Ample space to open and close door
	Handheld reachers	Sound-absorbing materials	Doorways at least 32 inches wide for a wheelchair or scooter
	Telecommunication device		

Lighting	Outside Environment	Personnel	Technology
Adjustable blinds	Sidewalks are smooth and in good repair	Adults 50+ advisory committee	Adaptive software
Task lighting	Doorways at least 32 inches wide for a wheelchair or scooter	Adults 50+ staff member	Adjustable computer stations
Window coatings to reduce glare		Staff training on working with adults 50+	Large monitor (at least 15 inches)
			Large print keyboards
			Mouse alternatives
			Web site meets accessibility guidelines

networking then having our own library social networks? We need to consider creating Facebook pages to display pictures and programs of events for others to comment on, as well as Twitter accounts and blogs for patrons to follow and communicate their thoughts and ideas. This will provide opportunities and practice utilizing social networks and encourage social interactions. The fastest-growing group of social network users is adults 74+. In 2008, 4 percent of adults 74+ used social networking sites, and the latest survey reports 20 percent of adults 75+ are using social media (Anderson & Perrin, 2017; Zickuhr, 2010). However, there are still large portions of adults 65+ not using social media. Creating training programs and our own social networks can provide opportunities for engagement and practice utilizing social networking sites. The following are a couple of social events contributors to this text mentioned that occurred at their libraries.

Kelly Martin Laney at Birmingham Public Library in Alabama: "Coffee, Conversation and Crafts is a weekly program from 11 to 1. . . . It is open to all adults, but because of the time period, most of the attendees are over 50. Planned in response to a report that seniors self-reported greater loneliness after social media became popular, this program offers free instruction and supplies for simple crafts. Puzzles are put out, along with light refreshments, and everyone is encouraged to make friends. The craft is an icebreaker; the real purpose is to build community and promote relationships."

Christy Wagner at ELA Area Public Library in Illinois: "An annual event jointly sponsored with ELA Township '55-Plus' the ever popular, 'Nightclub at Noon.' Traditionally we hold this event in midwinter to offer something special in that time when winter is beginning to drag on a bit! The idea is to transform the library meeting room into a 'Nightclub' atmosphere for a lunch and then special entertainment. All tables are draped in colorful tablecloths with accompanying decorations at each to match the theme for that year's entertainment. Wickless candles help to create the atmosphere and everyone is encouraged to dress up for the event. We have enjoyed Dixieland Jazz, an 'afternoon in Paris' with a sultry jazz singer accompanied by a pianist on the library's baby grand piano, 'Rat Pack' singers, and big band musical performances. Outreach and '55-Plus' staff serve our patrons at the tables. We break between lunch and the show to reset the room theater style. It's a fun distraction from the winter weather and has become a tradition we plan to continue due to its continual success. . . . We use a local caterer to provide a boxed lunch that includes a dessert. . . . The library provides hot drinks and water. We begin the lunch with a toast of sparkling grape juice served in champagne 'glasses' (plastic stemmed ware) and a toast! Every effort is made to transform the meeting room into a special venue! Total cost without including staff in-kind time for preparation and work on the day is usually in the $1,200 to $1,500 range. Costs are split . . . between my programming budget and '55-Plus' budget."

ASSISTIVE TECHNOLOGIES

Different types of assistive technologies will help adult 50+ patrons who have a physical challenge or issue viewing, hearing, or retrieving library materials. Some assistive technologies to aid individuals with visual challenges are magnifiers (handheld, electronic), yellow acetate sheets that enhance print (cuts down on glare from overhead lighting), screen reader software, text-to-speech software, a dedicated computer with magnifying options, and closed circuit television video displays (CCTVs) that enlarge text from a book or other items when placed on the platform (ASCLA, 2010). The American Foundation for the Blind (2017) has a link to a list of video magnifiers (see Appendix B). The systems range from tabletop devices, portable laptop versions, and items that can connect to your own laptops. Pricing varies, averaging $1,000 to $3,500 with handheld devices averaging around $300. In addition, the Library of Congress National Library Service for the Blind and Physically Handicapped (NLS) (2017) loans Braille and recorded books, magazines, religious publications, and audio equipment to individuals in the United States with a visual or physical impairment. Local cooperating U.S. libraries can mail the NLS items directly to enrollees at no cost. Equipment and items that are available will vary by state. For instance, the Wisconsin Talking Book and Braille Library has over 200,000 books and magazines in Braille and large print and audio-recorded books for adults, young adults, and children, as well as DVDs and videos. There are playback machines as well as accessories for the machines, including headphones, extension lever, amplifier, and breath switch (WDPI, 2017). Contact a state or local affiliate to find out more information.

Furthermore, hearing issues can occur as adults become older. Individuals who have a hearing loss can have difficulty hearing in a noisy environment and focusing on someone speaking to them (Harper, Yesilada, & Chen, 2011). Background noise has become a part of our library environment. Few libraries have a traditional, quiet atmosphere. This can make it difficult for an individual with a hearing loss. To help overcome a hearing impairment, consider adaptive computer software that provides visual cues to the audio such as Jaws or iCommunicator. Personal listening devices can also help tune out background noise and amplify the intended communication. For example, some of the libraries in this text (22 of the 1,317) have an audio loop that is in their meeting rooms to assist patrons who are conducting programs or meetings for their audience members. Other libraries explored in this text could have had this feature, but it was not listed on their Web site or Facebook page. Telecommunication devices for the deaf (TDD) or teletypewriter (TTY) machines can be used to type out in-person conversations. Relay services are also available for phone message communications. We need to consider designating a quiet area within the physical library to help decrease the background noise of computers and normal conversations.

Mobility issues are another concern for some individuals. We need to consider providing different technological devices such as joysticks, a larger mouse and keyboard, or computer workstations that adjust to wheelchair heights. Providing wheelchairs, scooters, or baskets on wheels will enable patrons who cannot carry items a place to store their materials and provide assistance for those who cannot walk very far around the library.

Providing different types of assistive technologies for adults 50+ who are having challenges fills an important need that helps breaks down barriers to access within our communities. Only a handful of the libraries (5 percent) examined in this text had information about the types of assistive technologies available at their library on their Web sites. However, some libraries only market their assistive technologies through print or within their physical library environment. With more adults 50+ accessing the Internet, we need to market our information in different ways to reach more of our library community. Knowing our adult 50+ library patrons will determine the types of assistive technologies needed and the best marketing strategy to use to make sure the community is aware of these services. The following are some contributor examples of assistive technologies offered at their libraries.

Assistive events. *Christy Wagner at ELA Area Public Library in Illinois:* "Low Vision Fair: This is an event we have done every few years and involves no real cost but intense planning and coordination. The idea is to provide speakers and resources for those patrons who have low vision issues and their family or caregivers. I work with the local Lions Club, various other agencies that provide services for people who have vision issues, a local optometrist or ophthalmologist who speaks on an issue such as Macular Degeneration Diagnosis and Treatment. In past years when our library had a Friends group, they sponsored this event, and it allowed me to advertise in local print media and offer a light lunch to participants. We had a booth-like arrangement in the room where the various agencies could explain their products and services such as the Talking Book Center, Second Sense, Center for Independent Living, a few low vision magnification companies as well. Outreach Services also had a 'booth' where staff explained our services. We created resource packets for each participant to take home, ensuring that the print on the information in the packets was large type format and in bold print. Planning for an event that involves several agencies requires you to begin several months in advance. Confirmation of each agency and presenter is critical. Reviewing any audio and visual needs they require, estimating space needs for the entire event also needs consideration and coordination with your in-house facilities staff. Publicity must also be done well in advance. The physical logistics need to be considered for those attending, sufficient parking, signs directing patrons to the event, extra space in the library parking lot for the Low Vision Screening Bus, etc."

Assistive kits. *Meryle A. Leonard at Charlotte Mecklenburg Library in North Carolina:* "We also use Bi-Folkal Kits. These kits focus on memory skills. Each kit is themed, and we add additional resources to enhance the program. Some of our most popular themed programs are Remembering the Fair, Railroads and Birthdays. (Makers of Bi-Folkal Kits, Bi-Folkal Productions, are no longer in business.)"

Assistive technologies. *Kathleen Handy, computer instructor at Saratoga Springs Public Library in New York:* "The computer classes we offer are geared for beginners, many of which are age 50 or older. We take time to consider hearing or vision issues (visually friendly keyboard and hearing assistive devices) and wheelchair or walker considerations."

Physical environment. *Yolo County Library Davis in California:* "I prepare for the Active Older Adult Circle with the following: reserving the meeting room monthly a year in advance, advertising by creating monthly flyers, a press release, and posting on our online Events Calendar. Checking in with the moderator before each program to see what is needed. On the day of the program, I set up the room with tables and chairs in a large square. I bring in soft seating for the members with arthritis. I set up the microphone, turn the heat up, and open the fire door so that members can enter from the parking lot. I set up the laptop, overhead projector, and get ready the Web site or YouTube video they will be watching and discussing."

MATERIALS AND SERVICES

As mentioned in Chapter 1, large print collections, audiobooks, and services to residential institutions and the homebound are important traditional services that are still needed for our adult 50+ library patrons. Collection development and the services we provide are shaped by our community's needs. Previous chapters mention how adults 50+ have diverse characteristics, and their interests will vary. For instance, an adult 50+ who is starting a second career could be exploring information on business opportunities and looking for guidance on résumé building, while another adult 50+ might want the latest best-seller for leisure reading. There are adults 50+ who are interested in gaming and technology, as well as others exploring eldercare information. Keeping our collection up to date with current titles is important, especially for individuals who enjoy reading printed text. However, our electronic collections also need to be kept current. American adults 50+ still continue to enjoy printed text (62.5 percent), though there are some who like to read an e-book (21 percent) or listen (12 percent) on a digital device (Perrin, 2016). Most electronic devices can enlarge print to some degree for easier reading. We need to consider having training classes on downloading electronic materials and the use of the various functions for different types of devices. Many individuals are not aware that our libraries have digital collections and the different types of materials that we have to offer (Horrigan,

2016). We need to explore ways to market these collections, especially to our adult 50+ technology users.

Large print books and magazines are still used quite frequently by our adults midlife and older and need to be kept current. Braille materials (see the earlier section) and talking books for the visually, physically, or learning disabled are available in every state. More information is available at our state libraries. Moreover, different types of audiobooks such as MP3 players, Playaways, and books on CDs, as well as digital recorded books, need to be offered in a variety of topics. In addition, past research reports DVD collections are borrowed frequently (40 percent) when individuals visit the library (Zickuhr, Rainie, & Purcell, 2013). We need to consider adding to existing collections foreign films, classic movies, and television series from different eras. These can be used for possible programs, discussions, or groups that adults 50+ might enjoy. We need to also consider having a number of captioned videos for community members who have hearing impairments. Likewise, popular music is widely collected in our libraries and needs to be in a variety of genres and performers. We need to consider creating collections that were popular from different time periods such as big band music, classic rock, or music and performers from the 1920s as well as other eras.

Furthermore, we need to consider creating or acquiring themed, memory, or reminiscing kits for our library collections. These kits encourage adults 50+ to discuss and share memories about the items within the kit. This creates an excellent social experience and also has cognitive benefits, such as helping with long-term memory (Howarth & Hendry, 2013). The kit can help individuals create stories around the items and build relationships among the group members. Kits typically include six to eight items geared toward a specific theme such as books, videos, photos, and objects. The items can be small and they work best with one item per participant. Craft stores, dollar stores, and other places can provide amazing finds for the kits. The possibilities are endless, so let your imagination soar! The following are some possible ideas for kits:

- Animals: small stuffed animals or plastic toys of dog, cat, turtle, bird, lizard, snake, hamster
- Beach: sand, shovel, pail, shells, suntan lotion, beach towel, beach ball
- Beauty: curlers, brush, comb, mirror, bobby pins, hairnet, makeup, barrette
- Gardening: shovel, trowel, dirt, gloves, seeds, flowerpot
- Holiday: small items for different holidays; ornaments, hearts, U.S. flag, candles, pumpkin, stuffed animal turkey
- School: pencil, pen, eraser, lunchbox, glue, chalk, small chalkboard, ruler
- Tools: screwdriver, hammer, nails, nuts and bolts, wrench, wood

In addition, we need to consider creating an area in the library that will have local, state, and government information and services for our adult 50+ community members. The space can include pamphlets and booklets on health issues, residential information, recreational and educational programs, financial services, and other information that can be helpful. Contact area organizations to provide materials. This can also open doors to future collaborations, as well as providing adults midlife and older the benefit of finding information all in one area of the library.

Depending on our communities, some library members could have English as their second language. This could influence the collection materials and the language offered on the library Web site. Some adults 50+ could have immigrated at various stages in their life and have various literacy skills in English. We need to consider adding collections with diversified materials, informational brochures, and documents in a variety of languages depending on the library community. Reaching out to community organizations to assist in translating the library's basic documents and Web site information can build relationships and encourage new partnerships and library members. The Nashville Public Library in Tennessee has the capability to change their Web site from English to two other languages to support their community members. Patrons can locate the different language links at the top of their Web page at https://library.nashville.org. Creating a Web site translated in another language will encourage all members of the library community to feel welcome, help with English literacy skills as they manipulate the Web site from English to their native language, and support digital literacy skills in their native language.

The following are a couple of examples from contributors to this text of services offered at their libraries.

Brianne Columbo at Fairfield Free Public Library in New Jersey: "The library offers our print collection in alternative formats that is often accommodating to seniors. We have an extensive physical large print collection and audiobook collection, as well as digital services, Hoopla and Overdrive, which offer e-books with font size modification settings, and audiobooks. We also actively promote the services of the New Jersey State Library Talking Book & Braille Center (TBBC), which serves New Jersey residents of all ages whose ability to read may be affected by a physical impairment, a reading disability, and a vision impairment. Seniors with vision or physical impairments may qualify for free services from the state library, including long-term loans of audiobook players and audiobooks."

Elizabeth Eisen, adult programming librarian at Appleton Public Library in Wisconsin: "I work with six retirement homes or apartment complexes to provide books for book discussions and I do monthly or quarterly presentations. These presentations incorporate Bi-Folkal Kits and age-appropriate books. I offer a themed slide show, sing-along (sometimes with my banjo or ukulele), skits, jokes, and crafts."

LIBRARIANS AND STAFF

Librarians and staff are always thinking about the needs of their library patrons and the best way they can reach and provide the right services and programs to meet those needs. We currently have guidelines (see Chapter 1) to assist us in providing services that are appropriate for adults 50+. However, we need to tailor our services to meet the needs of our individual communities and their diverse members. There is not a "one size fits all" (Cooke, 2016). We need to ask questions to become aware of the varying characteristics of our adults 50+ and learn what they want and how to reach them to provide innovative and engaging programs and services. Today's adults 50+ are more active, more involved, and using more technology. Our libraries are where they can engage, connect, learn, and imagine a variety of opportunities and experiences. We need to keep in mind that our libraries can play a pivotal role in helping to meet their informational needs.

Dedicated Position

Consider having a dedicated individual on staff to serve adults 50+. This can be an asset to the overall library team and to the aging community members. This also helps in ensuring that adults 50+ are thought about as a group in our planning and services. Some important aspects this position could undertake would be to become a liaison for the adult midlife and older community members and to the other librarians and staff. In addition, the adult 50+ librarian can develop midlife and older adult programs and services, attend appropriate conferences to stay current on trends, and develop training modules for other staff members.

Readers Advisory

Readers advisory is important to help determine the types of materials a patron is interested in acquiring. Asking questions and listening to community members will assist in providing for the needs and wants of the adult midlife and older patrons. This is especially important for individuals who are homebound or in residential facilities who are utilizing the outreach services at our libraries. Ahlvers (2006) mentions that adults 50+ are appreciative of the attention and service they receive from a librarian, especially because we live in a world that is fast-paced. Being patient, being respectful, and listening to all of our patrons can help us carry out our mission in service to all. It can also develop loyal library users as we satisfy their wants and needs. Readers advisory for adults 50+ is the same as for all of our patrons and, at times, can be outside of the physical library environment. We can talk about books at the reference desk, in the stacks, and on our social media accounts or outside of the library either within their homes or residential facilities or virtually by phone, e-mail, or other messaging formats. We need to consider creating different avenues for the readers advisory, which will provide alternative approaches to initiate conversations with many types of individuals.

Training

Libraries are in a critical position to serve our diverse populations, helping to overcome barriers that affect our library community in accessing and retrieving information. As we think about serving our adult 50+ library patrons, we need to break down stereotypes that can create issues and cause programming and services to not reach all our community members. We currently have many successful children, teen services, and adult programs within our libraries; however, few programs are specifically focused for adults 50+. Most of our adult programming is for individuals 18+ years of age. Some of these programs might not appeal to all of the ages that span at least three generations of individuals. Then there are also some adult 50+ members who do not want to be stereotyped and recognized as "old" within their community and will not attend programs that are specifically for adults 50+. Still others might feel intimidated by younger adults and will not join a program if it is offered to everyone and they feel they will be in the minority of attendees. The first step is to consider staff training workshops, webinars, or attendance at area conferences that have themes on 50+ programs and services. Enhancing our knowledge will help us better understand and serve the needs of this growing community. In addition, we need to survey and talk with our adult 50+ patrons to assist us in creating the types of programs and services they want and need. The following are some contributors' thoughts and some examples of how they keep informed about adults 50+ in their communities.

> *Marie Corbitt at Westerville Public Library in Ohio:* "Go to as many conferences as possible. Talk with other people who are doing or trying to do what you are. It's a great way to brainstorm, collaborate, and get new ideas."

> *Ocean County Library in New Jersey:* "OCL is active with advisory groups that have missions to serve the health and wellness needs of the adults 50+ throughout our county."

> *Yolo County Library Davis in California:* "I attend the Yolo County Healthy Aging Alliance collaborative meetings. It is at these meeting that I share our programs. This has been a big help in getting the word out."

CHAPTER SUMMARY

This chapter looked at the physical library environment and accessibility. Having adults 50+ on library committees can help with important decisions about the accessibility challenges individuals can experience as they age. Providing equipment and technologies that will assist in overcoming barriers to access and retrieve information is essential for a welcoming library environment. Learning about adults 50+ through training and workshops helps us understand the adult 50+ community and assists us in the creation of services and programs. A dedicated position serving adults 50+ ensures the needs and wants of the 50+ community are at the forefront when planning the physical library environment and our adult services and programs.

4

Ready or Not, Here They Come: What about Programming?

Programming for adults 50+ for most libraries typically falls under adult programming. Very few libraries have programming that is intended just for adults midlife and older. Based on the information gathered about the libraries in this text, only some (12%) had programming specifically for adults 50+. This can be due to varying reasons. Some of the contributors stated their patrons did not want to be singled out and would not come to programming that specified an age, whereas other contributors mentioned that, depending on the program, their audiences mostly were adults 50+. Therefore, they did not have to single out adults 50+ because they were already attending that particular program anyway. Surprisingly, some of the libraries only offered one or two programs a month for their adult patrons, and more than half of those libraries only offered a book club, a craft program, or a basic computer class for their adult patrons. Most of the contributing libraries that offered adult programming offered more than two types of programs. On average, five different programs are offered a month, with some libraries offering up to 15 adult programs. However, this number does not take into consideration if the program was repeated during the month.

In this chapter, ideas, suggestions, helpful tips, and some testimonials are included from the contributors to this text. Please keep in mind the following listed programs are offered by many of the libraries and that most contributors gave extra information during the interview process. However, not all information is included due to space limitations.

TIPS AND SUGGESTIONS

The following are some tips, suggestions, and ideas about programming and services for adults 50+.

Know Your Library Community

Knowing your library community will help determine the types of programs and services offered to suit their needs.

Melanie Wehrle at Pikes Peak Library District in Colorado: "While age and experiences growing up affect life expectations, values, and lifestyle, they do not determine when older adults will retire, experience an empty nest, or even when they have the time to participate in library programs. Many remain healthy and active, as well as working and volunteering, well into their 70s and 80s. . . . I have seen how libraries and other organizations use stereotypes of seniors to focus their senior services to only those who are elderly, frail, or disabled. The older adult demographic today includes a much wider group of individuals with varied sets of abilities, needs, and preferences . . . they do not want to be called 'senior' and . . . they will not attend programs identified as for only seniors."

Carroll County (MD) Public Library in Maryland: "Asks questions such as, How can we uplift the quality of the lives of our elderly residents through library services, collections, and programs? How can we serve the elderly community despite financial challenges to do more for other age groups? and How can library staffers develop pragmatic skills and a can-do attitude to think creatively to up the ante in serving seniors in our community? These types of questions help guide our services."

Tracy Trotter, library director at Adams Memorial Library in Pennsylvania: "I sincerely believe there isn't much need to target seniors as a distinct population. Just because someone gets older, doesn't mean their tastes change. If they liked history as a youth, they will continue to like it in later life. If crafts are enjoyable to them when they are 45, they will still be enjoyable at 65."

Listen to Your Library Community

Talking with our patrons formally and informally can help us gather information for future programs and services.

Richard Conroy at Essex Library Association in Connecticut: "It is extremely important to listen to your patrons to gain clues as to what their needs are. The casual conversations that take place at the Service Desk are an excellent means of doing so. For example, one of our regular patrons who had recently lost her partner was chatting with one of our staff members and mentioned that she was struggling with her loss, but was not religious, and was uncomfortable with the concept of formal grief counseling. That led the staff member (who happened to be the person who develops our adult programs) to contact the hospital hospice program, which, in turn, led to the creation of our highly popular drop-in Bereavement Counseling program. The takeaway is to listen first, think about how to meet an expressed need, and then develop an appropriate program that includes the use of partners and collaborators in the community if necessary."

Elizabeth Eisen, adult programming librarian at Appleton Public Library in Wisconsin: "If someone approaches staff regarding a four-part series with different topics, start with one program so you can gauge audience interest and speaker performance."

Kathleen Handy, computer instructor at Saratoga Springs Public Library in New York: "I think the success of the computer program, in particular, is that we modify classes to meet current needs. For instance, we started offering classes on iPads and iPhones over the past four years due to strong demand. MS Excel is another class that always draws lots of participants, so we increased that offering. . . . We listen to suggestions patrons have regarding classes to offer, as well."

Meryle A. Leonard at Charlotte Mecklenburg Library in North Carolina: "Before you jump into programs giving people what you think they want or need, take time to build a relationship, get to know them, and ask them what they want. Advising a 'KISS' approach: Keep It Sweet and Simple. Some of the best received programs have been the simplest ones."

Make an Impact

There are times when certain programs and services that are offered can make a difference in the lives of library patrons.

Fife Lake Public Library in Michigan: "A couple short stories on how important our senior programming is, . . . We hosted a presentation . . . after one of our luncheons, 'Keeping Your Aging Skin Healthy.' One of the attendees went to visit her dermatologist after she had some concerns from information she received at the presentation. She did have skin cancer. They were able to treat her and she is fine thanks to the information she received, . . . One of our seniors' husband had recently suffered a stroke. The stroke left him struggling to walk without assistance from a walker. We were having a special entertainer . . . playing her guitar and singing favorites of the past. Gradually, many of the seniors began to get up and dance to a favorite oldie. This couple also joined in with him being held up by his wife. It was such a touching moment. When they sat down, the wife leaned over to a friend and with tearful eyes whispered, 'I didn't think we would be ever able to do that again.'"

Programs for All Adults

Most of the contributing libraries, because of their community's needs, do not have programs for adults 50+ and instead provide programming for all age groups. Some of the libraries do not specifically target adults 50+ because attendance would be low for the program.

Lisa C. West at Homewood Public Library in Alabama: "I do the Adult Programming for all adults without often purposely segmenting 'senior' programming. Everyone who is an adult is free to attend."

Chad Robinson at Matheson Memorial Library in Wisconsin: "We don't really target adult programs to a specific age group, but the vast majority of our attendees are over 50."

New Durham Public Library in New Hampshire: "No programs are specifically for that age group; we have many programs that are labeled 'Adult,' but all ages are welcome. Traditionally, any program offered for that age group does not garner participants."

Use Staff as Presenters

Utilizing staff as presenters can be cost effective and can sometimes showcase a hidden talent, or a surprising program develops with a little investigating and imagination from other library staff members.

Meryle A. Leonard at Charlotte Mecklenburg Library in North Carolina: "Look internally at staff or volunteers who may be interested in offering a program. This could include sharing cultures, enlisting the help of a technology guru or an undercover chef who will offer healthy eating or cooking classes."

Melany Wilks at Pioneer Memorial Library in Kansas: "I have found that staff have been thrilled to put their gifting and abilities to work for serving and increasing the library programing. This has been in the area of computer classes, just add color, science fiction book club, and cell phone and tablet training. It adds a bit to the budget without breaking the bank, or it redirects maybe less than useful hours to something that helps us reach our goals."

Presenters Other Than Library Staff

Besides library staff, we need to look at our library patrons and the community to increase the types of programs that we can offer.

Simsbury Public Library in Connecticut: "This was a four-part program over the span of two Saturdays. . . . The second Saturday was also Connecticut Open House Day, a statewide tourism initiative, and the programs that day were part of that event as well. The first Saturday had a lecture by a local historian . . . followed by a guided hike. . . . The second Saturday began with a Teddy Roosevelt re-enactor . . . followed by a lecture by the CT Forest & Park Association . . . Another local historian gave a slide show . . . and following a lunch . . . in the 1820 House, we took a guided tour of the house. . . . We paid for the food using money from the Friends of the Simsbury Public Library. We secured a grant from CT Humanities . . . to cover honoraria, travel expenses for our re-enactor, and three large posters for the library and town hall."

Program Length and Scheduling

Scheduling a program at the right time and at the right length to garner enough attendees and keep their interest can be tricky. Consider offering the same program on different days, at different times, and even in a different month. This will enable all types of adults 50+ to come to the program. Keep in mind, there are adults 50+ who continue to work and will not be able to come during the day, and there are also adults 50+ who are retired and would rather meet earlier in the day. Many contributing libraries agreed about adjusting the time schedule of a program.

Having a secondary time may bring in individuals who might not normally come to the library programs due to the time constraints.

Athol Public Library in Massachusetts: "We sometimes adjust the times of our programs if we think the program will be of interest to older patrons."

Tamar Kreke, adult and technical services coordinator at Greene County Public Library in Ohio: "Seniors typically don't attend programs at night (they may not feel as comfortable driving at night)."

Try! Try! Again!

Just because a program did not have enough patrons to warrant interest does not mean next time the same number will be in attendance.

Lisa Prizio: "It is interesting that about five years ago we tried to start a knitting group and no one attended. We hired an assistant . . . and let her try again. . . . For whatever reason, it worked the second time."

Services and Thoughts

When examining our services for adults 50+, we need to think about our community's interests and the challenges they can face in accessing information to determine what best suits their needs. We can also offer special services to adults 50+ such as reduced or no fines.

Dan Hubbs at Saratoga Springs Public Library in New York: "Many services for seniors are more obvious, but should be noted. For instance, do we have the books and movies and other materials that seniors are looking for? Is the lighting in the building sufficient? Are the materials shelved in a way that people can easily access them? How is the seating? Is there access to the building for people with mobility issues? And so on."

Mary at Wilbraham Public Library in Massachusetts: "One service we offer once patrons turn 60 is no fines on overdue books. They still pay fines on videos and best-sellers."

PROGRAM THEMES

One important thing to remember when developing programming for our midlife and older adult community is to change, grow, and adapt to the library members' needs. Lear (2013) mentions how adults 50+ are more educated and healthier than previous generations. They are interested in meaningful work and in staying connected to their communities. Having a variety of programming and services will help fulfill our library's mission and can foster more library patrons in the future.

Look to many different resources for ideas and inspiration. We can gather ideas through our library staff. Some are communicating with patrons on a daily basis, giving a picture of what the community is reading, requesting, listening to, and viewing. Also, some staff could be of similar age (50+), inspiring different ideas as well. Network! Network! Network! Our peers are a font of information of creative ideas. A nearby library might exchange a staff member to come and present a program in exchange for a staff member at that library doing a class at their facility. Be creative and try new things. Some might work; others might not. The worst thing that happens is the program was not successful. However, the program could work in the future, so try not to cross it off the list. Offer it at a new time during the day or evening, change portions of it, or wait and offer it at a different time of the year. Many factors play a role in the success of a program. We have some great resources from the American Library Association "Keys to Engaging Older Adults @ Your Library" toolkit that gives advice on programming for adults 50+, and ALA Library Services to an Aging Population has *21 Ideas for the 21st Century*. Appendix B has these links and other resource links for further inspiration.

The following are some excellent ideas and tips to help inspire and perhaps encourage us to explore new avenues or expand our current offerings for adults and adults 50+ given from our library peers who contributed to this text.

Antiques and Collectibles

Consider having professional speakers or patrons who can talk of their expertise on different aspects of antiques and collectibles. In addition, many adults 50+ enjoy collecting and would like to share their collections (stamp collections, model trains, coins, etc.) with others.

This creates the opportunity for a wide range of topics and social interactions for adults 50+ and can possibly establish a new enthusiast on collecting in the younger generations.

- Restoration and preservation.
- Maintaining a collection.
- Value of items. (This could have a small fee depending on speaker or dealer.)
- Viewing different types of collections.

Arts and Crafts

Some adults midlife and older have a craft they love to do and share with other patrons. Different types of craft programs, however, can sometimes have a small fee for materials. This is usually not a deterrent because the attendees will be bringing home what is made. Having patrons pay the fee is good for the library budget too! In addition, consider asking for donations of craft supplies. Many adults 50+ have extra items in their homes they would love to give to a worthy endeavor. Many libraries have different craft clubs (knitting, crocheting, sewing, quilting, etc.) that meet weekly. This can be physically, cognitively, and socially beneficial for adults 50+ (McFadden & Basting, 2010), as well as creating intergenerational opportunities for learning and exchanging among attendees.

Adult coloring. Consider adding adult coloring as a program or just as a social event at the library. Coloring can have some health benefits, such as lessening anxiety in adults, and invites creativity as well as creating social connections.

Coffee and coloring club. Jenneffer Sixkiller: "I've had a great and regular turnout of mostly seniors. . . . I choose a different 'theme' . . . making photocopies from coloring books . . . and . . . pages from the Web. I purchased several sets of markers, colored pencils and pens, which are only used for the coloring club. I push together six tables, to make one long rectangle, put the coloring supplies in the middle, lay out coloring sheets at each seat, plug in the pencil sharpener, bring in . . . coffee . . . and pull up meditation music or instrumental music playlists on YouTube to pipe in."

Just add color. Melany Wilks at Pioneer Memorial Library in Kansas: "Drawing an over 50+ to 90-year-old crowd. We have one family of older children (over 50) bringing their father to the event. Together they color, talk, and fellowship with each other and others that attend. They say that it helps make sure that they are taking time with Dad and gets him to exercise his mind and function better."

Felt bags shaped like Yoda for Star Wars day. *Tracy Trotter, library director at Adams Memorial Library in Pennsylvania:* "The craft . . . can be demonstrated in a series of steps . . . can be completed in an hour and a half; is not extremely messy to transport home; does not cost a great deal to make . . . minimal assistance . . . and will allow the people to go home with something attractive and . . . a skill they can duplicate if they enjoyed it. . . . We also try to create an example of each month's craft to have sitting out at the circulation desk. . . . Seeing a craft on a poster is fine but seeing the actual finished result is even better."

Book Clubs and Authors

Consider having a variety of book clubs such as different genres (classics, history, romance, etc.) or a book club for a certain age group. Keep in mind that an adult book group could have someone who is age 18 and also someone who is age 68. That is a difference of 50 years, which could affect discussions, meanings, and interpretations. Some libraries have started book clubs specifically for adults midlife and older, as well as having ones with varying ages. Having an opportunity to engage with peers who might understand their challenges and references can create a more comfortable opportunity for some adults 50+ in your library. Also, consider having a book club in other locations around the community or, for the tech-savvy patrons, book discussions on the Internet or utilizing social media as part of the book club. Additionally, we can use many different facilitators for book clubs such as staff, patrons, and authors, who can be a nice low-cost or free option for the library.

Author events. Consider having popular, local, and unknown authors to garner interest and discussions on various topics.

Author programs. Ocean County Library in New Jersey: This can entail having an author present on a book recently published or having a monthly program featuring local authors in the community.

Author talks. Kathleen Handy, computer instructor at Saratoga Springs Public Library in New York: This can encompass panel discussions that can include three to four authors focusing on a theme such as local history, aging in place, or even authors in a certain genre. For instance, have a panel of mystery authors and discuss plot inspirations.

Book signings. John J. Trause, director at Oradell Public Library in New Jersey: "Picture This: For Your Eyes and Ears, reading, Q&A, and book signing."

Book clubs. *Mariel Carter, adult service reference librarian at Marinette County Consolidated Public Library Services in Wisconsin:* "Hosts two book clubs each month. One meets in the afternoon during the week and the other meets in the evening. . . . Each book club chooses their own books based on input from group members with the guidelines that there must be enough copies of the book in the library system . . . and the books must be old enough that they are not in high demand. . . . I find discussion questions online and tweak them for my group's use. I also try to pick books that are available on audiobook and in large print for people who are more comfortable reading larger text or like to listen to books."

Bookworms. Beth Neunaber: "A retired librarian . . . facilitates the . . . book discussion group."

Senior book club. Brianne Columbo at Fairfield Free Public Library in New Jersey: "Once a month in the afternoon, our adult events coordinator hosts a book club specifically for seniors."

Book club in a bar. Heather Johnson at River Falls Public Library in Wisconsin: "A very popular book discussion group." This entails having a book discussion at a local establishment outside of the physical library environment.

Cooking. Tracy Trotter, library director at Adams Memorial Library in Pennsylvania: "We ran a book club where instead of fiction, people checked out cookbooks. They read through the books and gave a review of how well-designed the books were, how easy they seemed to be to use, etc. In addition to their review, they were asked to bring in a sample recipe for the others to try. We themed each week with a different course."

Non-fiction book club. Elizabeth Eisen, adult programming librarian at Appleton Public Library in Wisconsin: This type of book group was led by two patrons that discussed various non-fiction books. Past titles include *Ike's Bluff: President Eisenhower's Secret Battle to Save the World* by Evan Thomas and *Blind Man's Bluff: The Untold Story of American Submarine Espionage* by Sherry Sontag.

Not your mama's book club. Lisa C. West at Homewood Public Library in Alabama: "Instead of all reading the same book, you get to do it your way . . . read a book or an article, listen to a podcast or an interview, or watch a documentary and then discuss."

Short story discussion group. Dan Hubbs at Saratoga Springs Public Library in New York: "The short story discussion group I lead is made up primarily of seniors and retired community members."

Summer reading club. Anonymous: A typical summer reading program encompasses children at the library. An adult summer reading program will promote adult literacy and encourage adults to interact more with the library. Consider having patrons write book reviews, having prizes, or creating workshops that adults can attend. The objective is for the adults to have fun reading as much as the children during the summer months.

Business

Consider contacting local businesses such as a local bank or a grocery store. These businesses can offer different types of programs, such as financial planning when you lose a spouse or stretching money in retirement.

Identity theft. *Kathleen Goodson at Wimberley Village Library in Texas:* "Presented by representatives of a local bank. Participants learned the warning signs of identity theft, what to do first if information is lost or stolen, and how to begin to repair the damage if it does happen."

Career Development

Some adults midlife and older are starting second careers. However, some have not constructed a résumé in a long while or need assistance when looking for employment.

Employment. *Simsbury Public Library in Connecticut:* "Job help for those who have lost a job, are looking for a new job, or are starting a new business, often people 50+who are experiencing unemployment for the first time." This program was presented by a career counselor examining age, career transitions, and employment gaps, providing insights and strategies to overcome challenges and achieve success.

Résumé strategies. *Terry Soave at Ann Arbor District Library in Michigan:* This program is part of a career development workshop, which encompasses making a professional résumé. Check out local career centers, work agencies, or universities for possible collaborations and resources.

Civic and Community Events

Consider collaborating with community partners and create forums about events or political issues, which allows for different views and perspectives to be expressed about a variety of subjects and also can be an avenue to learning about different cultures and issues within a safe environment. Additionally, some libraries organize bus trips to local businesses or special events within their community. Possible trips could include holiday shopping; nature tours to parks, preserves, or conservatories; trips to local museums; or local sporting events.

Civility speaks. *Mariel Carter, adult service reference librarian at Marinette County Consolidated Public Library Services in Wisconsin:* "Coordinated with a UW-Extension agent to help facilitate and lead the discussion, we pick discussion guides from pre-existing free guides like the National Issues Forum, or bring in specialists from the community. . . . We rely on the civility guidelines as outlined by the Civility Project to make sure that everyone listens with an open mind and everyone speaks with respect. The evenings start with an informal social and snacks; discussion takes up no more than 90 minutes. Prep work on this can be time consuming, but it is a very rewarding program to see people finding agreement and seeing another side of an issue. . . . Cost is minimal."

Chocolate and all that jazz. *Melany Wilks at Pioneer Memorial Library in Kansas states this program* "is a free community event that celebrates Valentine's Day. . . . The college jazz band and the college singers are the entertainers so it draws across the generations."

Civic engagement community service projects. *Meryle A. Leonard at Charlotte Mecklenburg Library in North Carolina:* "These projects are a great way for participants to make community connections and feel connected to their community. During this program, items are created for such groups as Chemo Caps, Project Linus, Quilts of Valor." Appropriate links can be found for these organizations in Appendix B.

Field trips to local events. *Fife Lake Public Library in Michigan:* "Annual bus trip to Comerica Park for Tiger Baseball games and Senior Expo in Traverse City."

Cooking

Some adults 50+ enjoy sharing recipes and trying new food creations. Consider professional chefs to teach how to roll sushi or practice knife skills. This also could be an area to learn about different cultural foods or a place for intergenerational learning for teens to learn basic cooking skills from culinary skilled adults.

Death and Dying

As we age, the prospect of our death or death of a family member or friend becomes more of a reality. Creating programs that deal with these sensitive subjects can help support adults 50+ with these challenges.

Bereavement counseling. *Richard Conroy at Essex Library Association in Connecticut:* "A drop-in Bereavement Counseling program that meets twice a month and is moderated by a chaplain for the hospice program at a local hospital."

Grief 101: What to expect when grieving. *Terry Soave at Ann Arbor District Library in Michigan:* This program was presented by Arbor Hospice's Grief Support Services, providing information and resources to cope with a loss of a loved one.

Discussions

Discussions can range from films, to political issues, to community forums, or to topics. Providing a meeting room and sometimes a moderator to keep discussions running smoothly can be helpful.

Film discussion. *Greenwood County Library System in South Carolina:* "The headquarters library offered a film discussion program this past winter." This event entailed viewing and discussing films around a given theme. For instance, the theme of the American Revolution in South Carolina with the film *The Patriot*, or the County Reads program themed, "The Distance between Us," with the following film screenings, *Tortilla Soup* and *Bless Me, Ultima.*

Great Decisions discussion group. *Matthew Riley at Friendswood Public Library in Texas:* Great Decisions is America's largest discussion program on world affairs. More information can be found on the Foreign Policy Association Web site at http://www.fpa.org/great_decisions/.

Books sandwiched in. *Leslie DeLooze, community services librarian at Richmond Memorial Library in New York:* "Features community speakers talking about new books or about books selected around a specific theme. . . . A committee looks for possible books and speakers and contacts them about three to four months prior to each series. . . . The time was selected to enable working adults to attend during their lunch hour, although the vast majority . . . are retirees. Coffee, tea, and cookies are served; participants are encouraged to bring their own sandwich. The programs are video-recorded, and DVDs are available in the library for borrowing."

Current events. *Simsbury Public Library in Connecticut:* "A series of programs on faith in the 21st century, programs, and community conversations on current topics such as immigration."

Eldercare

Many adults 50+ are taking care of their parents either at home or utilizing assisted living facilities and nursing homes. Consider offering programs and resources on caregiving to help individuals understand the challenges and the assistance that is available within the community.

Elder law workshop. *Debbi Gallucci:* This program entails having an attorney and counselor at law providing information about powers of attorney, living trusts, long-term care, healthcare proxies, and estate and financial planning. This information is important for individuals or caregivers who are making decisions for an aging person.

Estate Planning

A will is not enough in Oregon. *Adrienne Doman Calkins at Sherwood Public Library in Oregon:* "This program is one we offer about twice a year. The audience is often a mix of Baby Boomers, retirees, and new parents. It is presented by [an] attorney . . . free of charge . . . covering a variety of topics from wills to trusts and more. He provides one free hour of consultation to attendees by appointment, which ends up bolstering his business."

Getting the last word: Writing your own obituary. *Kathleen Goodson at Wimberley Village Library in Texas:* "Presented by a journalist whose career began by writing obituaries. This was a two-hour workshop for those who wanted to be remembered accurately."

Exercise

Offering a variety of fitness programs to keep healthy and active provides adults 50+ an alternative to stay physically fit at little or no cost.

All abilities chair exercises. *Kathleen Goodson at Wimberley Village Library in Texas:* "Classes that include breathing techniques, gentle strengthening exercises, and mild yoga stretches, all from a seated position or with the aid of a chair. . . . It is funded by our library and from used book sales."

Senior strength training. *Brianne Columbo at Fairfield Free Public Library in New Jersey:* "Held by a certified instructor. The library provides a safe space for seniors to warm up, learn and complete circuits, and cool down."

T'ai chi: Meditation in motion. *Kristi Haman:* "Reduces stress and increases balance and flexibility. This gentle martial art is offered by a trained instructor."

Bend and stretch. *Kelly Martin Laney at Birmingham Public Library in Alabama:* "Based on the National Institute on Aging's Go4Life program. Using the booklets provided (at no cost) volunteers or staff lead seniors through a gentle exercise routine, primarily sitting in chairs, to promote strength, flexibility, balance, and endurance. . . . Participants are cautioned to move slowly and to not extend any movement to the point of pain. We have a posted disclaimer stating that the program is led by volunteers who are not certified physical fitness trainers. . . . The exercise lasts for approximately 45 minutes, followed by a short period where participants can enjoy a cup of tea together."

Line dancing. *Simsbury Public Library in Connecticut:* "We held a line dancing class that was attended by children and their parents and seniors."

Films

Providing a venue to view movies can be an engaging way to bring intergenerational programming into our libraries. It is important to obtain a public performance license before having a film screening unless the film has public performance rights. When considering whether to get a license, contact the state library or state library organization for eligibility for a reduced rate in obtaining a license.

Weekly movie. *Quincy Public Library in Illinois:* "We choose movies that we think will be of interest, and supply popcorn and soda."

British mystery nights. *Tracy Trotter, library director at Adams Memorial Library in Pennsylvania:* "We watched the first episode of several TV series . . . that were in our collection. Then, if people liked the series, they could continue watching the rest by checking out the DVDs."

Classic movie night. *Matthew Riley at Friendswood Public Library in Texas:* "A large percentage of films selected are on the National Film Registry list. We subscribe to two licensing companies and search their databases to ensure we have the right to show selected films. We serve light refreshments. A library staff member will research the film and will provide a short introduction prior to the screening. We also have a film history trivia contest prior to the film and donated prizes are given to the winners. . . . Classic Movie Night (now called Friendswood Library Flicks) has been very successful and has created a social group of classic film enthusiasts who arrive as much as one hour before film time to discuss old and new movies."

Coffee and classics. *Muncie Public Library in Indiana:* "We have a 'Coffee and Classics' series . . . the first and third Fridays of each month, . . . It is not explicitly marketed to seniors, but it is in the middle of the day and features old movies, so that is our target audience. We provide coffee and popcorn . . . we also feature give-aways of donated books, . . . The movies are in our collection, and we have a movie license that covers the showings. The popcorn, coffee, and other supplies are covered by the library's regular programming budget, . . . Preparation is simply to develop a calendar of titles, produce a poster, place a hold on the film, and set the room up and show the film."

Gaming

Games in the library, such as video games, board games, and card games, are another form of providing information, stories, and entertainment to our patrons. Games can also provide literacy skills and educate individuals within a different format. Besides just putting games on a shelf, encourage card or board games at library tables by setting aside one specifically for games. Consider hosting intergenerational gaming nights and having experts explain different types of games and talk about strategies.

House of cards challenge. *Kate Skinner:* "Donated family games . . . as the prizes. Families and groups of mixed ages challenged other groups to build the best house of cards. Packs of cards were acquired free . . . from the nearby . . . casino."

Learn to play Mah-Jongg (an Asian, multi-player card game). *Terry Soave at Ann Arbor District Library in Michigan.*

Bridge card game. *Richard Conroy at Essex Library Association Connecticut.*

Bagels and Bingo. *Debbi Gallucci.*

Wii bowling tournament. *Tracy Trotter, library director at Adams Memorial Library in Pennsylvania:* "One of our more successful intergenerational programs . . . we registered teams of two players, one of which had to be 18 or younger and the other had to be 55 or older."

BrainHQ database. *Mary at Wilbraham Public Library in Massachusetts:* "We have a handful of databases that are of particular interest to seniors, including BrainHQ, which has games to keep your brain active and prevent cognitive decline."

Senior game day. *Beth Neunaber:* "All over 55 were welcome. We had tables set up for various games, including a bridge expert, who taught people to play bridge. We also had Wii set up for bowling. . . . We do now offer an assortment of games that people may check out and use in the library."

Live-action Clue. *Tracy Trotter, library director at Adams Memorial Library in Pennsylvania:* "As in the board game, players moved from room to room, but in this case the rooms were sections of the library such as the magazine area, the reference section, biographies, and fiction . . . the weapons were real-world objects from the library: a metal bookend, some poisoned White-Out correction fluid, a very heavy book, etc. The suspects were all famous mystery writers . . ."

Trivia game. *Melany Wilks at Pioneer Memorial Library in Kansas:* "Draws intergenerational participation."

Gardening

This type of programming can be an excellent opportunity for collaborations with a local gardening club, nurseries, and garden enthusiasts. Utilize books in the collection, and have attendees share tips and trade plants. Some libraries have even started a seed library where community members share and swap seeds.

> **How to build a better garden—fall garden planning.** *Lisa C. West at Homewood Public Library in Alabama:* "Once a month on various Saturdays we meet with Master Gardeners who will teach an hour program on various timely topics."

Health

Health topics are one of the top searches on the Internet by adults 50+ (Zickuhr, 2010). Consider topics such as diet and nutrition, heart health, stress, cancer, diabetes, and choosing a doctor. It is also important to address effective searching for health information online. Having health literacy programs on searching the Internet can be beneficial to find what is needed and to identify trusted sources.

> **Protein, carbs, and fats: Where do you get yours?** *Terry Soave at Ann Arbor District Library in Michigan:* This program examined dietary sources for a raw vegan diet given by a certified yoga teacher.

> **Wilderness hiking: Think globally, hike locally.** *Santa Barbara Public Library in California:* "Designed to encourage adults to get outside and enjoy the natural world while getting some exercise, which is good for mental health and physical health. . . . We have speakers on a variety of topics. . . . The California Coastal Trail: Oregon to Mexico in 96 days; Healthy People, Healthy Trails; Hiking the Northern Channel Islands; Historic Chumash Trails; How Not to Get Lost in the Woods; Ultralight Backpacking. . . . All speakers are volunteer."

History and Genealogy

Genealogy is a top hobby for many individuals, especially for adults midlife and older. Some possible examples to consider can be programs and resources on local history, how to navigate popular ancestry Web sites, or even how to begin looking for information. The Reference and User Services Association, a division of the American Library Association, offers guidelines and resources on their Web site. Some libraries have started memoir writing or recordings. This is when an oral history of a life event is recorded, such as the Veterans History Project. More information can be found on their Web site (see Appendix B). In addition, consider collaborating with a local historical society and have a guest speaker talk about local events or people, or ask if they have a traveling display. This can create ideas for new programs where adults 50+ can talk about their own experiences during a certain time period.

> **Genealogy discussion group.** *Mariel Carter, adult service reference librarian at Marinette County Consolidated Public Library Services in Wisconsin:* "Although

the reference librarian presents at some of these meetings, members of the group often bring their expertise to present different topics to the group. Topics covered include organizing genealogy research, using Ancestry.com, making a family newsletter, planning a family reunion, the usefulness of cemetery data, and findings from research trips."

Genealogy and local history presentation and workshop. *Muncie Public Library in Indiana:* "May include some sort of visual aid or slide presentation . . . hands-on, or sharing activity along with the speaker presentation."

Historical portrayals. *Tracy Trotter, library director at Adams Memorial Library in Pennsylvania:* "This month we are hosting a man who portrays General Ulysses S. Grant."

Local history. *Dan Hubbs at Saratoga Springs Public Library in New York:* "Many of our daytime programs are geared toward seniors, our very popular local history programs draw 100-plus folks on a regular basis." The Brown Bag Lunch Lecture Series is a program in collaboration with the Saratoga Springs Heritage Area Visitor Center, which focuses on local history. Past programs include discussions on the Saratoga Mineral Baths; Crime, Corruption, and Gambling, as well as Lillian Russell and Diamond Jim Brady. Special speakers including historians, local residents, and authors have presented the various programs.

Oral history. *Meryle A. Leonard at Charlotte Mecklenburg Library in North Carolina:* "Participants are interviewed and get to tell their story and leave their legacy. Those who share their information receive a DVD, and their stories are added to the North Carolina Room's archive collection. One participant shared she thoroughly appreciated being heard and she felt important."

Walking history. Consider having a library-led tour that involves local history, sightseeing, and walking around the community. This can encompass research, book, or film discussions, as well as a walking history tour to bring the stories to life. This type of program encourages mental and physical health for the participants as well as integrating different collaborators within your community.

Explore state history. *Meryle A. Leonard at Charlotte Mecklenburg Library in North Carolina:* "Participants get to dig deep into local history with resources from Main Library's North Carolina Room. They learn how information gleaned from personal belongings, government archives, and buried artifacts can paint vivid images of the past. This program contains premade kits on subjects such as Archeology: Buried History of NC and Hands-On History."

Holidays

Jingle all the way—Christmas songs and stories of the season with storyteller. *Lisa C. West at Homewood Public Library in Alabama:* "The storyteller [and] musical master mix traditional carols, jolly songs, and sweet stories to fill your holiday with spirit. . . . The library pays the storyteller and musician and the lighting person. We have this event catered as well but with [a] light hors d'oeuvres buffet instead of a meal. . . . Patrons pay $25 per ticket."

Holiday open house. *Heather Johnson at River Falls Public Library in Wisconsin:* "Features musical performances, holiday crafts, demonstrations by local organizations and businesses, and activities for all ages. This year we also had a local celebrity (who herself is 97 years old) and cookbook author at the event for a meet-and-greet and book signing."

Makerspace

Consider having a space within your library where people can gather to be creative. This can be a DIY project, sharing ideas to invent new projects, or offer resources such as a 3D printer, hardware, or craft supplies. A makerspace can be in any area of the library and can be as big or as small as you want it. Public Libraries Online (2017) has excellent links to different articles, and publisher Libraries Unlimited provides many useful books on makerspaces. See Appendix B for appropriate Web sites.

Make programming kits. *Melanie Wehrle at Pikes Peak Library District in Colorado:* "The makerspaces maintain traveling Make Programming kits that can be requested by the branches to offer classes. . . . Some of the kits are Fiber (knitting, crocheting, and weaving), Wood Burning, Mobile Kitchen, Robots, Snap Circuits, Sewing, and Jewelry. Branches only need to supply the space, including floor or table covers; staff time to supervise; and any consumables such as paper, fabric, and wood."

Maker Mondays. *Heather Johnson at River Falls Public Library in Wisconsin:* "Each month the library features an assortment of both high-tech and low-tech and no-tech maker projects that are family-friendly, hands-on activities in a pop-up makerspace environment. The adult-and-family-focused program takes place . . . with staff instruction and support along with a healthy snack and coffee included."

Medicare

Many libraries are providing assistance and guidance to patrons in navigating healthcare options. Providing seminars with featured speakers and trained professionals can help adults 50+ with their medical decisions. The Centers for Medicare & Medicaid Services provides a library toolkit to assist librarians in sharing information about Medicaid, Medicare, and other programs. More information can be found on their Web site (see Appendix B).

Medicare educational seminars. *Kathleen Goodson at Wimberley Village Library in Texas:* ". . . presented about three times a year. Facilitated by Medicare experts that help seniors understand and make informed decisions about Medicare."

National Events

There are a number of national events that we can celebrate in a variety of ways, depending on how big or small you want to make the program.

National Library Week. Consider having programs to celebrate libraries. This is generally held the second full week in April.

The Big Read. This program is designed to revitalize the role of reading and encourages individuals of all ages to come together, read, and discuss a single book.

One Book, One Town. *Debra DeJonker-Berry at Eastham Public Library in Massachusetts:* "Having said that our programs are well-attended by the over-50 age group, we have recognized that there are unique challenges facing adults as they age . . . this year's . . . is focusing on Aging in Place. In addition to the book itself, we always include a series of programs . . . addressing issues such as fraud, medicine, and legal issues."

National Puzzle Day. *Athol Public Library in Massachusetts:* "January 29 is National Puzzle Day, so we . . . have multiple tables of puzzles for a few weeks. People of all ages seem to enjoy spending varying amounts of time putting in a piece or many pieces. We also circulate puzzles and have accumulated a large collection just by asking for donations. Many older people are enjoying this large collection . . ."

Performers

Consider providing different types of performances such as music, singers, and theater groups. These can range from local students from area schools; patrons with musical talents; formal concerts; hands-on workshops; poets, singers, or instrumental performances; theater groups; reenactments; or dancers. Programs can vary depending on budget and the styles of music preferred by the community.

Music: Monthly friends coffeehouse. *Simsbury Public Library in Connecticut:* ". . . a variety of artists."

Music and memory. *Debbi Gallucci:* "Utilizes music therapy to help caregivers reconnect with their loved ones who are affected by dementia. . . . The caregivers are able to borrow an iPod shuffle which is loaded with a customized music playlist for their loved one. They can borrow it for as long as they need it. . . . It was an initial investment of $1,000 to purchase 10 iPods, headphones, and an iTunes account . . . we've had to purchase additional iTune cards to expand the music library to accommodate a wider range of music interests."

Mystery dinner theater. *Lisa C. West at Homewood Public Library in Alabama:* "Every year, we partner with a professional theater group here in town who puts on a play here at our library. We arrange for a local caterer to provide a full-course buffet meal . . . with the show following . . . Tickets are $30 for the buffet and show. . . . We pay the theater group, and the caterer, but usually end up making money on this event. We repeat this dinner theatre program in February and have a romantic-comedy in honor of Valentine's Day."

Poetry. *Melany Wilks at Pioneer Memorial Library in Kansas:* "Our Poetry Group draws mostly over 50+ for writing and sharing poetry. I have a leader who is over 50 and is a retired teacher."

Re-enactors. *Kathleen Handy, computer instructor at Saratoga Springs Public Library in New York:* "Visiting and sharing information." For instance, an event was held to remember veterans, and a local patron dressed up in WWII-era clothing and spoke at the event.

The arts: Old time radio show. *Simsbury Public Library in Connecticut:* "Put on by a local theater group."

Theatrical presentations. *Athol Public Library in Massachusetts:* This program entails performances given by a local theater company that involves stories, entertainment, and dialogue between the cast and the audience after the performance.

Photography group. *Lisa Prizio:* "No age required, but all are over 50."

Retirement

Consider having programs that adults 50+ can encounter before and after retirement. Various topics such as benefit calculations, investing, Social Security, and other valuable information can assist patrons in their finances and plan for unexpected events.

Mistakes 99% of retirees make when applying for Social Security benefits. *Lisa C. West at Homewood Public Library in Alabama:* "A local financial advisor with 30 years' experience. . . . Learn if you can retire and when, as well as filing strategies to maximize Social Security benefits."

Science

Programs on different science topics can include science experiments, hands-on activities, or information about our solar system. Consider collaborating with a local museum or university to bring in speakers or demonstrators on various science topics.

Lunch on the lawn—Solar eclipse. *Leslie DeLooze, community services librarian at Richmond Memorial Library in New York:* "For all ages, where participants will receive protective glasses, instructions on use, and information about eclipses."

Observe the moon night. *Simsbury Public Library in Connecticut:* "At a local private school's observatory, programs on astronomy presented by a local university professor."

Special Topic Speakers

Presenters on different or unusual topics can spark interest and gain new attendees, depending on their popularity, such as ghost hunting or penny pincher ideas.

Tracy Trotter, library director at Adams Memorial Library in Pennsylvania: "One of our most popular speakers is a man who is a paranormal expert. He speaks on UFOs, Bigfoot, ghosts."

Stories and Storytelling

Storytelling can connect the past to the future by recounting family memories, tales, and legends. This can also be a good cultural event. Some immigrants and refugees of diverse backgrounds can recount oral stories and tales that have been passed down through the generations. This can also be an excellent intergenerational project connecting teens and adults 50+. Stories can be digitally preserved utilizing social media, podcasts, video and audio recordings, or other online systems and software to help maintain history for future generations.

Adult story time. *Beth Neunaber:* "We are beginning an adult story time, where seniors for an assisted living group will be coming to listen to short stories read by staff. We are starting small . . . and will tailor the reading selections to the interests of the group. The participants have Alzheimer's. . . . We plan to monitor this, and perhaps open additional adult readings to other adult care facilities."

Technology

Technology is a big part of today's society. Computer classes can include basic use of computers to privacy and safety on the Internet. Being aware of keeping our personal information safe, viruses, scams, privacy, and more is important for adults 50+ with more information becoming available online. Additional information and programming ideas can be found in Chapter 5.

Basic computer class. *Beth Neunaber:* "Introduces people to using a computer, setting up e-mail, using a mouse, common terms, and tips and tricks to searching the Internet. Though this program is not limited to 50+, most attendees are in that age range."

Computer classes. *Greenwood County Library System in South Carolina:* "The Reference staff teaches the computer classes . . . the librarian teaching it sets up the auditorium with tables and chairs, sets up the laptops and places handouts at each seat."

Online security and scams. *Terry Soave at Ann Arbor District Library in Michigan.*

Technology: One-on-one. *Simsbury Public Library in Connecticut:* "Technology assistance, classes on Microsoft products (Word, Excel, PowerPoint)."

Travel

Many adults midlife and older enjoy traveling to different places, whether locally, within the United States, or to other countries. Programs can include how-to seminars, travel agent speakers, or people sharing their travels by bringing in videos, photos, and souvenirs.

Armchair traveler series. *Simsbury Public Library in Connecticut:* This series transports patrons to various destinations without leaving the library. Videos and discussions from presenters who have recently traveled to different areas share their experiences and popular places to visit, as well as provide some authentic snacks.

Virtual travel. *John J. Trause, director at Oradell Public Library in New Jersey:* "Virtual Tour of Hackensack River." This program was a slideshow and discussion about being a riverkeeper of the Hackensack River and watershed presented by a licensed U.S. Coast Guard captain.

Writing Groups

Consider having writing programs that can teach basic writing skills or how to write a novel. Creative writing, memoirs, and writing down local and historical stories can be beneficial to the individual, the library, and the community. Pick a theme and watch the creative juices flow. Look to community members and ask if they would like to pass along their expertise. There is a good possibility that the adults midlife and older in the community have many interesting stories to share about different life and historical events. An excellent time to garner interest is during National Novel Writing Month (NaNoWriMo) in November. The challenge is to write creatively from November 1st to November 30th. There are also virtual spaces to connect with other writers and to connect with other libraries and bookstores. More information can be found at the Web site https://nanowrimo.org/come-write-in.

Emerging writers workshop: How to publish and market your indie books. *Terry Soave at Ann Arbor District Library in Michigan:* Indie books are from independent publishers from concept to completion. These workshops were presented by local authors, author marketing specialists, and writing enthusiasts.

Graphic novel writing for teens and adults. *Simsbury Public Library in Connecticut:* "A two-part class for National Novel Writing Month." This was a workshop to help patrons with the elements of writing a graphic novel, including language to use in a graphic novel, as well as working with artists and plotting. It also included writing exercises and peer reviews. This was presented by a comic illustrator.

Writer's circles. *Ocean County Library in New Jersey:* This is a group of writers of all genres that meets to discuss writing issues and to critique their own and each other's work.

PEER PROGRAMS

Providing adult programming that is for adults 50+ can be challenging and rewarding. This can include presenters who are over age 50 or information and hands-on activities that will only involve participants who are adults 50+. Based on past research, social motivation by peers, such as encouragement and sharing of skills, provides comfort and is a factor in the learning process (Ng, 2007). Having an environment that has individuals who share many of the same life experiences, challenges, and issues can also be beneficial. Butcher and Street (2009) explain how adults 50+ did not want to appear foolish in front of others. Plus, some adults 50+ do not want to be labeled and therefore will not attend a program that was identified for adults 50+. Knowing our community needs will help us decide what is best for our library patrons.

A number of contributors to this text stated they typically did not have programs that were specifically for adults 50+ and specifically presented by adults 50+. However, some libraries did have various programs that were given by adults midlife and older, even though they did not have an age-specific requirement. The following are some examples from the contributors to this text. Most contributions came with more than one type of program that the adult 50+ was presenting. Along with the programs, some contributors mention the adults 50+ were library staff, various presenters, and volunteers in their library.

Muncie Public Library in Indiana: "Two of our book clubs are led by staff over 50, and the majority of the participants in both clubs are over age 50. We market the book clubs to everyone, but these two particular book clubs seem to attract seniors."

Jaci at Cranberry Public Library in Pennsylvania: "We do offer three book clubs . . . that are directed by adults 50+, and the majority that attend are over 50, but they are not specifically for that crowd."

Kathleen Handy, computer instructor at Saratoga Springs Public Library in New York: "Our iPad classes are led by a retired math teacher, and he also leads a casual weekly gathering of interested folks in the Library Bread Basket Café for iPads. . . . Another skilled retiree leads a session on Computer Crafts. . . . Another retired librarian teaches a class called 'Please Go Away! Travel Workshop' which is very successful, helping many retirees to find economical ways to travel."

Ryan Johnson at O'Fallon Public Library in Illinois: "One of our adult book clubs is led by a gentleman over 50, as is our Gentle Yoga class, and our T'ai

Chi class. We also have some cooking classes taught by a lady over 50. While these are open to any adult, it is mostly older adults who attend."

Anonymous: "We have had knitting, craft, bridge, Mah-Jongg, and other hands-on programs taught by adult instructors and librarians over 50 years of age, and many speakers fall into the 50+ age category."

Athol Public Library in Massachusetts: "The knitting group and mystery discussion are both led by adults over 60 years of age. None of our programs or offerings are restricted to 50+ adults, though."

Simsbury Public Library in Connecticut: "Many of our health and wellness programs are taught by adults in this age group. Our recent 'Transform Your Life' series, which was largely targeted to this age group, was put on by a presenter who is a senior. . . . We also have two 'Great Decisions' current events discussion groups led by retirees and largely attended by retirees."

Melanie Wehrle at Pikes Peak Library District in Colorado: "We have a number of art instructors who are 50+ that teach classes for us . . . a working painter who is in his early 80s . . . a drawing teacher who is in her mid-60s, and a photography teacher who is in his mid-50s. . . . It is obvious to the students that all of these artists not only enjoy making art but also teaching older adults. They have a way of encouraging everyone to find their creative sides in a nonjudgmental environment regardless of skill level."

Quincy Public Library in Illinois: "Our discussion groups have been led by an adult in his 70s who selects topics of interest and moderates the discussion. We had a computer tutor for several years who was in his 80s. He had to stop when his health no longer allowed it."

Christy Wagner at ELA Area Public Library in Illinois: "I am the facilitator for the Senior Book discussion group. . . . I am over 62! Our group ranges in age from early 50s to 92. A critical component of the group is that all of the titles we read MUST be available in large print, audio, and regular print formats. For the off-site book group, we've added another caveat, in addition to the above mentioned criteria, all books MUST be available through the Illinois Talking Book Center."

Fife Lake Public Library in Michigan: "Both Fitness and Yoga are led by senior volunteers. The Library Staff and Senior Network Staff do the majority of the organizing of the luncheons and events, but the seniors are encouraged to assist at the luncheon by helping with set-up, serving, paperwork, and clean-up."

Kathleen Goodson at Wimberley Village Library in Texas: "Our Senior Exercise classes are taught by yoga instructors and massage technicians who are 50+. Several of our Book Clubs are led by or facilitated by adults 50+. Our Documentary Film Night is managed by adults 50+. Almost all of our library volunteers are adults 50+ with one being in his 80s."

Chris Jackson, special audiences strategist: "Quite a few of our programming staff, myself included, are 50+!"

Heather Johnson at River Falls Public Library in Wisconsin: "The library director is 50+ and she does many of the programs for adults ages 50+. . . . One of the reference librarians . . . is also 50+ and she teaches . . . primarily . . . technology and electronic devices. This summer she will be teaching a few classes about online graphic design tools and a series of beer making classes."

Lisa C. West at Homewood Public Library in Alabama: "I often have presenters that are in the 50+ age bracket. For example, I am 50+ and I handle two of the book clubs, one is a book club at our local Senior Center as outreach, the other is in the library, and most of the participants are 50+."

Santa Barbara Public Library in California: "We also have a Computer Coaching program that is a one-to-one computer tutoring program and often the coaches are 50+. We also have a book club at a local retirement home organized by a staff person who is 50+."

Kate Skinner: "Computer training is currently taught by a 50+ staff member. The majority of attendees are 50+ though we do not specify an age. Free Yoga is taught by a 50+ staff member. We do not specify 50+ but 40% to 50% of attendees in any one class could be 50+."

Kelly Martin Laney at Birmingham Public Library in Alabama: "We have several volunteers who are over 50; they teach classes, lead programs, help with set-up for programs, assist with tasks in the children's department, recruit participants, and advertise library programs and resources."

INTERGENERATIONAL PROGRAMS

Public libraries are a perfect place to bring together different age groups to attend and participate in their programs. Intergenerational programs have many benefits, including saving on funds and fostering relationships between different aged individuals (Honnold & Mesaros, 2004), plus dual learning opportunities. Possible suggestions with younger children can be combined story times or having book buddies. This can be done at the physical library or as an outreach program at a residential facility. Teens and adults 50+ programs can involve teens conducting interviews of adults 50+ for local history stories or helping with community service projects. Consider crafts, songs, short stories, sharing of collections, and games. The best part about intergenerational programming is the conversation between the generations that might not be a part of the original program. The following are some examples of different intergenerational programs from the contributors to this text.

Athol Public Library in Massachusetts: "Most of our programs are intergenerational, since most are open to all. . . . One program that is definitely intergenerational is our annual Community Reading Day. The library organizes a day with the . . . schools when readers spend about one half to one hour reading a book, sharing the importance of reading, and often doing an activity with the class that relates to the book. . . . Most of our volunteer readers are over 50 years old, many are retirees, some retired teachers, and we also try to get community leaders like a fireman, policeman, the town manager, selectmen, and politicians (most of which except fire and police are over 50). This project brings community members into the school, and hopefully, reinforces the importance of reading as an important and lifelong activity."

Webster Public Library in New York: "Our Sit & Knit program is the only one I can think of that involves mentoring and teaching knitting skills to others."

Ryan Johnson at O'Fallon Public Library in Illinois: "We do often have grandparents bring grandkids to story times, tutoring sessions, or other events. We also have a few mother and daughter pairs come to the fitness classes we hold."

Muncie Public Library in Indiana: "We had an Adult Coloring Program that drew in a range of adults from early 20-somethings to retired ladies. Time to color and talk—[there were] some very interesting conversations!"

Ocean County Library in New Jersey: "Ocean County Library has a retired English teacher who offers a drop-in program for high school students to instruct them on how to gather and write their research papers."

Tamar Kreke, adult and technical services coordinator at Greene County Public Library in Ohio: "Types of intergenerational programs attended by seniors can vary. Grandparents often attend story times and special children-friendly programs for all ages (ex: magic show, reptile presentation, music program)."

Melany Wilks at Pioneer Memorial Library in Kansas: "We produce a Tic Tac Toe Game for adults and youth."

Kristi Haman: "We also have family programs that grandparents bring their grandchildren to. Examples are Family Movie, Scrabble Play Day, Story Times, and Puppet Shows."

Yolo County Library in California: "Since programs that are aimed towards adults seem to draw less than 20 participants, I have started opening up programs to all ages. These programs include quarterly cooking demonstrations, a maker-studio that meets every three months, and fun programs such as Hogwarts School of Witchcraft and Wizardry, which is run by science graduate students."

Kathleen Goodson at Wimberley Village Library in Texas: "The Wimberley Apron Society meets twice a month to share gardening experiences, cooking, preserving, and fermenting recipes and to share healthy food. . . . Young moms, grandmothers, and both young and older men look forward to attending this friendly gathering."

Simsbury Public Library in Connecticut: "Here are some examples of intergenerational programs . . . Biking in Simsbury. . . . Patrons from age 8 to 70 explored the bike paths in town with two leaders from the biking community; Wii for Teens and Seniors. The seniors whipped the teens at Wii bowling three years in a row; Arm Knitting for teens and seniors."

Kelly Martin Laney at Birmingham Public Library in Alabama: "Reality Check. We randomly assigned middle school–aged participants a 'lot in life,' which included their education level, marital status, number of children, and income. They were required to take the monthly income and visit tables manned by the seniors in order to negotiate housing, transportation, groceries, insurance, purchase a set of clothes for a family member or themselves, charities, tithing, educational opportunities, part-time work, child care, and other expenditures. The seniors were told to upsell the students as much as possible. They had certain purchases they were required to make, but they had to stay in budget. I had a 92-year old who demanded to see a young lady's budget list to make sure she had enough money to make a clothing purchase. When she saw that the girl hadn't bothered to subtract her expenditures, she told her that if she '. . . wrote me a bad check I'll call the sheriff and have you arrested!' The kids came out shell-shocked and the seniors had a ball."

Heather Johnson at River Falls Public Library in Wisconsin: "The story times for babies and toddlers often include grandparents and other caregivers who are 50+."

Leslie DeLooze, community services librarian at Richmond Memorial Library in New York: "We occasionally have intergenerational programs. These include things that are of interest to a wide age range, like an Anne of Green Gables Day, Harry Potter Day, Star Wars Day."

Quincy Public Library in Illinois: "Coloring club is intergenerational. . . . We have about half older and half younger participants. All find things in common to discuss as they color."

Jenneffer Sixkiller: "All of our adult programs are intergenerational. We recently held Escape Rooms in our library and had participation from ages 18 to seniors."

Beth Neunaber: "We held a Wii Bowling tournament with teens and seniors on teams."

Adrienne Doman Calkins at Sherwood Public Library in Oregon: "DIY Craftshop series is our most successful intergenerational program. Each month is a new craft, taught by two librarians on staff who are avid crafters. . . . The ages are 12+ for the program, and we often see mothers, daughters, and granddaughters attend together. We also have mothers and sons, fathers and daughters, neighbors, school friends, and people there to meet new friends. We provide all the supplies and expertise. We set up the room with about six large tables, allowing people to mingle and chat. Attendees spend the next [one to two] hours making a craft from start to finish (no kits!) that they can be proud of. We hear many stories of attendees teaching their families and friends the craft at a later date. Recent crafts have included flower crowns, snow globes, glitter houses, hidden book safes, origami string lights, and peg dolls. This program is a monthly series offered on a weekday afternoon. . . . That is a sweet spot time for us to get a mix of after-school attendees and older adults who want to be home before dark."

Chris Jackson, special audiences strategist: "We've had a successful intergenerational gardening program for many years, a one-day event where children and adults 60 and over replant flowers and vegetables in raised beds on the library grounds."

Mariel Carter, adult service reference librarian at Marinette County Consolidated Public Library Services in Wisconsin: "The intergenerational programs are the Yoga Stretch, Science Fest, Art Shows, Holiday Open House, Summer Reading Club, and Winter Reading Club. . . . Our Summer Reading Club for adults runs concurrent with the children and teen Summer Reading Clubs so that adults may participate with their children or grandchildren or do it just for the fun of completing puzzles, brain teasers, activities, and reading during the summer."

Terry Soave at Ann Arbor District Library in Michigan: "Tie-Dye Workshop for Teens and Adults."

Kate Skinner: "Our Free Yoga . . . classes are totally intergenerational teens and adults . . . in one of our classes we had three generations: grandmother, daughter, teen granddaughter doing yoga alongside each other."

Lisa Prizio: "The Knitters group meets weekly . . . where they work on their own projects and visit. Two teens have joined the group, and the women are teaching and sharing their skills as well as sharing extra yarn and needles with them. Both groups are receiving benefits from each other."

CHAPTER SUMMARY

This chapter showcased different programs and services for adult 50+ patrons. Peers in the field gave us practical advice and ideas that we can use to develop and enhance our own adult 50+ programs and services. Having different types of programs available at different times will provide multiple opportunities for a working or retired adult 50+ to attend.

5

Computers, Facebook, and the Internet: Technology and Social Media

Technology is changing and growing everyday in today's society. Adults 50+ have a variety of capabilities when accessing and retrieving information from a computerized system. It is important not to generalize and make assumptions about their digital literacy skills and abilities to use technology (Decker, 2010).

DIGITAL LITERACY

It is important and essential for individuals to have the knowledge and digital literacy skills to access, find, evaluate, create, and communicate information effectively from a variety of formats (ALA Digital Literacy Task Force, 2011). When examining adults midlife and older, there are some individuals who are comfortable with technology, whereas others are afraid to use online systems. Adults 50+ were born when some technologies had not been created, and some did not use the technology available. This can make some adults 50+ more uncomfortable using computerized systems. Unlike today where computers are prevalent in high school, there is a gap where Baby Boomers and some pre-Boomers did not use computers when they attended high school. However, there are some adults 50+ who have used a computer at home or at work in the 1970s and 1980s (Salkowitz, 2008). Keeping all the different possibilities of technology use and nonuse in mind, we need to understand that this causes a digital divide of technology exposure and usage between generations. However, as stated earlier, it is important that we do not make assumptions about technological abilities or skill level for this age group due to their varied characteristics. Age does not prevent learning, and based on recent research, adults 50+ are increasing their use of the Internet. Pew Research reports that 67 percent of adults 65+ are using the Internet on different technological devices, though a digital divide with regard to using technology still exists. However, the research notes that 71 percent of adults midlife and older who are Internet users go online every day or almost every day after learning the necessary technological skills (Anderson & Perrin, 2017; Smith, 2014).

Adults 50+ need to acquire digital literacy skills due to the increase in digital content on the Internet, such as health information, government documents, educational opportunities, entertainment resources, financial records, and leisure reading activities. In addition, communicating with family and friends is becoming more prevalent on a computerized device (Madden, 2010). Digital literacy skills will give an individual the knowledge to be able to search for information and resources, find and be provided entertainment, and have the ability to interact with others in an online environment. The public library is an excellent place to learn digital literacy skills, especially during a library media program. Bennett-Kapusniak's (2013) research on 50 U.S. public libraries found only half of the libraries offered a basic computer program and only a handful of libraries had a computer lab to practice computer skills. When examining the 1,317 in this text, almost a third of the libraries (32 percent) provided a basic computer class and very few (5 percent) had a room or computer lab where patrons could practice their computer skills. Most of the libraries that offered a basic computer class also offered other different types of technology classes such as learning about various technological devices, how to set up an e-mail account or how to use Microsoft Publisher and other advanced classes. The lack of computer or technology programming within many of the public libraries examined can be discouraging for adults 50+ who rely on their public libraries to assist them in accessing and retrieving online information. In addition, not having the time to practice skills in searching for information can increase anxiety and reduce the comfort level in adults 50+ who are using technology (Butcher & Street, 2009). Patience and repetition are important when learning how to use a computerized device. Just because one person is successful and understands the process does not mean another will be at the same level. Having the time to go over and repeat what has been learned on a regular basis will help in retaining the new digital skills and create more confidence when using an online system. The information on the computer or technology programming offered by the public libraries examined in this text was gathered from their library's Web site. Therefore, the percentage found for computer or technology programming at these libraries could be higher if the classes were marketed to their patrons using print or other forms of marketing besides their library's Web site.

WEB SITES

When individuals search for information on the Internet, different factors play a role in the success and use of the online system. The Web site design and the visual display are important for an individual to navigate through the information presented on the Web site (Wolfram & Zhang, 2001). Creating a Web site that is user friendly for adults 50+ is important because more information and communication with others is online, and as adults age, certain challenges and issues can affect the use of technology (Fisk et al., 2009).

The National Institute on Aging provides a checklist for Making Your Web Site Senior Friendly (2002) (see Appendix B). The checklist provides information on designing readable text, presenting information, incorporating media, and increasing ease of navigation. The information also provides an example of a Web site that was developed in accordance with the guidelines specified. In addition, there are several Web sites on the Internet that can check your Web site for accessibility. Plus, asking a nonstaff adult 50+ patron to look at the Web site will help in locating any issues and determine the site's ease of use for midlife and older adult patrons. In a previous study examining the challenges Baby Boomers can face using mobile devices, Bennett-Kapusniak (2015) created a list of helpful suggestions for Web site design (see Table 5.1). Small changes can be helpful, such as the capability of changing the font size or limiting the items on the Web page, or increasing the space between items for easier viewing. Creating a Web site where all types of patrons are able to navigate will help us fulfill our mission of providing accessibility to information and resources to all library users.

Links

In addition to creating a user-friendly Web site, some public libraries have provided links on their main Web page or on a separate page within their Web site of resources that adults 50+ may find useful. These resources can contain local, state, or national information such as links to area centers or institutions, Social Security, volunteer or educational opportunities, social events, or caregiver information.

There are many interesting and helpful sites that we can link onto our library Web sites that can be beneficial for adults 50+. Appendix C has a list of possible Web sites that can be of interest for the adult 50+ library patron. Creating a page of resources, including local resources and information, will let our communities know that our library Web sites will have the information they need without having to scour the Internet for a particular resource or information. This will especially assist some adults 50+ who are overwhelmed by the abundance of information on the Internet. For instance, Tech-Boomers (2017) is a free site licensed under CC by 4.0 where an individual can learn how to use popular Web sites such as Facebook, Netflix, PayPal,

TABLE 5.1. Technology Challenges and Web Site Design Suggestions

Challenges	Web Site Design Suggestions
Inability to Establish a Connection	Create short videos for faster downloads and easier access
	Expand 3G services
	Offer continuous service coverage
	Enhance mobile traffic capacities
Inability to Search for Information	Have options for increased font sizes
	Provide eye-catching icons and use consistently
	Double-space text and ensure it can be adjusted by the patron
	Avoid low-contrast backgrounds
	Create brighter screens
	Have visual, auditory, or text choices
	Create an intuitive interface design
	Provide more natural-language features
	Provide easy-to-follow directions
	Limit items on the screen, background music, pop-ups, and moving logos
	Minimize scrolling in programs
Inability to Solve a Problem or Find Information	Provide visual, animated, and text tutorials
	Build in instructional procedures
	Create better organization and flow of information
	Provide information on a Help system
	Provide examples for dealing with unsatisfying interactions
	Provide more interactive feedback
	Provide feedback right away

and many others. Public libraries can partner with TechBoomers to help with teaching digital literacy skills. More information, including a webinar, can be found on their Web site (see Appendix B).

Furthermore, consider providing a link or an icon on your library's Web site that enables patrons easier access to the library's OPAC. Creating a recognizable link that is prominently displayed will help adults 50+ find the catalog page right away, especially if there is a lot of information displayed on the Web page. Based on prior research, some adults 50+ can experience cognitive overload when searching for information on an online system. Computer Web sites need to be simple and easy to use so it requires less mental effort for adults 50+ to seek out information (Czaja et al., 2006). Creating useful links not only provides adults 50+ just one Web page to look for and access information, but also provides them with quality information that they can find trustworthy.

Tabs

Some public libraries dedicate a Web page for their adult 50+ community members. Depending on the Web site design, some libraries have created a tab at the top of the Web page drawing attention to their adult 50+ patrons to click on it for more information. Other library Web sites have a link on the side of the Web page with other linked resources. The tab or link name varies from Seniors, 50+, Mature Adults, 55+, 65+ and others, depending on the library. Many adult 50+ pages have specific resources, information displayed in a larger font, outreach services, assistive technologies available, materials available at the library that they might be interested in, tutorials, and other articles of interest. We need to consider creating a separate Web page for our adult 50+ community members, which can foster connections and establish the importance and value of the library, the community, and the adult 50+ library patrons.

Ease of Use

Adults midlife and older can use different types of systems to access information online. This can be a factor in the digital literacy skills an individual needs to utilize the various systems and may present challenges due to the different system variables in effectively accessing and retrieving information. Most adults 50+ want a system that is easy to use to gather information (Martyn & Gallant, 2012). The diversity in adults 50+ can be a factor in the way they seek information in an online environment, especially in the comfort level in utilizing a computerized device. As stated previously, research indicates many adults 50+ are on the Internet every day and are using various devices to go online. However, Rainie (2012) notes that adults 50+ search for information differently depending on their age. We need to provide a simple Web site that is easy for our patrons to navigate. This will allow for more comfort in using our system in finding information and will determine if we will have a returning patron to our library Web site.

An area that sometimes is overlooked with regard to adults 50+ is how some public library patrons are checking out materials. This is changing as we become a more technological society. Some libraries have self-checkout stations where patrons need to read the screen to perform the necessary functions to check out library materials. We need to consider the instructions and the size of the font on the screen, especially with regard to our adult 50+ library patrons. Some experience vision challenges, and others do not have the digital literacy skills to work with a computerized system. Taking the time to patiently advise and walk through the self-checkout steps, sometimes on a regular basis, creates an atmosphere of comfort and welcome for all.

BARRIERS TO ACCESS

The role of the public library has become more crucial in providing programs and services that encourage this diverse 50+ age group to continue utilizing and partaking in areas they feel will satisfy their information wants and needs (Honnold & Mesaros, 2004). Our role is to try to alleviate the barriers that some disadvantaged patrons have to accessing and retrieving information.

Affordability

As mentioned in Chapter 1, some adults 50+ have economic issues. This can affect if they are able to afford computerized devices, if they can afford a Wi-Fi connection, or if they can upgrade to receive a strong enough bandwidth speed for effective downloads. Economically disadvantaged populations utilize the public library to build their knowledge of technological devices, as well as to utilize the library for their computers and Internet connections to access and retrieve information online. Anderson and Perrin (2017) have noted that household income is a factor in broadband adoption, with only a little over half (51 percent) of the adults 50+ in their survey having high-speed Internet.

Geographic Regions

Having better broadband infrastructures will alleviate insecure connections. However, sometimes due to budget issues, it is difficult to upgrade to receive better bandwidth. Broadband connections in a public library environment needs to be a major priority, because community members look to libraries to provide consistent and stable access as more information becomes more prevalent on the Internet. According to the Institute of Museum & Library Services, public libraries reach almost all of the U.S. population and most of our libraries (98 percent) have a Wi-Fi connection (ALA, 2017). Previous research has shown that our population relies on their public libraries to provide a stable broadband connection (Saunders, McClure & Mandel, 2012). However, public libraries have varying disparities in terms of Internet access and broadband connectivity (Jaeger, Bertot, McClure, & Rodriguez 2007). The American Library Association is continuing efforts to ensure libraries have access to broadband that will serve their communities, and the Federal Communications Commission has developed an e-rate funding program to help boost library and school broadband access (Wapner, 2014; Wright, 2014). However, the application process and other issues such as hardware and hook-up costs still remain challenges for some rural and small libraries (Thiele, 2016). The broadband issue is a continuing process that is changing on a daily basis, and we need to continue to advocate for our library patrons so we can provide this valuable service.

Race and Nationality

Our society is culturally diverse, with a number of individuals who have English as a second language. According to the Population Reference Bureau (2013), one in eight Americans age 65+ are foreign born. Some of the immigrants came as young children, whereas others arrived in America much older. This will affect their English-language capabilities, digital literacy skills, and exposure to technology. Public libraries are a space where we can help play a role in engaging immigrants by providing English-language learning, training, and resources in a safe and welcoming environment.

Other Challenges

Some adults 50+ have other challenges that create barriers to technology use, which have been discussed previously. These challenges can include overcoming the fear of using technology. Some adults 50+ feel that they might break something if they touch a computerized device or that they might put in information wrong, thereby not making the computer work correctly. Some fear that they will not remember what to do to use the online system, and others fear that once they learn one device, they will have to learn another one because of the changing technology. Some have issues understanding the different terminology, and others are anxious they will not find the right information because they are overwhelmed by the amount of information that is showing up on the screen. Public libraries can address these challenges by offering different types of classes to suit individual needs.

Overcoming Barriers

Public libraries can help in overcoming some of the barriers adults 50+ might face with technology by designing functional and senior-friendly Web sites to help make navigating and finding information easier online (Hart, Chaparro, & Halcomb, 2008). We can also provide technology training either in classes or through one-on-one help to alleviate fear or anxiety while using technology. To create a productive learning environment for adults 50+, Speros (2009) recommends the following strategies for instructors:

1. Create a comfortable learning environment that conveys respect and support.
2. Schedule short sessions at various times to decrease fatigue from information overload.
3. Allow enough time for patrons to understand the information before moving on to the next concept.
4. Link new skills with past experiences to help patrons retain information.

5. Express the practicality of learning the skills to assist them in their daily lives, thereby increasing motivation to learn.

6. Minimize distractions to help patrons stay focused.

7. Present clear information by speaking concisely and facing the patrons using familiar words, and explain technical terms such as "icon" or "scrolling."

8. Provide printed handouts of instructions with visual cues or screenshots to help guide the patron outside of class.

9. Give specific directions and encourage patrons to keep instructions in a location at home that will be seen for effective use.

10. Encourage interaction throughout the session by demonstrating and then having the patrons practice the skill.

11. Suggest practicing the skill on a regular basis to help retain information.

12. Recap essential information frequently and have patrons repeat the information in their own words to help with processing and recalling the information.

To assist adults 50+ in overcoming their anxiety and become more comfortable with using technology, Singer and Agosto (2013) created a list of suggestions:

1. Small class sizes to give more one-on-one instruction.

2. Offer written guidelines and tip sheets.

3. Offer contact information for future help.

4. Provide hands-on training in a computer lab so participants can interact and engage with the technology while they are learning.

5. Receive social and emotional support during the training process from their peers and instructors, which will help alleviate anxiety.

6. Try to give individualized attention to get to know the participant's knowledge and experience and also to encourage interactive engagement if problems arise while learning the technology.

Adults 50+ are capable of learning and enjoy trying new things (Nycyk & Redsell, 2010). Try to allow time for questions and answers and be enthusiastic, positive, and encouraging. We need to consider training library staff on different devices so they are comfortable utilizing technology. This will help patrons when they come in with a new device or if they have questions about technology. Knowing how to use a device in addition to searching and downloading information are important in today's society.

To help reach some disadvantaged areas in our communities, some public libraries have bookmobiles and techmobiles that are supplying a Wi-Fi connection and computerized technology. Techmobiles are similar to the concept of bookmobiles, but instead have computers and other technology gadgets, plus they offer programs within their vehicle. Some of the bookmobiles and techmobiles also provide Wi-Fi hotspots in areas where it is difficult to find a stable Internet connection. In addition, they can travel to residential areas where adults 50+ cannot travel to the physical library to access the Internet for needed information. Furthermore, more than 80 percent of Americans age 65+ use a mobile device to get their information, and a large majority of low-income individuals do not have a broadband connection at home (Lu, 2017). We need to consider leaving the wireless connection on after hours to help individuals who might have a wireless device but cannot afford a broadband connection.

TECHNOLOGY AND SOCIAL MEDIA

Adults midlife and older are adopting technology, and their Internet activity has been steadily increasing. Different types of computers and mobile devices are being used to access the Internet, and research reports that e-mail and social networking sites are a top activity when communicating with family and friends (Perrin & Duggan, 2015; Zickuhr & Madden, 2012).

Adults Midlife and Older Web Sites

As mentioned previously, some libraries create a dedicated Web page for their adult 50+ library patrons. When examining the 1,317 libraries in this text, very few (2 percent) have a Web page specifically for adults over 50. Santa Barbara Public Library in California has an excellent example of providing a Web page of resources for seniors located at https://www.santabarbaraca.gov/gov/depts/lib/default.asp. To find the Seniors Web page on their Web site, patrons need to look under the Collections & Resources tab, scroll down the list, and click on the link for Seniors. Under this link, adults 50+ can find library resources that are available for their age group; volunteer and educational opportunity links; and local, state, and national resource links, as well as end-of-life resources. Providing various links on a number of topics that adults 50+ could be interested in strengthens our support for these library patrons and increases our value and impact within our community.

Another option to consider for our library Web site that would be beneficial for adults 50+ or to individuals who have vision impairments is the ability to change the font size on the library's Web page. Changing the font size on the interface page, event page, or calendar page can ensure that programs and services can be seen clearly on a computerized system. Simsbury Public Library in Connecticut provides a wonderful example of this opportunity at the top of their Web site landing page located at http://www.simsburylibrary.info.

Programs and Services

Many public libraries, as mentioned earlier, offer a variety of technology programs to their community. These programs vary but can include everything from basic computer classes to learning about social media sites and more advanced classes such as digital photography or navigating and using Microsoft Excel spreadsheets. Some of the libraries examined in this text conduct programs or classes with a group of patrons, whereas others (17 percent) have one-on-one training. Most of the library contributors that discussed their computer training stated that they preferred teaching one-on-one with adults 50+ because it helped with the variations in skill levels and they are able to give more attention to the individual patron.

Public libraries in the United States offer digital content to their patrons such as e-books, music, videos, and audiobooks that can be downloaded onto their computerized devices. Some public libraries (4 percent) in this text had e-readers that patrons could check out of their library. Most of the e-readers were preloaded with books already on them. They were by genre or had a random selection of best-sellers. Other libraries let their patrons check out mobile devices. This can be helpful to adults 50+ who cannot afford a mobile device but want to keep up to date with technology. Also, having e-readers available to check out provides an individual the opportunity to investigate the mobile device before purchasing it. The e-readers that were offered by the libraries included Kindles, Nooks, and tablets (iPads or Samsung Galaxies). According to Perrin (2016), less than a quarter (21 percent) of Americans over age 50 have read an e-book in the last 12 months and even less (13 percent) have downloaded an audiobook. This low percentage could be due to a variety of reasons, such as not having the knowledge or skills to download electronic materials onto a mobile device, not having a device to download materials to, an unawareness that the library has electronic materials available to download, or the patron just prefers printed text to an electronic format. A number of public libraries in the United States offer their electronic media in a variety of formats through Over-Drive. To help spread the word about electronic media, OverDrive has a digital bookmobile, which is a 42-foot vehicle that is traveling across the United States, providing libraries an outreach center for individuals of any age to learn how to download e-books as well as the opportunity to explore different gadgets, trainings, and workshops. Check out the OverDrive Digital Bookmobile Web site at https://www.digitalbookmobile.com to determine the latest schedule and state.

Social Media

Individuals are increasing their use of social media to find news and entertainment, to share information, and to connect with family and friends. Pew

(2017) has found about half of all American adults 50+ (49 percent) use some type of social media, with Facebook having the most visits on a daily basis. Keeping in touch with family and friends is important either through face-to-face communication or by using technology. With the majority of younger adults (83 percent) utilizing social media and electronic devices to communicate, more midlife and older adults are wanting to explore and learn how to use the different types of social media that are available.

Learning how to use YouTube, blogs, Skype, wikis, and podcasts, as well as others and learning how to create a Web site are some of the areas that can be beneficial for adults 50+ (Martyn & Gallant, 2012). For instance, learning how to create their own podcasts or blogs, perhaps on local histories or stories, can be beneficial for the local community and for individuals interested in genealogy. In addition, learning how to Skype can open up a new way for grandparents or great-grandparents to communicate with their grandchildren and great-grandchildren. As technology advances and patron interests change, offering a variety of programs will provide a valuable service supporting lifelong learning, connecting others in different ways, and gathering new patrons for our public libraries. The following are some examples of technology programs from contributors to this text.

COMPUTER EXAMPLES

One-on-one classes. *Athol Public Library in Massachusetts:* "We offer one-on-one computer help right now, but have offered classes for up to 10 participants in the past and hope to offer them again. This is done by staff members and available to anyone, but is most requested by older adults."

One-on-one for non-English speakers. *Adrienne Doman Calkins at Sherwood Public Library in Oregon:* "We formalized this offering fairly recently to make it easier for patrons and staff to handle sign-ups. It's been very successful, especially for seniors who are struggling to keep current with technology. A patron can book up to two 30-minute sessions a month with a librarian. Patrons sign up with staff in person or over the phone, or can fill in a form on our Web site. Currently two librarians share responsibility for the sessions, and one is available for Spanish sessions. We schedule about three to six sessions a month."

Group classes. *Kathleen Handy, computer instructor at Saratoga Springs Public Library in New York:* "We typically get anywhere from 2 to 15 attendees at a time. I also prepare handouts, and people can opt to pay a small printing fee for them. They can alternatively use our website from home or anywhere and read most of the handouts online and opt to print at home if they wish. Our classes encourage interaction and participation, with hands-on access to up-to-date computers and software, thanks to a forward-looking administration and Friends organization. I prepare for classes by reviewing handouts and considering past class questions and concerns that could be addressed. I also research many activities that can be done on computers (visiting sites such as jigzone.com so participants can practice mouse skills while doing something fun such as putting a jigsaw puzzle together). We have more 'meatier' mouse skills tutorials such as Mousercize, too."

Melany Wilks at Pioneer Memorial Library in Kansas: "Computer classes: We did not develop them for the over 50 group, but about three-fourths of our participants have been the ones to take the class. They are also the largest completers of the class. Cost was originally just using our patron desktops. . . . We wanted more programing options, so we sought a grant to purchase laptops for patron training."

Online tutorials. *Kelly Martin Laney at Birmingham Public Library in Alabama:* "We have one-on-one computer training that utilizes the Learning Express database, and a lot of our seniors love it. We set an appointment to see what they want to do with a computer, what equipment they have, and what they already know, then put them on the tutorial program that matches their needs. They maintain contact with 'their' staff person if they have questions. Most of these are done by staff over 50."

MOBILE DEVICE EXAMPLES

Staff instructors. *Brianne Columbo at Fairfield Free Public Library in New Jersey:* "Each Thursday morning, our adult events coordinator hosts Bring Your Own Device (BYOD). BYOD allows patrons to bring in their personal devices (e.g., laptops, cell phones, tablets, etc.) and ask any questions they have about the use of their device. It also allows the library to feature, promote, and teach free services we offer for library patrons (e.g., Hoopla, OverDrive e-books and audiobooks, Zinio, e-magazines, etc.). This does not require much preparation, but does require the instructor to have a broad knowledge of devices, their use, and a full understanding and working knowledge of the library digital collections and databases. The program typically lasts for an hour, dependent on the amount of patrons who drop in for assistance. We are happy to work with patrons for as little or as long as necessary."

Local collaborations. *Melany Wilks at Pioneer Memorial Library in Kansas:* "Cell phone and tablet training cost for staff to teach or have [a] local company come and teach. The local tech company now offers lunch to participants who sign up and attend. It is free and open to all but mostly over 50s attend."

Lisa C. West at Homewood Public Library in Alabama: "Get the Most Out of Your iPad and iPhone! . . . This workshop is geared towards casual users . . . certified trainers . . . answers . . . questions . . . (once a month series, free to library and patrons, audience primarily seniors)."

COMPUTER LAB EXAMPLES

Public spaces. *Adrienne Doman Calkins at Sherwood Public Library in Oregon:* "Computer classes (Excel . . . Word . . . Power Point). These are taught by a librarian on staff in our computer area before the library opens. We don't have a separate classroom with computers, so this is the only way we can really make this sort of program available to the public and it works really well. We wheel in a giant big-screen TV to mirror the instructor's demonstrations (with Microsoft Office settings changed for larger font and higher contrast). . . . Attendees can stay and practice and ask questions. . . . Many attendees take multiple classes, including many employees from our city, which has been great for building connections and fostering respect."

Separate computer lab spaces. *Christy Wagner at ELA Area Public Library in Illinois:* "We are fortunate to have a lovely 15-station computer lab which provides a quiet learning environment."

EBOOK EXAMPLES

Mariel Carter, adult service reference librarian at Marinette County Consolidated Public Library Services in Wisconsin: "Assistance borrowing e-books: My library system belongs to a statewide consortium that allows library card holders to borrow e-books and download audiobooks. Because downloading the correct app or figuring out the borrowing process can be difficult at first, my library offers one-on-one sessions with a librarian to help patrons get started. The librarian helps patrons download the app to use the library's e-book and downloadable audiobook borrowing system; helps get the app set up; and shows patrons how to navigate the Web site, check out materials, and use the app to read or listen to the books . . . there is no prep work for this service. There is no additional cost, except for staff time, to make this program work."

SOCIAL MEDIA EXAMPLES

Kelly Martin Laney at Birmingham Public Library in Alabama: "The main library has a newsletter and online calendar of events, as well as Twitter, Instagram, and Flickr accounts . . . Facebook page. I'm not sure how many of my seniors find out about our programs through them, but I know they LOVE having their pictures on Facebook."

Chad Robinson at Matheson Memorial Library in Wisconsin: "Every community is different, so I think the challenge is finding what your population is passionate about and planning your programming accordingly. One thing that has helped greatly is nurturing our Facebook page so that it has become vibrant enough to attract a wide population of frequent visitors."

Social media safety. *Jenneffer Sixkiller:* "We offer computer and technology classes during the spring, autumn, and winter seasons . . . and typically the attendance for those classes are adults 50+. These are new this year, and we're still figuring out what types of classes work with our library technology and our community. So far, we've offered classes on Facebook, social media safety, Flickr and photo organizing, and Microsoft Word. We've also acquired Gale Courses, available on our Web site."

Meryle A. Leonard at Charlotte Mecklenburg Library in North Carolina: "Participants learn how to navigate the popular social networking [sites] like Facebook with confidence and safety."

Specialized classes. *Ocean County Library in New Jersey:* "Throughout the branches, OCL offers numerous computer programs for adults 50+ both in a small group setting and one-on-one. These include basic computer skills, accessing and downloading e-books, basic tablet instruction, job search assistance, information on how to access the numerous databases offered free on the Library's Web site, and advanced computer classes."

Meryle A. Leonard at Charlotte Mecklenburg Library in North Carolina: "Coding: We take the fear out of technology and let our 50+ friends know they are capable of using and enjoying technology. Participants learn about coding, how it is used and we use . . . small robots to give participants the opportunity to code. Many of the participants said they felt more comfortable using technology."

OUTREACH EXAMPLES

Individualized. *Lucine Kauffman, SAGE coordinator (Services to the Aging in Genesee County) in New York:* "SAGE staff and volunteers 'deliver' tutorials for computer and mobile devices. Not many SAGE patrons have these electronic devices, but we offer the service and expect the requests to increase in the future."

Marie Corbitt at Westerville Public Library in Ohio: "Borrow a librarian. We provide one-on-one technology help to people in their homes since they cannot make it to the library. We have helped with e-readers, computers, e-mail, and printers. We even check out and help set up CD and DVD players. . . . There is no cost for general help besides staff time. But we do purchase DVD players and CD players to check out to people who would otherwise not have access to them."

Organizational. *Marian Christmon, manager digital inclusion at Nashville Public Library in Tennessee:* "The Nashville Public Library's Digital Inclusion Team (team members are all adults 50+) is working to address this critical need. . . . By partnering with other agencies, the team is able to reach the 50+ population where they are already receiving services. Partner organizations include Fifty-Forward, National Council on Aging [NCOA], recreation centers, and senior housing properties. The team takes mobile tablet and laptop labs to agency sites and provides training for the agency's patrons. Classroom instruction and activities are customized for the various audiences. For example, activities for participants who are seeking to reenter the job market include guided labs and classroom instruction focused on improving workforce development skills, while activities for others may be focused on developing basic digital literacy skills and accessing relevant online resources. All training programs include information on library digital services. Sessions generally conclude with information on low-cost devices and Internet services available in the area."

Marie Corbitt at Westerville Public Library in Ohio: "I do another program called iPals. This program is for people with memory difficulties. It is designed to allow older adults to interact with simple applications in an iPad in the hopes that they will become engaged and active. These apps include music, simple art, and simple puzzles. I do this program once a month at a memory care unit . . . We did purchase an iPad to do this program, but so far I have only been using free apps. Some of the most successful apps include Tozzle HD Lite, ShapePuzzle, Baby Animals, Pocket Pond, Fingerpaint, Pottery, ilovefireworks, Virtuoso Piano, a xylophone, and Touch the Sound."

CHAPTER SUMMARY

This chapter examined technology and social media and how adults 50+ have varying capabilities and skills when using computerized devices. Providing various technology classes can help adults improve or enhance digital literacy skills, which is needed with more information becoming more online. Plus, it assists adults 50+ in becoming more comfortable using technology and gives another avenue to communicate with family and friends. Libraries can help individuals access and retrieve information by providing a steady Wi-Fi connection or having computers available for Internet use. Creating an easy-to-use Web site and providing links to important resources for this age group will increase the possibility that adults 50+ will use the library Web site as the place to find the information they need.

6

Fostering Lifelong Learning at Any Age

Libraries provide a physical or virtual environment that fosters informal and formal learning. They are places that are free and open to everyone that offers significant sources of knowledge and different skill development for all types of individuals. Reading and listening to stories, looking at art and photography books, and experiencing poetry, as well as engaging with our nonfiction and vast fiction collections can assist and inspire our patrons. An accessible collection in a variety of formats (print, audio, and electronic) is important to reach all types of adults in our library communities.

SKILL AND LITERACY DEVELOPMENT

Age does not prevent us from learning new things. However, the way adults midlife and older learn and store information can be different from individuals of other ages due to cognitive changes within the brain. Acquiring new skills and having intellectual stimulation can be beneficial for adults 50+. Keeping the brain active builds new brain cells and maintains healthy brain connections (Alzheimer's Association, 2017). Pursuing lifelong learning opportunities can help an adult 50+ to remain active and healthy socially, physically, and mentally.

Fostering effective literacy, or the ability to read and write in adults, is essential to gathering and learning information. Literacy challenges can be attributed to different factors such as age, having English as a second language, a lack of education, or a disability (IMLS, 2014). Adult literacy skills, which include digital literacy, are important in pursuing lifelong learning opportunities due to the abundance of information online. Public libraries can assist and create opportunities for adult literacy and lifelong learning. The ALA Office for Diversity, Literacy, and Outreach Services provides links, resources, materials, and information to support literacy programs (see Appendix B). Literacy, in this text, was determined by if a library offered programs for English as a second language or other literacy programs, if continuing education classes were offered at the library, or if there was a specified link on their Web page to work on educational skills (math, English, etc.) or to take educational classes. Less than a quarter (19 percent) of the contributing libraries offered some type of literacy program or link for their library patrons. Keep in mind, however, that this percentage is derived from information taken from their online information, and literacy programs can be offered "in-house" or displayed within their physical library environment.

Many adults 50+ are lifelong learners and enjoy different types of engaging activities. However, their interests and skills will vary. For instance, there are adults midlife and older who are working longer, starting second careers, or are retired. These adults might want to take enrichment classes or learn a new skill. We also need to remember that many adults 50+ have English as their second language and others have not been able to finish their schooling due to different life circumstances. In addition, there are some adults 50+ who just want to pursue leisure activities. Leisure reading provides informal learning opportunities about people and relationships and other countries, cultures, and time periods and gives different perspectives and can enrich life (Moyer, 2007). These opportunities can be found in our print, audio, and digitized collections.

When promoting lifelong learning, we need to remember to collaborate with other organizations and agencies to expand and carry out our mission to our library patrons. Partnerships with local agencies can foster civic engagement with adults 50+ and their community. We need to consider organizing tours of collections for literacy groups or tutors, or provide a meeting space, or an area to showcase literacy materials. Partnering with museums can also offer a broader range of experiences and potentially have a greater impact on the learning experience. The Institute of Museum and Library Services created a framework of 21st-century skills and a self-assessment tool to aid and support libraries in their lifelong learning endeavors (IMLS, 2017). See Appendix B for appropriate links. There are many lifelong learning opportunities that we can offer to adults 50+. The following are a few categories, including some examples from contributors to this text and their ideas, tips, and lifelong learning programs offered at their libraries.

CREATIVITY, CULTURE, AND THE ARTS

There are 56 humanities councils throughout the United States. They provide cultural education, offer grants to develop cultural programming in the library, and provide contacts to various artists such as music groups, theater performers, and other individuals (National Endowment for the Humanities, 2017). There are also various ethnic and national organizations that can speak on various topics such as their cultural background and their place in society. Several states have theater groups that are for, by, and about adults over 50 years of age. We need to consider contacting various organizations in our communities to provide different types of experiences to suit a variety of needs.

The National Institute on Aging (2013) explains that there are many benefits for adults midlife and older who are involved in the arts. These can include positive cognitive and social relationships, which can lessen the effects of dementia (McFadden & Basting, 2010). The organization Lifetime Arts (2017) provides consulting and programming services to help fund, design, and implement creative arts programs for midlife and older adults. Currently, there are 20 public library systems in 12 states with creative aging library projects. Lifetime Arts also provides an online Creative Aging Toolkit for public libraries to help plan and implement creative aging programming (see Appendix B).

Offering a variety of cultural events, visiting artists, poetry readings, and theater troupes, as well as opportunities for discussions and creative expressions, are just some of the many lifelong learning services and programs we can provide for our adult 50+ community. Many libraries participate in programs that are community wide whereby patrons read the same book and then participate in a wide variety of programs around the same theme. Some libraries offer a variety of programs involving different ethnic experiences such as food, history, or traditions. Other libraries consider intergenerational programming involving adults 50+ and their younger patrons. The following are various ideas, programs, and tips for lifelong learning from contributors to this text.

Creating life stories. *Wallingford Public Library in Connecticut:* "As part of its 2017 community-based story telling initiative, the Wallingford Public Library sought to collaborate with the Wallingford Senior Center on a workshop series whereby older adults will develop new skills to document and share their life stories. The program . . . comprised seven workshop sessions and one culminating event. This skills-building series . . . based on the principles outlined by Lifetime Arts, Inc., in its Creative Aging Toolkit for Public Libraries. . . . Teen volunteers (relatives of participants as desired) . . . partner with participants throughout the program . . . the last part of each session . . . devoted to giving participants the opportunity to share with the group what they created that week and what the process was like for them . . . Total cost $2,380."

Socrates café. *Melanie Wehrle at Pikes Peak Library District in Colorado:* "One of our most successful programs whose attendees are almost all older adults . . . meets weekly . . . to discuss all kinds of subjects such as philosophy, religions, politics, morality, and the common threads among humanity. All adults are welcome to attend this well-moderated and thought-provoking group. The moderator is a longtime volunteer who does an excellent job of ensuring that the discussion stays civil, on topic, and that everyone gets a chance to participate. Since many of the regular participants are retired military, they have the discipline to have a civil discussion of highly sensitive topics without verbally attacking each other's views. They know how to agree to disagree with each other! The weekly discussion topic is chosen by the group a week in advance. . . . The only library preparation for this group is to set up the meeting room with the chairs in a large circle and to provide water and coffee."

River Falls Reads. *Heather Johnson at River Falls Public Library in Wisconsin:* "An annual program that encourages the community to read the same book and to participate in a wide variety of programs, author visits, and activities that promote lifelong literacy and encourage community conversations."

Origami group. *Yolo County Library in California:* "We offer . . . [a monthly program] that is also attended by adults 50+." The Origami group teaches the art of Japanese paper folding to all ages and levels of abilities with the first hour dedicated to beginners. The group learns how to fold paper into various shapes such as making pumpkins, bats, and unique napkin folds shown by an origami artist.

Korean culture program. *Simsbury Public Library in Connecticut:* "A free Korean culture program attended by patrons from preschool age through seniors. It included a full Korean meal."

Experience painting. *Melany Wilks at Pioneer Memorial Library in Kansas:* "For ages 11 and up had drawn grandparents and grandchildren together during the summer. Also, parents and children, or just middle age to over 50 with youth helping each other in the workshop. Very successful." This program was funded by a grant, which enabled patrons to learn to paint on canvas.

Black history. *Simsbury Public Library in Connecticut:* "Film screenings followed by moderated community discussions on civil rights." Past films include documentaries such as *The Untold Story of Emmett Louis Till, Alice's Ordinary People,* and *Freedom Riders.*

In stitches. *Heather Johnson at River Falls Public Library in Wisconsin:* "The River Falls Public Library . . . provide[s] . . . gallery exhibits . . . that enrich, educate and entertain people who pass through the space. Many of these exhibits provide adults ages 50+ with the opportunity to participate in programs that partner with the exhibits . . . the annual spring quilt show . . . includes many quilts that are on display in the exhibit that have been made by adults ages 50+ in the community. Programming opportunities for adults ages 50+ with this show included an author book talk and signing . . . a paper-piecing quilting workshop, and an opening reception."

The art of deduction. *Matthew Riley at Friendswood Public Library in Texas:* "An all-ages Sherlock Holmes book and art club. . . . We will read a story and create a work of art based on that story. Each meeting will be a different story and art project."

Viva Vallenato! Folk music from Colombia. *John J. Trause, director at Oradell Public Library in New Jersey:* "A World Music program for adults and children . . . we had a packed house of all ages celebrating with music, dancing, and Colombian cuisine."

Culture exploration. *Meryle A. Leonard at Charlotte Mecklenburg Library in North Carolina:* "This program was developed out of necessity. When a staff member was asked, 'Are you a terrorist?' because of her heritage, we decided to bring the Indian culture to our 50+ crowd. Participants enjoyed the photos, artifacts, and even food from Gujarat. They learned about customs, culture, and traditions. We shared all the resources the library offers to explore different cultures. The participants also had the opportunity to wear a sari. After the program participants shared they had a much better understanding of the culture. Other Cultural Exploration programs include Thailand, Venezuela, Spain, Mexico, and African American culture to our audience. These programs are presented by staff members."

LANGUAGES

If we examine our communities, most will find a variety of individuals from different ethnic and racial backgrounds. There are some adults 50+ who have likely immigrated themselves or have parents and grandparents who immigrated to the United States from a different country and, therefore, English is not their first language. Having materials in other languages available in our collections offers patrons items in their native tongue, but also opportunities for other patrons to learn another language and about other cultures. In addition, there are different Web sites that offer courses to learn a language online, such as Mango Languages, that public libraries can subscribe to for a fee, and Duolingo, which is a site offering free lessons and projects to learn a variety of languages. Almost a quarter (23 percent) of the contributing libraries offered language classes other than English to their library patrons or had a link to learn another language online. Some of the libraries also offered programs such as basic computer skills in another language. There were also a few that offered discussion classes for adults who spoke another language other than English so they could practice their English-speaking skills. We can also consider having our own Web site translated into other languages. This can be helpful to our library patrons who have English as a second language. Chapter 3 discusses the Nashville Public Library's Web site, located at https://library.nashville.org, which gives patrons the ability to change the language in which the site is displayed. The following are contributor examples of some cultural programs at their libraries.

Foreign film series. *Heather Johnson at River Falls Public Library in Wisconsin:* "Runs twice a year and offers adults . . . the experience of viewing a diverse selection of foreign films in the library."

Conversation club. *Meryle A. Leonard at Charlotte Mecklenburg Library in North Carolina:* "This program is targeted for our 50+ participants who don't speak English as their first language. Program participants practice their English speaking and listening skills in a relaxed group environment. No lectures in this program, just conversation."

Odissi dance. *Terry Soave at Ann Arbor District Library in Michigan:* "Temples, sculptures, ritual dances, stories and rhythms of Eastern India,"

Language. *Simsbury Public Library in Connecticut:* "English, Spanish, and French conversation classes. Spanish and French are attended largely by the 50+ age group."

LEISURE ACTIVITIES

Leisure activities are how individuals spend their time outside of a work environment. Most adults, as we age, spend less time working and more time pursuing leisurely activities. According to the Federal Interagency Forum on Aging-Related Statistics (2014), adults 55+ spend about a quarter of their time during an average day in leisurely pursuits. Some midlife and older adults want to be involved in meaningful activities and are looking to libraries for enriching opportunities among their collections and services to satisfy their need for lifelong learning. The more active an individual is in different activities, the greater the chance their informational needs will be met (Hales-Mabry, 1993). Leisure activities are linked to better health and improved well-being in adults midlife and older. Drawing from scholarly research, the more adults 50+ are involved in mental, physical, social, and productive leisure activities such as reading, discussions with others, and creative projects, the more it increases their healthy behaviors and the greater the satisfaction in life (Chang, Wray, & Lin, 2014). The following are a sampling from contributors to this text of some leisurely activities provided at their libraries.

Active older adult wisdom circle. *Yolo County Library in California:* "This group meets monthly and is moderated. . . . It is a meeting of elders exploring together aspects of the conscious aging movement, seeking to mine the wisdom from their long lives and to find effective ways to share and pass on their legacy. Most members are over 80."

Classical music in the afternoon. *Simsbury Public Library in Connecticut:* "We do a . . . series with . . . the Hartt School at the University of Hartford. They provide musicians from their Community Division for a very reasonable price, paid for through our Friends of the Simsbury Public Library."

Adult learners series. *Elizabeth Eisen, adult programming librarian at Appleton Public library in Wisconsin:* "We offer lectures, field trips and workshops on a variety of topics. Examples of some of the topics have been The Electoral College, Artic Exploration, Astrology, and Diet. These are patterned after the adult [learning] opportunities offered at local universities, but our programs are free of charge."

Creative expression. *Heather Johnson at River Falls Public Library in Wisconsin:* "Each year the library sponsors annual contests for the community to participate in. Adults are able to use their creativity and submit entries into the Peeps Diorama Contest, the Summer Flower Show, and the Gingerbread Competition."

Local history discussions. *Anonymous:* "Brown Bag Lunch series that our local history librarian does in conjunction with the Visitor Center. This long-standing program features local history speakers." This annual series is an educational program meant to highlight the rich history, culture, and traditions of the local city and its heritage.

EDUCATIONAL EXPERIENCES

Creating educational programs can involve different types of educational pursuits. Some adults 50+ are looking to further their education in scholarly activities. According to the Population Reference Bureau (2017), 25 percent of adults 65+ in 2014 completed a bachelor's degree. Besides furthering their education, there are other adults 50+ who need classes to increase a particular skill or learn a new language. There are some who were not able to finish their education due to life circumstances, and as they have gotten older, are able to go back and finish their education. Still others immigrated to the United States and want to take classes to assist with their English-language development. There are different programs and services we can offer to help adults 50+ with their educational endeavors. It is important to keep in mind that returning to school for some adults midlife and older can be stressful and intimidating. Collaborating with schools and higher educational institutions and providing educational courses at the library might help alleviate worries about academia and financial fees, as well as providing a familiar environment with resources that support their learning (Schull, 2013). For the adult 50+ who utilizes technology, online courses are available for individuals to learn something new or to sharpen known skills. At Universal Classes, we can gain access to over 500 different types of courses through a subscription (see Appendix C) that our patrons can then access for free. The Osher Lifelong Learning Institute, supported by the Bernard Osher Foundation (2005), is an organization currently at 100 universities and colleges in the United States that supports lifelong learning by offering noncredit courses for adults 50+. Various colleges and universities also offer classes in certain subject areas for a reduced fee for adults 50+. We need to consider contacting a local institution about collaborating with the library on specific topics and asking about their policy on costs for educating midlife and older adults.

Another educational area that we are starting to provide in our libraries are makerspaces. Makerspaces are places in the library for creative, hands-on activities, including activities involving technology. Offering makerspaces can provide a physical space that would be beneficial for inquiry-based educational learning, fostering a collaborative environment and creating enriching projects (Kurti, Kurti, & Fleming, 2014). The makerspace allows patrons to take control over their own learning, generating opportunities to experiment with different options or endings for a project. The Web site *Make It @ Your Library* is an excellent resource to get started (see Appendix B). The following are a few contributor examples of what their libraries are doing in terms of educational programming.

OLLI presents. *Lisa C. West at Homewood Public Library in Alabama:* "Osher Lifelong Learning Institute (located at the University of Alabama) is leading the way in lifelong learning for mature adults in Central Alabama. OLLI provides members with the opportunity to learn new things, make friends, travel, and embrace life. Special semester classes are taught at senior centers for a membership price of $25. We have partnered with OLLI to present their bonus programs at the library, which are free to everyone, but geared toward seniors at libraries."

Osher lifelong learning. *Terry Soave at Ann Arbor District Library in Michigan:* "We regularly collaborate with . . . the University of Michigan's OSHER Lifelong Learning series." Ann Arbor had a series of lectures that included a talk on voting by the League of Women Voters, a political science professor speaking on democracy, and a psychology professor speaking on brain aging.

Makerspaces. *Melanie Wehrle at Pikes Peak Library District in Colorado:* "Two of our regional branches now have makerspaces. In conjunction with these spaces, we have a Maker and Artist in Residence program . . . the makerspaces have the equipment, such as laser engravers, 3D printers, various power tools, and sewing machines. . . . These programs are held at all times of [the] day, including evenings. They attract a large number of older adults who are looking to rediscover their creativity or learn a new creative skill. The funding for these programs is included in the budget."

CHAPTER SUMMARY

This chapter discussed lifelong learning and how beneficial it is for the brains of adults 50+ to remain active. Creating different types of formal and informal learning opportunities can provide adults 50+ different areas of interests to pursue. Collaborating with other institutions and organizations can lead to a wide variety of programs enriching and inspiring our library communities.

7

Community Collaborations

Creating partnerships with outside organizations and institutions will enhance the value of the library and also increase its profile and value within the community. When we collaborate with outside agencies, there is also the potential of broadening the amount of adults 50+ we can reach. Collaborators can bring their expertise on certain subject areas and assist in the workload, share any possible expenses, and help with the publicity of the event, depending on the program or service. In addition, building ongoing relationships can free up planning time for other programming throughout the year. For instance if a program was a success, ask the collaborator to come back on a regular basis (Lear, 2013). A successful partnership benefits everyone, including our library community members. In this chapter, different organizations are mentioned as possible collaborators for the library. Appendix B has links to the appropriate Web site for more information.

ESTABLISHING PARTNERSHIPS

The first step in establishing a relationship with future collaborators that will benefit our adult 50+ library patrons is to examine the organizations and agencies within the community that offer services and programs to adults midlife and older, such as a local community senior center or the local Agency on Aging. In addition, consider exploring potential partnerships with organizations that have various types of information that can provide lifelong learning opportunities or informational programs and entertainment possibilities. Collaborating with other partners around the community will expand the types of programming and services we can offer at the library. The following is a list of potential partner organizations:

- Community senior centers
- Scout troops

- Religious organizations (churches, synagogues, etc.)
- Agency on Aging (local and state affiliates)
- Recreation departments
- Support groups (Alzheimer's, Caregivers, etc.)
- AARP (American Association of Retired Persons)
- Fitness organizations (local gyms, YMCA, YWCA, etc.)
- Theater groups and music associations
- Educational institutions (local schools, universities, and colleges)
- Civic organizations (Lions Club, Knights of Columbus, etc.)
- Military and veteran organizations (VFW posts, VA hospitals, etc.)
- Local businesses (pharmacies, grocery stores, merchants, funeral homes, etc.)
- Charitable organizations (American Red Cross, Volunteers of America, Meals on Wheels, etc.)
- Local hospitals
- Nursing associations
- Financial institutions
- Legal agencies
- Museums
- Mental and health associations
- Travel agencies
- Insurance companies
- Social Security Administration

We can reach out to potential partners by phone, e-mail, or face-to-face communications. We can offer to have meetings at the library for future discussions, and we can strive for a long-term relationship instead of just a one-time meeting. To help build a relationship with potential partner organizations, start by asking questions to determine what types of programs and services they offer to the 50+ adult community. Examine if they have speakers on certain topics or information they would be willing to share. It is a nice idea to ask if the library can be of service to them, such as providing a meeting space for their organization or providing a space to display their literature either within the physical library or on the library's Web site. Open communication and establishing the mutual benefits of a collaboration will create successful community partnerships supporting the library's mission and vision. These partnerships will help increase community involvement, promote healthy aging, and create beneficial services to enhance the well-being of adults midlife and older in our communities. Consider creating a list of partners and contacts with the programs and services they provide for easy reference for developing future programs.

TIPS AND IDEAS

The following are some helpful tips, ideas, and suggestions from contributors to this text about collaborating with other partners for programming and services for adults 50+. Creating effective partnerships can help meet the needs of more adults midlife and older in our communities.

Lisa C. West at Homewood Public Library in Alabama: "My advice is to look for program partners in your own community and surrounding areas. These folks are eager for the advertising and recommendations their programs will bring . . . collaborate specifically with AARP, OLLI (Osher Lifelong Learning Institute), they are specific groups that do exclusive senior programming."

Marie Corbitt at Westerville Public Library in Ohio: "Partnerships and good relationships with activities directors at senior facilities is key. They will be your advocates, the ones telling the residents about your program and encouraging them to go. It makes life much easier when they are on your side. And the trick is to make it easy for them to like you. Instead of contacting them each month to schedule a program, suggest doing a program every first Monday or third Tuesday of the month, or whichever day works best. A repeating program that they do not need to think about scheduling each month works out the best."

Chris Jackson, special audiences strategist: "Partnerships can be wonderful ways to reach this audience, since there are many organizations out there serving their needs. In addition to bringing outside funding and presenters, most partners have their own marketing mechanisms, allowing us to reach audiences we might not connect with otherwise."

Brianne Columbo at Fairfield Free Public Library in New Jersey: "Collaborate with local businesses, organizations, individuals, and groups. Many businesses are open to providing free lectures, programs, and other event contributions. We partner with several local businesses, (e.g., grocery stores, medical centers, doctors, authors, restaurants, etc.) in order to provide free programming for adults and seniors. In exchange, we promote the given business [or] organization in our promotional material, social media, and Web site."

Webster Public Library in New York: "The bulk of our programs are offered by outside groups (AARP or volunteers) so other than booking the room, taking registration (if required), and any technical assistance needed for the presenter, there is little work involved."

Quincy Public Library in Illinois: "We offer meeting space for several support groups such as Parkinson's, Alzheimer's, brain injury, and Retired Senior Volunteer Program."

Ryan Johnson at O'Fallon Public Library in Illinois: "Always try to find partners in the community. We make it very clear that any business we partner with cannot make sales or a sales pitch when they present at the library. They can, however, provide brochures or business cards for people to take. The business donates their time and gets free PR out of the event. We get experts' help to inform and educate the public, which is part of our mission."

Melany Wilks at Pioneer Memorial Library in Kansas: "It has taken years to draw different representative[s] into cooperation and collaboration. Start small and allow for growth to happen. . . . Reaching out with others to collaborate extends the number of persons serving the community through the library."

John J. Trause, director at Oradell Public Library in New Jersey: "We work with many groups, so it is essential that I, as library director, the library staff, the Friends of the Library, and the members of the Oradell Public Library Foundation maintain connections to all the other groups in the area."

Anoka County Library in Minnesota: "It is important to know and work with agencies in your community that already work with your target audience. Even if other agencies are not a partner helping to create programs, they are a great source of information and are a great venue for promotion. Who better to know a best time of day or optimal length of a program for seniors than your local senior center coordinator? How better to promote a service for homebound persons than to slip a brochure in with Meals on Wheels deliveries?"

MUSEUMS

According to the Institute of Museum and Library Services (2017), there are over 35,000 U.S. museums that include art, history, science and technology, children's museums, historical societies, tribal museums, planetariums, botanical gardens, and zoos. Museums have similar missions and values as libraries, which will assist in the planning and the process of a joint collaboration. Partnering with museums can bring in associates to speak about different items they have currently in their collections, create a class on preservation of materials, or bring about the creation of new innovative programming. Consider asking the museum to share a part of their collection to highlight certain materials they currently have on display to inspire interest and future visits to learn about the whole collection. A mutual collaboration has the potential to create new opportunities for outreach and extend the number of new members enjoying what the museum and library in the community has to offer. Consider the types of partnership by examining goals and resources for mutual collaboration. Building on the skills and practices that the library and museum already have will create a more sustainable and effective collaboration (Kulpinski, 2009). The following is an example of a contributor collaborating with a community member who has connections with a local museum.

Webster Public Library in New York: "Collaborations are key . . . the class we offer on Ancestry.com is conducted by one [of] our board members who happens to not only have a great interest in genealogy but also volunteers at the local historical museum in town."

LOCAL, STATE, AND NATIONAL COLLABORATORS

There are many institutions and organizations to explore partnerships with to expand and create new opportunities for our adult midlife and older library patrons. Collaborations can be at the local, state, or national level. Exploring different options opens up new avenues of possibilities that might not have been thought of before. Many organizations can have affiliates that are part of the larger association. As librarians, we are always asking questions and searching for information for our library patrons. We need to look at finding partners for our programs and services with the same determination and process. If a collaboration seems out of reach, build a bridge, ask for other possible avenues to explore, bring in other partners, and examine if a future partnership is a possibility. We need to consider keeping a file of partners and representatives with dates and notes from our communications. This list can be beneficial to follow up with potential partners or with future prospective endeavors. Establishing partnerships builds relationships with our communities and benefits your midlife and older patrons. Partner organizations can also have more extensive demographic information that can be of value in creating library services and programs. In addition, some could have mailing lists or individuals who have not been reached through the library, creating potential new patrons.

Furthermore, when exploring potential collaborators, remember to ask library patrons. There are many adults midlife and older who like to volunteer and share their expertise and knowledge (Roberts & Bauman, 2012). Plus, a connection or contact can be made by a simple conversation. In addition, most communities have an area Agency on Aging, and different local community organizations have adult 50+ services. We can also look to neighboring communities if something in the area is not offered. Contact other libraries to obtain ideas or to exchange services and programs. When exploring possible partners and conducting a search on the Internet, remember that many names can be used for "adults 50+". Try all possibilities (senior, elderly, older adults, etc.) to increase your chances of finding information. Sometimes the right word will bring up a new area that had not been previously discovered.

The possibilities of having different collaborators with our libraries are extensive. For instance, most states have a department of health and senior services, and some states have individual departments on the county level. Here we can find representatives who can come out and speak on a variety of topics such as interviewing techniques and resume building, housing, volunteering, nutrition, and many others. Ask local universities or colleges for volunteers, faculty, or students to talk on certain subject areas such as creative writing, or art students to showcase their own artwork and teach their technique. The Library of Congress Center for the Book has affiliates in each state that sponsor various programs. These affiliates carry out the national center's mission in their local areas; sponsor programs that highlight their area's literary heritage; and call attention to the importance of books, reading, literacy, and libraries. On their Web site you can find a list of states with appropriate links (see Appendix B).

Furthermore, ALA has traveling exhibits, and you can apply to have the exhibit come to your library. It is important to take note of application deadlines for each exhibit and check back on the Web site for changes and a list of new exhibits. There are eight traveling exhibits as of November 2017. Other organizations also have traveling exhibits. Keep in mind that some organizations have various fees. This could include the exhibit, the components, shipping and handling costs, setup instructions, and a press kit for promotion of the exhibit. Some interesting sites to check out are Traveling Exhibits, The Gilder Lehrman Institute of American History, the Smithsonian Institution Traveling Exhibition Service, and the Lunar and Planetary Institute. The Library of Congress also has exhibits available for travel. There isn't a fee for the exhibit. However, the library is responsible for recording photography, mount preparation, packing, crating, shipping, insurance, and any possible courier costs. See Appendix B for appropriate links.

Furthermore, we need to take into account that time management is important with our partners. Programs can be quite involved, taking a lot of time and planning, or they can be very simple with little preparation or materials. It will take time to plan and schedule an event and also time to set up and take down presentations and displays. We do not want special guests to feel rushed to remove their items or that they have to leave a room because of an upcoming program. In turn, if we are visiting another institution, work time in to arrive and leave on time and make preparations if programs run over the time allotted. We need to create a calm atmosphere by being prepared and organized, whether hosting or as a guest, which will forge better relationships for future collaborations. The following are contributor examples of different collaborations with local, state, and national organizations as well as individuals in the community.

LOCAL EXAMPLES

Arts councils. *Anonymous:* "Our Artist in Action series brings a local artist into the library . . . every month to do a demonstration. We originally used a 'pop-up' space for this, moving aside bookshelves near the circulation desk on our main floor so that the demonstration was very visible. Eventually, we needed to move the demonstration into a regular meeting space because our moveable bookcases started falling apart from all the moving. We partner with . . . our local arts council, and that group recommended the first two artists to give us a start. At this point, we tend to find the artists on our own. We offer a standard $50 honorarium. During the years that I have done this program, we have featured a wide variety of artists, including painters, print makers, potters, collagists, art quilters, wood carvers, musicians, and even a fly tying artist who used his skills to make jewelry."

Caregiver organizations. *Anoka County Library in Minnesota:* "Anoka County Library also collaborates with the Anoka County Family Caregiver Connection to present Dementia Dialogue. Dementia Dialogue is a book and film discussion group that explores dementia through stories both real and fictional. Both agencies provide input into the title selections and staff to lead the discussion. The Family Caregiver Connection is helpful in offering suggestions to make the programs 'caregiver friendly,' promoting the programs to caregivers and other interested persons, and offers valuable information and referral to participants after the discussion. Their participation has truly enriched the discussion group."

Kathleen Goodson at Wimberley Village Library in Texas: "Powerful Tools for Caregivers helps family caregivers reduce stress, improve caregiving confidence, establish balance in their lives, communicate their needs, locate helpful resources, and make tough decisions. Provided by AGE of Central Texas from a generous grant from St. David's Foundation." (AGE of Central Texas is an organization for caregivers.)

Civic engagement

Chamber of commerce. *Beth Neunaber:* "Seeking partners and collaborators is essential. As the Adult Services Supervisor, I attend community meetings, such as the . . . Chamber of Commerce and Service Clubs to meet people in the numerous professions that are represented in these groups."

Environmental committees. *John J. Trause, director at Oradell Public Library in New Jersey:* "A Walk in the Sun (walk around Oradell Reservoir) . . . co-sponsored with Oradell Environmental Committee."

Elizabeth Eisen, adult programming librarian at Appleton Public Library in Wisconsin: "I collaborate with the local Sierra Club to offer documentary film discussions." The Sierra Club is a local affiliate of a larger organization in the state of Wisconsin concerned about the natural environment.

Santa Barbara Public Library in California: "We partner with local Trails Organizations. Those people know other people and have an existing community to draw speakers from as well as help promote the event to their members."

Local clubs. *Christy Wagner at ELA Area Public Library in Illinois:* "Outreach also works with our local Lions Club to bring low vision services to our patrons such as the vision screening bus. We view all community organizations and some businesses as potential partners for programming."

Local events. *Mariel Carter, adult service reference librarian at Marinette County Consolidated Public Library Services in Wisconsin:* "In partnership with the Wisconsin Science Festival, we hold an annual Science Fest to encourage an enthusiasm for science. This event attracts adults with science hobbies to bring them to show budding enthusiasts. It is a great way to help children find out about different aspects of science by working with older people who are enthusiastic about ham radios, composting with worms, bike repair, simple machines, beekeeping, etc. . . . This event does not have to cost much money, but can if purchasing special materials for the science experiment tables."

Parks and recreation departments. New Durham Public Library in New Hampshire: "Our cribbage program is sponsored by the Parks and Recreation Dept. and held at the library. As it is during the day, most participants are retired and 50+."

Community members. Mariel Carter, adult service reference librarian at Marinette County Consolidated Public Library Services in Wisconsin: "We invite professionals and locals to present to an adult audience as often as these people are willing to do it. . . . Presenters include authors to tell about their latest books, travelers describing their latest trips, horticultural experts teaching a specific skill or providing education on a particular topic, meditation or yoga leader, and local experts talking about community programs and initiatives. Prep work includes scheduling the event and making sure that each event is well advertised. Depending on the expected audience, we may provide coffee, tea, and a light dessert. Otherwise, these events do not cost the library anything."

Educational institutions

Elementary schools. Fife Lake Public Library in Michigan: "We collaborate with our local elementary school and credit union to host a Smart Money program. The elementary students come over and learn about money with the seniors. During the holidays, the students come over to carol during lunch and visit with Santa. The seniors love seeing the school children and are so good with them. You can see their faces brighten when they come in. We usually have a light snack and drink for these programs as well."

Marie Corbitt at Westerville Public Library in Ohio: "Leaping Letters . . . a letter writing program between seniors and an elementary school class. This is a great way to connect two parts of the community who may otherwise not get a chance to know each other. We use Library Link (our school delivery program) and our own Outreach delivery service as a means of delivering the letters back and forth. We also try our best to bring the two groups together to meet at the end of the school year. We have done this twice, with much success! They love getting to meet each other in person. Prep for this program includes trying to get seniors involved. It has proven a bit difficult to find seniors to write letters . . . I also organize when letters need to be written and returned and keep things on schedule. There is no cost for this program since we do not need postage. We deliver all letters ourselves."

High schools. Jaci at Cranberry Public Library in Pennsylvania: "Recently, we partnered with a local high school teacher and Classrooms Without Borders to present . . . the last surviving . . . Holocaust survivor . . . We had 170 people attend (adults as well as students), which maxed out our meeting space. To prepare, we created promotional material such as press releases, e-mail blasts through Constant Contact, and flyers to distribute within the library. As with most of our programs, participants were required to register. Because we maxed out on our registration, we developed a number system for those people that came the evening of the program and were not able to register in case we had room available after those that registered had checked in."

Simsbury Public Library in Connecticut: "Simsbury High School. We have done 'Sweet Saturday Morning' baking programs with their culinary arts department about half of the attendees 50+."

Financial Institutions. *Lisa C. West at Homewood Public Library in Alabama:* "Investing in the 21st Century Lunch and Learn Taking Control of Your Retirement Workshop and Luncheon. . . . This workshop is a partnership between Merrill Lynch and the Homewood Public Library. (No cost to library or patron. Merrill Lynch provided the food.)"

Ryan Johnson at O'Fallon Public Library in Illinois: "We also partner with local financial advisors to provide information surrounding Medicare, Social Security, retirement planning, and the like . . . these are educational events only. We never charge a fee for patrons to attend."

Historical societies. *Simsbury Public Library in Connecticut:* "History: 'Victoria' a lecture by a professor from Trinity College . . . followed by a Victorian tea at the Simsbury Historical Society Tea Room."

Chad Robinson at Matheson Memorial Library in Wisconsin: "We have frequently partnered with our county historical and genealogical societies to offer genealogy workshops and speakers on local history."

Mariel Carter, adult service reference librarian at Marinette County Consolidated Public Library Services in Wisconsin: "When we get the honor of hosting traveling displays from the Wisconsin Historical Society, many adults come to the library to see the displays. These events take time to coordinate schedules with artists and can also take 30 to 60 minutes to put up and take down the display. These displays do not cost the library anything."

Health organizations. *Richard Conroy at Essex Library Association in Connecticut:* "We collaborate with various other nonprofits such as the VNA, as well as private entities like the assisted living facility." (VNA is Visiting Nurse Association.)

Beth Neunaber: "We have partnered with chiropractors, nurses, and other healthcare professionals to offer programs such as Healthy Heart, Healthy Body; Solutions for Low Back Pain."

Legal agencies. *Beth Neunaber:* "We've had legal advisors come to share expertise [on] writing wills, living wills, and power of attorney."

Local businesses. *Lisa C. West at Homewood Public Library in Alabama:* "We partner with a shredding company who sends their truck to our site to destroy . . . sensitive documents and files. . . . This event is a cooperative program of the Homewood Library, the Homewood Chamber of Commerce, Secure Destruction, Protec Recycling, and Homewood Rotary."

Simsbury Public Library in Connecticut: "Metro Bis Restaurant . . . We do a cookbook author program with them, they bring in an author who will be doing a program that night at their restaurant, and they come to the library during the day for a lecture and free samples made by the restaurant."

Lisa C. West at Homewood Public Library in Alabama: "Dixie's Pet Loss Support Group. . . . The death of a pet can be one of the most devastating events that can happen to a person, yet one of the most misunderstood, too . . . (partnered with the Greater Birmingham Humane Society, this is a free program to library and the patrons. Many senior participants)."

Media (television, radio hosts, and newspaper reporters). *Fife Lake Public Library in Michigan:* "We also do programs that are just for fun. Our local TV station's weatherman . . . will call bingo."

Neighboring libraries. Lisa Prizio: "For the last two years the . . . library has partnered with . . . (another) library (which is the neighboring town) to provide a Memory Café. It serves people with Alzheimer's disease and their caregivers. We meet once a month, first at one library and then the other. We provide coffee, tea, and cookies. . . . We visit and chat and have provided music programs, documentaries, and games. We visited the historical societies in both towns and have picnics and small hikes. These afternoons are very enjoyable. It's more like having company over than working."

Lisa C. West at Homewood Public Library in Alabama: "Genealogy 101: Introduction to Genealogy Series of 10 programs provided by Birmingham Central's Southern History Dept. . . . Various staff members of the Southern History Department will . . . cover such topics as vital records, courthouse and church records, and the Federal Census."

Retirement communities. *Carroll County (MD) Public Library in Maryland:* "We specifically have partnerships with the two largest assisted living nursing homes in Carroll County. . . . Over the last couple of years, we have developed and presented several local author programs and programs about local history. The key is to complement what the centers are currently providing while creating experiences that are unique and exactly what folks want to come to. No one is ever done learning."

Kathleen Handy, computer instructor at Saratoga Springs Public Library in New York: "We could say that doing outreach for . . . a community for assisted living retirees . . . we collaborate to bring library services to the residents there, where we answer computer and device-related questions twice monthly. Interestingly enough, I have a 90+ year-old resident who is very proficient on her iPhone. I help her with questions on the device. Many others have laptops or iPads that we help with."

Senior centers. *Anoka County Library in Minnesota:* "Anoka County Library partners with several community senior centers to provide support with technology-related issues. Once a month, library staff visit senior centers to provide one-on-one assistance with downloading library e-books, setting up an e-mail account, using social media, or any other technology question. The senior centers provide space, promotion, and take registrations for the sessions. These have been good partnerships . . . the senior centers are able to provide a welcomed service to their clients, and the library is able to reach seniors that may not be able to get to the library for in-house tech assistance."

Athol Public Library in Massachusetts: "The Athol Senior Center shows movies each month, and the library recommends and provides these movies to them."

Mary at Wilbraham Public Library in Massachusetts: "Our previous outreach librarian had some times that she would drop in at the senior center and show people how to use Overdrive, one of our resources for downloadable library e-books. She only had one or two people drop in at any given time, but a few people came into the library later asking about downloading e-books because they'd heard of that program and just hadn't been able to reach it."

Christy Wagner at ELA Area Public Library in Illinois: "I collaborate with the ELA Township '55-Plus' program (our local 'senior center') such as the annual 'Nightclub at Noon,' Courageous Decisions, Tough Conversations series, the monthly senior book discussion group as examples."

STATE EXAMPLES

Civic engagement. *Tracy Trotter, library director at Adams Memorial Library in Pennsylvania:* "Shortly we will be offering assistance for seniors in filling out PA Rent Rebate forms, which are to be taught by our state representative at his suggestion (we think it's a brilliant idea!)."

Simsbury Public Library in Connecticut: "Simsbury and the History of Land Conservation. . . . This program generated a lot of civic pride as our attendees . . . discovered that people associated with our little town were instrumental in starting both the state and federal land conservation movement. . . . We collaborated with our local land refuge, a state forest and park group, our local historical society, the staff of the historical inn, and a local restaurant. Because it was part of our statewide Open House Day, we advertised through the state Web site . . . the Web site of our funding source and through all the organizations we collaborated with. We also publicized programs through local newspapers, TV and radio, area land trusts, conservation organizations, other area libraries, the Senior Center, the Friends, our state representatives, schools, and local tourism organizations. We marketed it to all ages, but the 50+ age group represented the largest group of attendees. My main tip for a program of this magnitude is to have plenty of volunteers lined up to help move people smoothly between events."

Educational institutions

Universities or colleges. *Tracy Trotter, library director at Adams Memorial Library in Pennsylvania:* "Later this year we will be hosting programs for adults as well as ones for children on the subject of the upcoming solar eclipse, for which we are partnering with a local college that has a planetarium. They are sending astronomers at no cost to give talks on the topic."

Kathleen Goodson at Wimberley Village Library in Texas: "Texas Agri-Life Extension agents have come to make presentations on everything from harvesting and preserving the garden to feral hogs in Texas."

Melany Wilks at Pioneer Memorial Library in Kansas: "Adventures in Wellness: Discusses ways for enhanced wellness. The program was written by a person [working] for the K-State Extension Center through a grant. Our K-State

Extension office here advertised it as 'Keys to Embracing Aging.' She had no one signed up. We talked about it and I suggested a name change to 'Adventures in Wellness' so that we might draw a broader base of people. Plus, people don't like to admit they are aging. Now . . . with the new title . . . we had 10 attend plus 2 who said they could not that week. It is the same program promoting things like positive attitude, eating smart and healthy, Physical activity, brain activity, social activity and tuning in to times . . . (12 sessions for 12 months)."

Lisa C. West at Homewood Public Library in Alabama: "We have partnered with The UAB (University of Alabama) Neurology Dept. who provide doctors and researchers from an area of their expertise who talk about common ailments and explain what research and treatments are in development for these [common health] problems. We have had programs on dementia, depression, arthritis, epilepsy, changing eyesight, blood pressure, and many other diseases."

Heather Johnson at River Falls Public Library in Wisconsin: "Exercise Your Imagination . . . a creative bookmaking workshop for those 60+ . . . with support from the Helen Daniels Bader Fund, a Bader Philanthropy (presented by the UW-Milwaukee Center for Community-Based Learning, Leadership, and Research) . . . storytelling and bookmaking in a supportive environment while celebrating 75 years of Little Golden Books. . . . Led by specially trained art students from UWM's Peck School of the Arts."

Debra DeJonker-Berry at Eastham Public Library in Massachusetts: "We have offered programs (training on our assistive technology) partnering with . . . statewide groups such as the Perkins School for the Blind and their Talking Book and other services."

Chris Jackson, special audiences strategist: "Caregiver University is a new series of programs designed to help those addressing the needs of a family member or friend who needs significant care support. Often this is one spouse caring for another whose health is in decline, or an adult child caring for an elderly parent. The series is [a] partnership between the library, a local healthcare provider . . . and a local extension office of a state university."

Mariel Carter, adult service reference librarian at Marinette County Consolidated Public Library Services in Wisconsin: "The UW-Extension Agricultural and Horticultural Agent presents programs on gardening techniques (including ways to help reduce gardening strain on a body)."

Health agencies. *Beth Neunaber:* "Once or twice per year, we partner with the Senior Health Insurance Benefits Advisor . . . a state agency. The representative is available to assist with the complex task of signing up for Medicare."

Wallingford Public Library in Connecticut: "'Lunch & Learn' is a monthly healthcare presentation given by various professionals, after which a light lunch . . . is served. . . . The program is sponsored by the not-for profit organization Masonicare, Connecticut's leading provider of healthcare and retirement living communities for seniors. Past topics include sleeplessness, insights into the aging eye, living with congestive heart failure, pain management, and

memory loss and dementia. . . . There is no cost to the library or the participants. The speakers and the lunch are provided by Masonicare."

Kathleen Goodson at Wimberley Village Library in Texas: "'Latest Research on
the Aging Brain' presented by . . . professor of psychology at Texas State University. This was an extremely well-presented and educational lecture that
packed our small lecture room."

Melany Wilks at Pioneer Memorial Library in Kansas: "Operation Red File:
Collaboration through health department and community coalition. Targets
older adults to organize their health information in one place in case of an emer-
gency. Was very successful for the over 50+ group. Cost to library was flyers and
meeting room. Each organization brought their input and supplies that were
needed. A grant was written to help with this."

*Lucine Kauffman, SAGE coordinator at Richmond Memorial Library in New
York:* "SAGE (Services to the Aging in Genesee County) coordinates library services to senior (60+ years old) residents of Genesee County who are unable to
visit the library due to an illness, disability, or lack of transportation. SAGE staff
and volunteers deliver library services to . . . individuals in their private homes.
Plus, every six weeks, SAGE staff delivers a rotating large group loan to . . .
senior resident facilities. . . . Delivery to individual SAGE patrons in their private homes is tailored to their needs and preferences. New SAGE patrons are
given a preference survey to complete. The survey asks what media they are
interested in receiving and the genres and artists they prefer. Some patrons prefer to choose their own materials either by putting a hold on items through their
online library account or calling SAGE staff with their requests. Some patrons
prefer to have staff choose materials for them (based on their completed preference survey), and a few volunteers choose the materials for their assigned patron.
Some patrons receive materials 'on demand' and some have regularly scheduled
visits from their assigned volunteer . . . SAGE partners with the other five programs funded by . . . the Aging in Genesee County . . . SAGE staff also attends
monthly meetings of the Genesee County Interagency Council to network with
all of the other human services agencies in the county. SAGE buys an ad in the
county's Office for the Aging newsletter where SAGE staff also writes an article
each issue."

NATIONAL EXAMPLES

AARP (American Association of Retired Persons). *Webster Public Library in
New York:* "Our programs are open to everyone but the most popular for this
specific age group is the AARP Defensive Driving Class, this is held in our meeting room, we don't conduct the class."

Meryle A. Leonard at Charlotte Mecklenburg Library in North Carolina:
"Affordable Care Act and Older Americans: How the ACA Affects Medicare
and Older Adults: This program is a collaboration with AARP. AARP representatives visit our branch and outreach locations to help participants understand
the implementation of the Affordable Care Act. This program pushes politics
aside and helps people get answers about how this law will impact them."

Administration on Aging. *Santa Barbara Public Library in California:* "We have HICAP do informational programs about Medicare." (HICAP is a Health Insurance Counseling and Advocacy Program.)

Tamar Kreke, adult and technical services coordinator at Greene County Public Library in Ohio: "We work closely with the Greene County Council on Aging to make sure we are meeting the needs of the county's seniors. We participate in their meetings, and they often invite us to their health fairs, informational sessions, etc."

Muncie Public Library in Indiana: "We have had success partnering with Life Stream, the local Council on Aging. Last summer, we partnered with them on a program 'A Matter of Balance,' which was a multiweek program aimed at fall prevention."

Alzheimer's Associations. *Chad Robinson at Matheson Memorial Library in Wisconsin:* "We have recently been partnering with community members and organizations that appeal to this age group. Examples include providing space for our local Alzheimer's Association to host a monthly Memory Café."

Lynn Harthorne: "Memory Café is brought to the library once a month by Alzheimer's and Dementia Alliance.... The goal of the Memory Café is to provide a relaxed environment in which persons with mild cognitive impairment and their family members can enjoy the company of others facing similar challenges and learn, laugh, and visit together. Activities are chosen (and sometimes led) by participants; some with the whole group and some in smaller groups depending on interests. Examples include t'ai chi to improve balance, discussing artwork, creative projects, games, guest presenters on an array of subjects, storytelling, and simply sharing among friends."

Beth Neunaber: "Enjoying the Holidays: Tips for Those with Loved Ones Who Have Alzheimer's wellness program with the Alzheimer's Association."

Meryle A. Leonard at Charlotte Mecklenburg Library in North Carolina: "Alzheimer's Association Western Carolina Chapter: free guest speakers, topics include but are not limited to healthy eating, aging diseases, and legal planning."

Kathleen Goodson at Wimberley Village Library in Texas: "As part of the Alzheimer's Foundation of America's National Memory Screening Program, we offered discreet, noninvasive tests consisting of questions and tasks designed to gauge memory, and thinking and language skills administered by a doctor. In addition there were information tables, games and activities about successful aging, and chair massages."

Health organizations. *Adrienne Doman Calkins at Sherwood Public Library in Oregon:* "Death & Dying Series.... Many times patrons come to both Estate Planning and Advanced Directives.... This particular program is in partnership with Oregon Health Decisions and is one of their 'Key Conversations' programs."

League of Women Voters. *Santa Barbara Public Library in California:* "We partner with the League of Women Voters on civic engagement topics and the audience is nearly all 50+."

Meals on Wheels. *Ocean County Library in New Jersey:* "Ocean County Library has partnered with the county's Meals on Wheels program to provide their clients with information on the library's services."

National Endowment for the Humanities. *Rebecca at Guthrie Public Library in Oklahoma:* "Another program that is well used by our seniors is Let's Talk About it, Oklahoma! (LTAIO), a project from the Oklahoma Humanities (the state affiliate of the National Endowment for the Humanities). It is a book club with the discussions led by a scholar from the community! Preparation is mainly used in keeping track of where the books are, finding scholars, scheduling the building, setting up the space, preparing refreshments for the break, and cleaning after the program."

World affairs. *Marie Corbitt at Westerville Public Library in Ohio:* "Great Decisions is our country's largest discussion group on world affairs. It is designed as a forum to allow older adults to become familiar with and discuss their views on global topics. It is a program through the Foreign Policy Association, and you can purchase a booklet with eight articles for the year as well as a DVD with short documentaries to go along with each article. So this program would involve purchasing those items. Some examples of topics include Digital Privacy, Human Trafficking, and Trade Policy. . . . The booklet and DVD together cost $70. Prep time is reading the article and watching the documentary beforehand."

CHAPTER SUMMARY

This chapter explored the benefits of collaborating with individuals, organizations, and other associations to help expand the experiences of our library patrons and to increase the amount of adults 50+ we potentially can reach within our communities. Partnerships can include local, state, and national affiliates that also provide benefits to the library and to the partner organization.

8

Don't Just Sit There: Reach Out!

Outreach provides services to individuals in the community who cannot physically visit the library due to an illness or limitation. These services can deliver information and recreational enjoyment that can assist in alleviating loneliness and depression (Honnold & Mesaros, 2004). Outreach can be offered in many forms to our adult 50+ community members: materials delivered by mail or personal home delivery, visits to institutions such as assisted living or nursing care facilities, drop-off or deposit collections at institutions, and having bookmobiles or techmobiles available for our community members. We also can consider offering programs through online social networking sites such as podcasts and YouTube videos, live streaming of programs, or creating DVDs of popular programs to share the experiences with patrons unable to physically attend at our libraries. Outreach services can increase the library's value to the community because the service depicts how the library is meeting all the population's needs within the community.

A key role for the outreach services provider is to know the library patrons' wants and needs who are receiving the services. Choosing the materials is especially important. We need to keep in mind that large-print books can be heavier than regular-print items for some adults midlife and older. We need to consider offering book holders, magnifiers, and page turners as part of our loan materials. Audiobooks such as books on CDs, Playaways, and downloadable MP3 options, as well as e-book selections in a variety of genres, are also important. It is an excellent idea to bring an assortment of materials and media, as well as asking questions to gauge interests while describing the available resources and services. Keeping records on interests, types and number of materials borrowed, and the number of visits or mailings for each outreach patron is vital. This will help with readers' advisory for your patrons and show how well the program is being utilized for library administration and for any future grant opportunities.

We need to ensure that the local community knows about our outreach services. Having different avenues of marketing our services is important. We need to consider marketing our services in-house and also on our Web sites. Advertising outreach services on our Web page can attract new patrons who searched electronically to determine if the library has what they need without having to physically enter the library. Birmingham Public Library in Alabama has an excellent example of marketing outreach services that are available at their library depicted on their Web site at http://www.bplonline.org. Patrons can click on the Services tab at the top of their Web page, which will navigate them to the outreach services offered at their library.

Besides marketing outreach services on the library Web site, we need to think about other marketing strategies such as advertising on local cable stations, newspapers, or radio stations. We need to consider creating flyers or bookmarks that include outreach information and leave them near checkout stations or reference desks for individuals who have family members, friends, or neighbors who might need the library services. Make sure to include a phone number, e-mail address, and Web site to apply and note that the service is free to help alleviate cost concerns.

Outreach services for the public libraries in this text were determined by examining their library Web sites. Some of the contributing libraries (15 percent) were noted as having outreach services that included personal home and institutional delivery of materials as well as mail service. Very few (5 percent) libraries had a bookmobile, and only a handful of libraries had a techmobile.

HOME SERVICES

Home delivery services can encompass materials sent via the U.S. Postal Service (USPS) or by personal delivery. Deliveries can range from once a month to every couple of weeks. Libraries are charged a reduced rate to mail items, and the patrons typically receive this service free of charge. More information about library mailing rates can be found on the USPS Web site. Sending materials by mail can save staff time; however, personal contact is lost and more personalized service is generated by delivering the materials in person.

Library staff, family members, or volunteers can deliver outreach materials. In addition, we can consider partnering with other local community agencies, such as a visiting nursing service or a local religious group's visiting ministry. Having these organizations possibly deliver materials along with their regularly scheduled visits can increase the number of patrons receiving library services. Try to keep records and statistics, including stories or comments from patrons, to help garner support for the program. We need to consider being consistent in using the same individual who personally delivers outreach materials to help establish a comfortable relationship. Outreach services can encompass other types of services besides just delivering materials: answering questions, providing companionship, or assisting with technology. Discuss a delivery schedule and note any special instructions. The following are some examples from contributors to this text of the outreach services they have at their libraries.

Mail delivery—books by mail. *Anoka County Library in Minnesota:* "Anoka County Library's most popular outreach service. . . . The library mails materials free of charge to persons who cannot get to their community libraries. The service is open to anyone who is temporarily or permanently unable to get to the library due to winter weather, recovery from surgery, inability to drive, or permanent disability. The library will mail any circulating items that the patron requests, including ILL [interlibrary loan] materials."

Yolo County Library in California: "We offer an important outreach service 'Books by Mail' which delivers library materials to county residents who are homebound due to disability or lack of transportation. All of the participants are 50+."

Personal delivery. *Jenneffer Sixkiller:* "Our circulation department takes books to homebound senior citizens on a monthly basis."

Kate Skinner: "We do not have formal outreach services: outreach is done as and when necessary. . . . If we hear of someone in our community who is temporarily unable to get to the library and has no one to help them, we will make a personal trip to exchange material."

Debbi Gallucci: "We provide library services to our homebound patrons. A staff member visits with our patrons and brings them large-print books, movies, magazines. I also visit the local senior nutrition center monthly to bring our seniors large-print books, magazines, coloring pages, and we have started to do crafts with them."

Quincy Public Library in Illinois: "We have a very active delivery program to individuals who are unable to come to the library due to either a temporary or permanent physical disability. . . . We will deliver any items that can be checked out at the library. We keep very careful records of each patron's likes and dislikes, as well as records of all titles we take to them. Staff does all the selecting and most of the delivering, but we also have a group of volunteers, mostly seniors, who do deliveries as well."

At-home program. *Findlay-Hancock County Public Library in Ohio:* "There are . . . patrons, unable to come to the library, who receive a variety of items (books, movies, books-on-CD, music, magazines) from the library once a month. The items are delivered to where the patrons' live."

Van service. *Chris Jackson, special audiences strategist:* "We have a van service that makes biweekly stops at local senior living, assisted living, and nursing home facilities, providing both lobby stops and deposit collections."

VOLUNTEERS

Utilizing volunteers can be beneficial when providing outreach services. Volunteers can be a welcome addition, especially if the library is short on staff due to budget constraints or time because of programming needs. Volunteers should be carefully screened and interviewed with background checks, especially if they are representing the library and visiting homebound individuals. We need to consider creating policies for volunteers and training if at all possible. Volunteers for delivery of materials can be any age. However, many adults 50+ are trying to find ways to use their free time and also create a difference in their communities (Roberts & Bauman, 2012), which makes them ideal helpers for outreach services. The following are some examples from contributors of outreach services utilizing volunteers at their libraries.

Jaci at Cranberry Public Library in Pennsylvania: "We do have volunteers and the majority of them are retired and over 50. However, anyone over 18 can be an adult volunteer."

Athol Public Library in Massachusetts: "We provide home delivery of materials each month. A volunteer chooses books, based on a conversation or information provided on the sign-up form, and checks the materials out. A second volunteer, CORI checked, delivers the books and picks up the old books. The library also provides book deposits when requested to area nursing homes." (CORI is criminal offender record information.)

Service to senior citizens. *Carroll County (MD) Public Library in Maryland:* "Bringing together the library and senior facilities via a volunteer corps. A library staff member prepares plastic tote boxes of books, magazines, and books-on-CD to be delivered by volunteers monthly to assisted living homes, adult day cares, and nursing home facilities. The volunteer will visit with senior residents individually, discuss books, swap family stories, and even play a game of chess together. The library staffer supervises 35 volunteers, coordinates their schedules, supports discussion program opportunities, and collaborates closely with staff of 30 senior facilities. The goal is to connect the elderly to the lifelong enjoyment of learning."

Beth Neunaber: "Currently, we do not have staff doing outreach to seniors. Two retirement centers have volunteers who monthly come to the library and check out a selection of books to be used by their residents. The library offers these materials at a 6-week checkout period, rather than the standard 4-week period."

BOOKMOBILES AND TECHMOBILES

A bookmobile is a mobile library vehicle typically in the form of a van, large truck, or sometimes a bus. Some mobile libraries carry large-print books, audio books, and other media in addition to a full selection of books. Materials are shelved inside the bookmobile so patrons can browse the selection when the bookmobile is parked (Reitz, 2017). They serve special groups and patrons who have difficulty traveling to a traditional library such as occupants of nursing homes and assisted living facilities. A techmobile, as mentioned in Chapter 5, has computers and other technological gadgets in a motorized vehicle that can visit different areas or institutions. Their purpose is to offer individuals the opportunity to familiarize themselves with different types of technology, take classes using the technological devices, or use the Wi-Fi hotspots. The following are bookmobile examples from contributors to this text.

Carroll County (MD) Public Library in Maryland: "Bookmobile service was transformed in 1986. Service priorities changed from a general community bookmobile focus to one targeting child care centers, afterschool programs, and senior communities and neighborhoods."

Anonymous: "We have a bookmobile and it stops at all county senior centers, nursing homes, elder complexes, and senior living housing. We maintain 'honor' book shelves with rotating titles in many of these locations."

Findlay-Hancock County Public Library in Ohio: "The bookmobile travels to nine different Hancock County communities year round and offers many of the same library amenities; and it's been said the bookmobile has app. 3,000+ items on board to choose from. Twice a month the bookmobile stops at . . . a retirement community."

Greenwood County Library System in South Carolina: "The Library's bookmobile goes to Active Day (an adult day center for seniors) and three assisted living residences once a month. Library staff works with the activities directors at each site to plan short programs (15 to 20 minutes) during each visit. Following the program . . . residents may get materials they requested, choose from a selection of materials brought inside, or go out to browse items on the bookmobile. Programs include music, silly jokes, short stories . . . poems. Handouts may be adult coloring pages downloaded from the Internet."

Tracy Trotter, library director at Adams Memorial Library in Pennsylvania: "We also have a large bookmobile that has regular stops at senior care facilities and assisted living locations. For these, we provide all standard library services and we make sure we have plenty of large-print books and audiobooks on board for those days."

RESIDENTIAL SERVICES

The library can be a part of an assisted living residence or nursing home by providing programming delivered by library staff, volunteers, or the residential facility staff. Outreach library programs take a little more planning because materials and supplies need to be brought to the facility. Coordinating with residential staff can be beneficial with regard to supplies needed and the wants and needs of attendees. Having a variety of programs can create interest and broaden the number of attendees at the programs. Some program examples are music, book discussions or storytelling, memory kits, or technology training. Memory kits help some adults 50+ reminisce and share stories around a common theme (county fairs, pets, school days, train rides, etc.). When examining the libraries in this text, 4 of the 1,317 libraries have Bi-Folkal or memory kits to borrow in their library systems.

Furthermore, establishing a small rotating collection that is at the outreach institution can allow residents to have access to different materials on a regular basis. These collections are checked out on an institutional library card. In addition, a bookmobile or lobby stop can allow patrons to access materials on rolling carts to be checked out on their own individual library cards with a library member or volunteer. This can be done with a computer and a Wi-Fi connection. We need to keep in mind that when we bring our services to these outreach organizations, they have their own set of policies and procedures. It is a good idea to sit down with their administration to establish a collaborative agreement. The following are some contributor examples of outreach services at residential facilities in their communities.

Art. *Terry Soave at Ann Arbor District Library in Michigan:* "A program an AADL staff member recently facilitated at a local senior residence brought focus to a variety of art books from our collection as a sample of what they have access to borrowing from the library. Participants were provided supplies and were encouraged to practice drawing, utilizing the art books as inspiration. Having presented at this site before, this staff person was familiar with some of the residents' abilities. He made sure he had a backup plan, with tables and chairs, paper and drawing utensils at each place, as well as background music to listen to while they drew. These preparations were valuable, since they were very interested in the books, but they did not wish to discuss any of the artists with the group. As about 15 people began to draw, the remaining 5 continued to browse the art books, making interesting comments as he and a residence staff person circulated among them. It's always recommended a residence staff person be on hand, someone participants know. The staff person also brought a humorous storybook to read and sing. . . . When they finished drawing, some of the participants described their images and several of them said they enjoyed the activity. The activity director, who couldn't be there, sent the staff person an e-mail a few days later saying she heard from the residence staff person that it went very well. Our staff person, in turn, set up a time for the activity director to bring her residents to the main library on another date for a tour and craft activity. This program was successful in highlighting the library collection and portraying AADL as a welcoming place for the residents."

Book clubs and discussions. *Santa Barbara Public Library in California:* "We have just started outreach to adults. We have a book club at a local senior housing location."

Mariel Carter, adult service reference librarian at Marinette County Consolidated Public Library Services in Wisconsin: "Books Outside the Box is a booktalk program at an assisted living facility open to residents and the public. I pick out a theme (like Westerns, Award-Winning Books of 2016, or Real-Life Mysteries) and find books in my library that fit that theme. I write up a program guide with a list of titles and authors featured in the book talk for the audience to take with them. When I go to the assisted living facility, I bring my box of library books to show each title while I talk about it. I give a bit of background on the genre or why I decided to pick the topic and proceed to tell the audience about each book and author. The people who have library cards and are able to bring the books back the next time (or independently drop them off at the library) will often check out one of the books. Any books not checked out after the presentation go on display at the library for others to check out if they have missed the book-talk session. Prep work on this is extensive. It takes time to think about a theme, gather the books, put them on a display status so that library staff can find the books when they come back to the library for display, research each book so that I can talk about it or the author adequately, and design the program guide. . . . Cost is minimal, just mileage for driving off-site."

Lisa C. West at Homewood Public Library in Alabama: "We have partnered with our local senior center and do a book club once a month at the senior center as part of our community outreach. The library supplies the books, and everything is free."

Richard Conroy at Essex Library Association in Connecticut: "We currently have . . . a book discussion group moderated by myself (our library's director) that meets each month at an assisted living facility. I am in my mid-60s and am comfortable working with that population. . . . I think the fact that I am the moderator and over age 60 helps them to feel more comfortable than might be the case with a younger person. . . . Over the years I've become familiar with the group's literary tastes, though they do subtly change from time to time depending on the participants. Two or three times a year I prepare a list of between six and eight book titles that I think may be of interest to them. They may choose which books will be discussed from that list, but they are also encouraged to make their own suggestions. It is important for there to be at least two or three titles lined up in advance at any given time so that we have time to obtain extra copies through interlibrary loan and that they have time to read them. I, of course, read the books beforehand myself and prepare a few remarks to get the discussion started, as well as some open-ended questions to keep things moving when the conversation inevitably starts to lag. . . . However, though I do try to keep them on topic, they sometimes tend to veer off on tangents. . . . Periodically I find it necessary to remind myself that this is primarily a socialization opportunity for them, so if they do wander off the subject at hand that's not really a bad thing as long as the group as a whole is engaged."

Community residents welcome. *Alexandra Annen:* "We work with the local senior homes to present programs at their facility. One of the senior homes allows local seniors (outside of the facility) to come to their programs."

Computer skills. *Matthew Riley at Friendswood Public Library in Texas:* "We outreach to local senior and assisted living facilities to teach basic computer skills and other library service topics."

Library materials. *Jeannine:* "If someone has a disability (vision, mobility, etc.) that makes it difficult for them to come to the library, I go to visit them, bringing any items that can be checked out. I go to senior living, independent, and assisted living facilities, as well as individual homes that are within the school district. My patrons are almost all 50+, even 90+."

Library program and materials. *Heather Johnson at River Falls Public Library in Wisconsin:* "Once a month, the librarian from the RFPL will go to the location and conduct a program (chosen by the staff and residents) and have library resources to check out. Each resident has their own library card. These cards are linked to a noncharging institutional card. The individual patron cards have a HOMEBOUND status. . . . Residents . . . feel a sense of renewed independence by having their own library card. They are also told that they will not be financially responsible for any damages . . . or lost items. The patron library cards are kept in clear sheets in a three-ring binder and are brought to each location each month. . . . For each visit, resources (relevant to the resident interest surveys) are pulled from the library shelves and are brought to the location using three large courier bins and a fold-up pushcart. An additional three-shelf cart on wheels is brought to unpack the items onto . . . for the residents to browse. . . . Resources . . . are generally large-print books, audiobooks, DVDs, and nonfiction titles that are not new or that have holds. . . . This solves any problems with items being out of circulation for extended checkout periods or that will be a major loss to the library if they are damaged or lost. This has been added into the program as calculated and anticipated losses. Residents at each location are interviewed to learn more about their interests and hobbies. . . . The types of materials brought to each location are also individualized based upon physical needs. . . . Items are checked out using a staff laptop equipped with a barcode scanner and a mobile version of the circulation software. A library hotspot is brought along to ensure consistent and reliable access to the Internet. Due dates are preprinted onto bookmarks that remind the residents as to when their items are due and when the next library visit date will be at their location. Residents are able to return their library materials to a separate bin and these items get checked in on-site. This allows for the librarian and the staff to inquire about anything that might still be checked out on a patron's card. Items are either renewed or returned at this point. Monthly programs at each location have been created in collaboration with the staff persons . . . in charge of residents' activities and enrichment services."

Reading Collections. Ocean County Library in New Jersey: "At the independent and assisted living facilities, a browsing library is set up in the facilities for residents to have the full library experience of selecting their own materials. During the library's visit, real-time circulation and reference services are provided."

Chad Robinson at Matheson Memorial Library in Wisconsin: "We offer reading collections to several of our senior living facilities."

Memory programs

Bi-Folkal Kits. Meryle A. Leonard at Charlotte Mecklenburg Library in North Carolina: "Our outreach services to the target population are geared for people who can't use library services in a traditional manner. Staff members visit numerous organizations providing literacy, educational, or economic opportunity programs. . . . We have offered intergenerational programs, and they were always [a] success. We coordinated a day care center visiting an assisted living facility. Children were ages four to five, and we encouraged the adult care staff to invite participants who would be able to interact safely with the children. All children had to have signed permission slips to participate in the program. (The day care was responsible for the children, transportation, and monitoring the children during the visit.) We offered the Bi-Folkal Kit called "Remembering Birthdays." The children and adults took turns sharing how they celebrated their birthdays. They sang birthday songs and listened to picture books about birthdays. The group also made birthday cards together."

Memoir writing workshop. Lynn Harthorne: "Palm of the Hand Memoir workshop is ongoing at a local assisted living facility. . . . The residents have notebooks where they write their stories, and we share them at our meetings." (See Appendix B for Palm of the Hand Web site information.)

Remember when story times. Marie Corbitt at Westerville Public Library in Ohio: "Basically, I pick a theme for each month. . . . There is a magazine . . . that I use for short stories and it's a really good resource. It has great stories from the times most people aged 50+ will remember. And they are well written. In my experience, funny . . . heartfelt stories are the best. So I choose around three stories and one to two songs to go along with the theme. Sometimes it can be tricky to find songs that go with the theme that they would know. . . . Then I also try to do some type of interactive activity, especially something sensory because I go to some places for people with dementia. . . . Another successful story time was about national parks. I made button trees out of pipe cleaners with them for that. I also did one about happiness and filled balloons with different materials to be like stress balls and they had to guess what was inside the balloons. I also did one about Black History Month and we made a Freedom Quilt together out of paper."

Program collaborations. *Kelly Martin Laney at Birmingham Public Library in Alabama:* "We are just beginning collaboration with a local senior citizen center which is located in our service area, but is actually a separate municipality. I am anticipating that they will transport seniors to some of our programs and I will do book talks and promote reading at the center."

Story times. *Carrol County (MD) Public Library in Maryland:* "Presented by staff from the Eldersburg Branch Library. The program runs once a month in the spring and fall. . . . Families meet library staff at the . . . assisted living center. . . . The elderly residents of the . . . senior facility gather together with us to join in the program. We set registration for 12 children. We usually have about a dozen residents join us. Activities include what you would expect at a children's story time with a lot of manipulatives such as shaker eggs, scarfs, and copies of board books for choral reading for all present. The children love interacting with the residents by passing out and collecting these items. Songs and rhymes that the residents would know, such as Row, Row, Row Your Boat and The ABC Song, are used so that the residents are comfortable joining in the fun. The residents light up when they see the children and love spending time together. After the story time portion of the program, it's play time where we use a bin of toys that are stored at the facility. The kids will sometimes play with the residents and pass out stickers to everybody. One resident has put the stickers on her walker from each of our visits. The residents really look forward to future sessions and remember some of the children who come repeatedly. The kids and parents have a great time too. Some have said that they don't have grandparents in the area so this is a nice way for their children to feel comfortable with the elderly. Most of the residents use walkers or wheelchairs, and the children get exposure to these items when they may not in their everyday life. We have had infants attend and this is super special. Parents will talk to the residents about how old the baby is and if they have any siblings and the residents eat it up; who doesn't love a sweet baby? Librarians who have presented this program all report a deep sense of satisfaction for feeling they have really made a positive difference in their community and touched lives by connecting the very young with the elderly. The program not only brightens up the day for everyone attending story time, but the monthly experience has created friendships, beyond story time, between some of the young families and . . . residents bringing joy to all."

Rebecca at Guthrie Public Library in Oklahoma: "Most of the programs at our library focus on the nursing homes in our service area. We outreach to them . . . for an adult story time once a week. I go to the nursing home and read for 30 to 55 minutes, while residents are encouraged to exercise or knit or even eat a meal. The activity directors . . . have noticed that participants are more active and some have a better grasp on reality."

OTHER OUTREACH SERVICE IDEAS AND TIPS

The following text has additional information and suggestions from contributors about other types of outreach services at their libraries.

Know your community. *Marie Corbitt at Westerville Public Library in Ohio:* "I think the three most important things when it comes to doing outreach programs are simplicity, patience, and compassion. Keeping things simple, especially when relating to technology, is super important; otherwise, they can get overloaded and overwhelmed. Patience is also important because you will repeat yourself over and over and over. Be prepared for that. And compassion is important for all people, but especially seniors. They may be scared or worried to ask a question or participate in a program. Be encouraging and find out what's going on, let them talk and know you care."

Community and civic engagement. *Kathleen Handy, computer instructor at Saratoga Springs Public Library in New York:* "We also outreach to the Shelters of Saratoga, helping those living there with technology-related questions and needs, such as resumes. . . . We . . . distribute books to doctor's offices and still deliver recycled books to places like a local swimming pool for interested readers to enjoy."

Kristi Haman: "We visit senior communities, fairs, festivals, rallies, farmer markets, homes for adults with development disabilities, book stores, craft groups, hospitals, churches, and any place that requests an outreach visit."

Santa Barbara Public Library in California: "We . . . go to the Senior Expo once a year." (This is an active aging fair held yearly for seniors and caregivers.)

Ann Arbor District Library in Michigan: "Has an Outreach & Neighborhood Services (ONS) department . . . present throughout the community visiting housing communities, staffing fairs, and other similar events, supplying new and withdrawn materials to social service agencies. . . . ONS also coordinates the day-to-day operations of the Washtenaw Library for the Blind and Physically Disabled at AADL, a subregional library of the National Library Service for the Blind and Physically Handicapped."

Ocean County Library in New Jersey: "The library provides talks at various adult communities and at functions throughout the county, including health and wellness fairs. Each branch is charged with identifying the older adults in their community and providing a vast variety of outreach participation both in the community at adult communities, senior centers, township government meetings, and community events."

Attendance at meetings and conferences. *John J. Trause, director at Oradell Public Library in New Jersey:* "Regularly attend the meetings of the Oradell Chamber of Commerce and have addressed the two Rotary Clubs in town. We participate in Oradell Family Day in autumn each year to engage with all members of the community."

Simsbury Public Library in Connecticut: "Simsbury Public Library's Head of Adult Services serves on the Town's Aging and Disability Commission so the library may be part of the conversation and play a prominent role in serving the needs of that population."

Brianne Columbo Fairfield Free Public Library in New Jersey: "Our adult events coordinator handles outreach to seniors 50+. This includes attending 'Golden Agers' meetings . . . a senior citizen organization, to promote new events and services."

Promoting services. *Yolo County Library in California:* "I travel to aging summits as well as Yolo County retirement communities to advertise the service."

Mary at Wilbraham Public Library in Massachusetts: "Our assistant reference librarian coordinates outreach: delivery of materials to homebound patrons by himself and volunteers, and delivering a regular monthly drop-off of large-print books to the four nursing homes and assisted living centers in town. He also has begun scheduling presentations to some of the residential centers to promote our services to older patrons: home delivery, large-print books, books on CD and Playaway, phone reference, movies, online offerings and try to get them to sign up for library cards."

Resources. *Christy Wagner at ELA Area Public Library in Illinois:* "We provide a Caregiver's Kiosk that is stocked with resources for those who are in a caregiving role of any kind, books, DVDs, community resources. and information on local support groups, etc. . . . Outreach Services is charged with providing resources to those who have special needs such as low vision issues or some other condition that may prevent them from being able to read or even hold a book or tablet. We connect patrons with the Talking Books program and can also lend small handheld magnifying equipment."

Trips. *Anonymous:* "We have 12 bus trips . . . per year. . . . We try to do as many community outreach programs as possible, as our budget is limited."

CHAPTER SUMMARY

This chapter examined outreach services for adults 50+. We need to have different types of outreach services to provide for the various types of individuals in our library community. Services can be provided by staff or volunteers and can be in-house where residents can be transported to the library for a program, or services can be brought to their place of residence. Marketing is key to outreach so our community members will know what services and programs are available for individuals who might need these supportive services.

9

Not Just Books Anymore: Marketing Strategies for Your Library

We need to know our library community members when we promote and advertise our services and programming. Typically, we market to adults 50+ using a variety of approaches, which includes print, media, and technological methods, as well as speaking about our programs during face-to-face interactions. We need to consider and continue to use multiple marketing strategies because some adults 50+ can be experiencing challenges such as visual or hearing issues. In addition, some adults midlife and older can have difficulties using a computerized system, or they might not own a technological device. However, some adults 50+ are increasing their use of mobile devices and are utilizing social media more often to find news and information (Anderson & Perrin, 2017). These varied characteristics are important when determining how to market services and programs to adults midlife and older in our communities.

PRINT

Creating printed materials that advertise our programs effectively to adults 50+ are excellent methods to acquire information about our program and services. Many adults 50+ still enjoy printed materials over utilizing an electronic device. We need to be creative visually and factually to grab their attention with short informational sentences. The most common forms of advertising used are flyers and posters. Lear (2013) outlined some strategies to consider in creating effective flyers:

- Prominently display the program title
- Include a brief description
- Consider including an author quotation

- Provide the day, date, and time of the program
- Include wheelchair accessibility and note if you offer interpreters or other services
- Include a phone number and e-mail address for more information
- Mention if advanced registration or tickets are required
- List presenter(s)
- List program address
- Include a library logo
- Place the word "Free" on the flyer

Along with these steps, consider making the print at least 14-point font for easier reading, as well as providing a graphic to attract attention related to the event.

Besides flyers and posters, other print materials such as banners, newsletters, brochures, and bookmarks can be helpful in advertising programs and services. These can be distributed at senior facilities, churches, synagogues, funeral homes, grocery stores, salons or barbershops, doctor offices, coffee shops, and other places around the community. Remember to check with the organization before leaving information or posting on a bulletin board. In addition, creating bookmarks with program information will likely stay and be viewed longer than a typical flyer that is displayed on a bulletin board that has rotating information. Most patrons like to have a bookmark to maintain their space in a book they are currently reading, and a bookmark with a nice graphic will be a steady reminder of services and programs held at the library.

Furthermore, consider providing marketing materials in another language depending on the library community needs. Look for volunteers to help with the translation of the text to ensure correct interpretation. Interpretation, correct spelling, and grammar are important so the information is accurately delivered and the meaning is not misinterpreted by mistake.

Once the type of print advertising is determined, have the bookmarks, flyers, brochures, and newsletters available at check-out desks and other areas where promotional materials for adults 50+ are displayed in the library. We need to also consider placing them in windows or on different bulletin boards to catch the eye of patrons coming in or when patrons are moving around the physical library. Plus, newsletters, brochures, and pamphlets can be created and marketed in electronic formats. Utilizing both formats would increase the number of individuals reached because some adults 50+ do not like technology, whereas others utilize technology for all of their information needs.

TECHNOLOGICAL

Promoting marketing and advertising programs electronically, as stated earlier, can spread the word faster and market to individuals who might not enter the physical library environment. There are also some patrons who do not like a physical paper product that they might have to carry or hold on to as a physical reminder. This can be due to different reasons, such as the information might get lost because they already have too many printed materials around their house, or the individual just simply wants to reduce the amount of paper used and therefore chooses to receive the information electronically. According to Anderson and Perrin (2017), many adults 65+ (67 percent) are going online for information, and this number of online adults keeps steadily increasing. Utilizing different ways to advertise electronically has the potential to increase the number of patrons at our programs and using our services in the community.

Most public libraries today have a Web site or a Facebook page. We need to consider creating on our Web site a tab or link specifically for adults 50+ that can explain library services and announce programs available to them. This is also an excellent space to put links to resources available in the community. Some Web sites can have a lot of information displayed on the landing page, which can be overwhelming to an adult 50+ (Zheng, 2013), making it difficult to find the correct information. Creating a direct link or tab on the library Web site will provide adults 50+ a Web page that can be more user friendly and easier to navigate to find useful information.

Furthermore, utilizing social media can bring added attention to library programs and services to the tech-savvy adult 50+ library patron. Twitter, Facebook, YouTube, blogs, podcasts, and Flickr are some of the many possibilities that can promote and showcase library programs. These social media platforms can provide instant access to patrons, creating excitement about what is happening at the library, as well as the opportunity to provide commentary and build a connection with our library community members. We need to encourage our patrons to follow the library and to ask questions, make comments, and leave suggestions. This will help build stronger relationships by creating conversations that are beyond the physical library building. An added bonus is that it will help increase the usage of technology, especially for those adults midlife and older who do not use it often, giving them added practice. Based on prior research, social media platforms are being used by adults 65+ (34 percent), and Baby Boomers are using social media as one of their top searches on their mobile devices (Anderson & Perrin, 2017; Bennett-Kapusniak, 2015). In addition, if you have a multilingual community, consider adding software to change languages from English on the library Web site page. This will help market programs and services to library patrons who have English as their second language.

MEDIA

Contacting local media can be beneficial in advertising library services and reaching adults 50+ in our communities. Check with radio and cable stations for free public service announcements or press releases. However, it is possible that only some of the information will be mentioned or the information could be changed due to time limitations or because of other information being announced. Using paid advertising is a viable solution, but costs can vary. Paying for advertising will determine when your advertisement will run and that changes will not be made in the announcement. An advertising budget will help determine how programs are promoted and announced to the library community. Advertisements in newspapers are another avenue to pursue. They sometimes publish a community calendar or have announcements to adults 50+ in local sections. Some libraries also have their own radio station. These stations vary in terms of ownership, if they are community sponsored, and if they have special licenses. The radio stations also vary on content that is spoken, from readings, to announcements on programming, music, and special guests, as well as programming, news, and information.

COMMUNITY

Public libraries are a significant part of the community. Marketing outside of the library and participating in local fairs and other events can expand the library exposure. We need to look at different venues to market our programs. However, make sure marketing is publicized in the areas that will generate interest in the programs. This can also be a great opportunity for library volunteers who are connected to the community to create more interest by talking about the library and the programs.

In addition, we need to consider creating a mailing list, both for e-mail and mail via the U.S. Postal Service. This can consist of local newspapers, assisted living and nursing homes, local businesses and organizations, and individuals who requested to receive information about upcoming programs. Collaborating with local businesses can be mutually beneficial. For instance, a business can market library programs in exchange for the library advertising their information. This can heighten exposure and value of the library and the local businesses to the adult 50+ community members. Please refer to Chapter 7 for a list of possible businesses and organization partners.

The following are examples from contributors to this text about their marketing strategies for adult and adult 50+ programs and services. Almost all of the libraries market to their adult community members and not specifically to adults 50+.

Matthew Riley at Friendswood Public Library in Texas: "We do not specifically market to 50+. We market to the adult community but the majority of attendees are 50+."

Melany Wilks at Pioneer Memorial Library in Kansas: "We do not just market to over 50s but we don't exclude them either. Normal social media like

Facebook is the best. E-mail is used for some and, of course, announcements in the newspapers and in flyers."

Wallingford Public Library in Connecticut: "We market to adults 50+ the same way we market to other age groups: printed flyers posted in the library; print newsletter that is mailed or e-mailed to members, and posted in the library; an e-mailed list of upcoming events; and Facebook postings."

Most contributing libraries use many of the same marketing methods. However, the following list was created of different types of marketing strategies for easier reference. Please note that other types of methods might be included in the contributors' examples as well as the one referenced for added suggestions because most libraries use more than one marketing strategy to advertise their library programs and services to their community.

Bookmarks. *Kathleen Goodson at Wimberley Village Library in Texas:* "Online calendar of events. . . . Notices in the local papers in their events column, VIP ads in our local newspaper, on our Web site, posters, flyers, bookmarks, table talkers, through our Friends newsletters, Facebook, quarterly ads in magazines, on our scrolling monitor."

Muncie Public Library in Indiana: "We have developed special bookmarks and handouts and delivered them to the . . . county senior center. They had an annual fundraising dinner themed around 'White House Dinners' and we developed a bookmark of titles the library has on the topic."

Brochures

Print. *Terry Soave at Ann Arbor District Library in Michigan:* "Through traditional promotional channels, including a printed monthly brochure, advertising in local monthly magazines of happenings in the community, our Web site, and a variety of social media."

Local businesses and institutions. *Yolo County Library in California:* "Most 50+ members of our community read the local newspaper. . . . Our programs are listed in the 'weekly happenings' column, and this is where I notice most 50+ library users finding out about our programs. I also visit retirement communities and other county offices to leave brochures and talk about library services. Lastly, Facebook, flyers and handouts, a monthly programming calendar, an online events calendar, and a local community calendar all advertise our programs."

Calendars, electronic. *Kristi Haman:* "Marketing is key. We do just about everything to get the word out through posters in the library and around town, social media (Facebook, Nextdoor, etc.), media outlets, Web site updates, online and printed calendars, e-newsletters, and word of mouth. . . . We market to everyone."

Simsbury Public Library in Connecticut: "We use the traditional marketing tools to market to this demographic: newspapers, community TV, radio stations, paper calendars, flyers, online calendar, Facebook, and a weekly e-newsletter.

We have also developed some targeted marketing based on e-mails collected from registration sign-ups at our programs for that age group. In addition, we cross-promote with our partner organizations and with senior and 50+ residences in town. . . . Our staff regularly attends events in town. We invested in a tent with our logo on it and a large sign describing our services (paid for by the Friends)."

Community associations

Community advertising. Anonymous: "We market our programs in the local paper, on the local radio show, we share a REACH advertising system with the city, chamber of commerce, and school that helps keep the community abreast of what's going on around town."

Community calendar. Elizabeth Eisen, adult programming librarian at Appleton Public Library in Wisconsin: "I use our Web site calendar of events, Facebook, flyers, downtown association, local newspaper and magazines, and the visitors bureau online calendar."

Community guides. Heather Johnson at River Falls Public Library in Wisconsin: "While the trend is moving away from print publications as the preferred method of information delivery, many of the adults ages 50+ still prefer to get their information in a print format rather than a digital format. Based upon our current information, we market our programs to adults 50+ in our community in the following ways: newspaper articles, ads and columns, local print resources for community programs . . . the Parks and Recreation Guide (biannual), the Community Events Catalog (triannual), church bulletins . . . posters and flyers hung in the library and throughout the community (churches, stores, restaurants, nursing homes, food pantry, assisted living facilities, etc.), personal mailings . . . word of mouth and announcements at community events. Social media postings (Facebook, Instagram, and Twitter) . . . announcements on the local radio station, the library Web site and on the library OPACs. . . . In a very digitally dominated society, it is crucial to think of those persons not using online marketing to learn about programs."

Community newsletter. Webster Public Library in New York: "Flyers, articles in the town newsletter, articles in the local newspapers, Facebook, Twitter, Instagram. . . . We have a speaker feature on our Web site and regularly write articles for the town newsletter and local newspaper advertising that staff is eager to speak to outside groups on topics of interest."

Email. Carroll County (MD) Public Library in Maryland: "In a recent strategic planning survey . . . when we asked how folks heard about library programs and events . . . respondents ages 46 and over identified the library newsletter . . . library Web site . . . friend or family . . . library staff . . . and library Facebook page . . . as the top channels. Folks also identified library displays . . . library flyer or sign . . . library e-mail . . . and newspaper . . . as other ways they find out about library programming. In line with current trends, we are finding that each individual really has their own distinct marketing mix that works for them. . . . There is no one secret sauce to getting information to our customers, instead

there are many different sauces. . . . At CCPL, we utilize a few different strategies to amplify our marketing efforts . . . Friends of CCPL, our Friends group is
predominantly made of folks 60+. . . . We have a special e-mail list for them.
One benefit of being a member of the Friends is advance notice of our high-
profile, best-seller author events. These events sell out quickly. We often see the
same group of folks at each one. They help us spread the word about the library.
At a recent WWI-themed tea, we overheard one of our library ambassadors state
that she keeps applications for the Friends in her purse and tells everyone about
us and that they NEED to join. This type of authentic communication and tes-
timonial does more and says more in telling our story than any ad the library
could place."

Flyers

Print. Adrienne Doman Calkins at Sherwood Public Library in Oregon: "Local
print newspaper comes out once a month and continues to be the best way to
reach adults, especially those 50+ . . . book displays . . . where we have a poster
and small take-away fliers. . . . We make announcements at programs about
upcoming programs for similar audiences . . . posters to . . . businesses and
agencies in town, which helps get the word out . . . monthly e-newsletter."

Electronic. Muncie Public Library in Indiana: "Digital flyers and social media
posts can be circulated via social media or email to other organizations that
would be interested in sharing and attending."

Interlibrary. Lisa Prizio: "We just put it out there in the paper, on our Web site,
on Facebook, interlibrary flyers, and just telling our patrons what we are doing."

Magazines. *Terry Soave at Ann Arbor District Library in Michigan:* "Through
traditional promotional channels, including a printed monthly brochure, advertising in local monthly magazines of happenings in the community, our Web site,
and a variety of social media."

Movie Theatre. *Tamar Kreke, adult and technical services coordinator at Greene
County Public Library in Ohio:* "We attend fairs and festivals, publicize in the
local papers, get on local electronic signage, and have radio and TV spots, as
well as advertising at the local movie theater (before the trailers)."

Newsletters

Adult section. Anonymous: "We have an Adult Section in our library newsletter, plus we make up Adult Program flyers that are displayed throughout the
library."

Electronic. New Durham Public Library in New Hampshire: "E-newsletter,
newspaper, outside sign, upcoming events bookmarks, hard-copy newsletter
shared with Recreation Department, posters."

Print. Christy Wagner at ELA Area Public Library in Illinois: "Our library has
graphic artists and Public Information staff who create fliers, posters, participate in social media forums, maintain our Web page and electronic sign. . . . I
work extremely closely with this department to ensure that our events receive

coverage. Our community newsletter is a major PR vehicle and a beautiful four-color glossy magazine–type quality piece that comes out three times a year."

Newspapers. *Chris Jackson, special audiences strategist:* "E-mail and print newsletters, local newspaper, social media."

Tracy Trotter, library director at Adams Memorial Library in Pennsylvania: "Since we do still market using older forms of media, you could say that this is how we market to seniors. Program info running in newspapers and advertised on the radio will likely reach older people more than it will younger people. As for social media, our audience is a true mix of all ages, just as many seniors follow us on Facebook than younger folks. . . . For programs that feature outside speakers rather than library staff, we do put forth a greater effort to have a full house, which means in addition to our usual media releases to newspapers, radio, and social media, we also distributed posters and flyers in locations outside the library. We prepare posters and quarter-page handouts for people to take home as a reminder that they have already registered or wish to register. We do these using Publisher, and we can print up to 11×17 size posters in-house."

Free local paper. Mary of Wilbraham Public Library in Massachusetts: "We are fortunate that our town has a local, free paper that gets delivered to every resident in town. It is one of the biggest ways I get the word out about all adult programming, and I send press releases to other local papers as well."

Personal communication

Advocates. Kelly Martin Laney at Birmingham Public Library in Alabama: "Word of mouth is our best marketing tool, along with a printed calendar that lists all the programs monthly. We also post on Facebook, but the participants take extra calendars to doctors' offices and churches to post on their bulletin boards. They also invite people (sometimes, actually quite often, strangers) to attend. I call them my Silver Swarm because they are the best ambassadors for the library of all our patrons."

Community events. Muncie Public Library in Indiana: "We have booths at events specifically for seniors."

Face-to-face. Jeannine: "The outreach program is advertised on our website, and there are fliers on the first floor. Other than that it's word of mouth. Circulation co-workers may recommend someone they feel could benefit."

Muncie Public Library in Indiana: "Word-of-mouth promotion goes a long way, so networking in person and providing outreach to groups that serve and are of interest to that age range is also important."

Kathleen Handy, computer instructor at Saratoga Springs Public Library in New York: "In-class publicity and word of mouth and reputation is important."

Organization visits. Beth Neunaber: "Beyond the advertising methods we consistently use, when we have programs, events catering particularly to 50+, we have staff e-mail, phone, or visit the various senior centers and retirement centers. . . . Also, since most our Friends of the Library are 50+, we regularly share our programming with them and encourage them to help spread the word. This has actually had about equal success with our efforts to make contact with senior service agencies regarding the effect on attendance."

Phone calls. Fife Lake Public Library in Michigan: "Robo calls are sent out for registered seniors as reminders and corrections to events. Many times it is word of mouth."

Posters

In-house. Findlay-Hancock Public Library in Ohio: "We market all of our programs through press releases, posters in house, and social media. There is not a separate marketing campaign for 50+."

Local businesses and institutions. Richard Conroy at Essex Library Association in Connecticut: "We do make sure that our posters and other publicity materials are distributed to places where seniors are likely to see them but, other than that, we do not specifically target that age group."

Presentations. *Kate Skinner:* "Hand selling, word of mouth works very well for us, small community, letting staff at the Senior Center know what is available in the library, making presentations at the Senior Center, participating in the Senior Center events, using the local print media, an advertising broadsheet which gives us free classifieds."

Press releases. *Alexandra Annen:* "Same as all library programming: newsletter, press release, social media, and fliers."

Radio. *Lynn Harthorne:* "We use Facebook and our library Web site, as well as posters in the library. We also use the local newspaper and radio."

Interviews. Ocean County Library in New Jersey: "We market through social media, traditional print media, attending county functions, strategically placing marketing materials throughout each branch, initiating radio and print media interviews, and offering instructional and informational speaking engagements to organizations that have adults 50+ engaged in them."

Signage

Electronic

CIVIC INSTITUTION. *Jaci at Cranberry Public Library in Pennsylvania:* "The same as we do with any of our programs. We have a newsletter that patrons can get online or in the library. We promote programs by sending out press releases to the local newspapers, e-mail blasts through Constant Contact, flyers are available in the library, and we have digital signage screens in both the library and municipal building."

IN-HOUSE. *Anonymous:* "We have a quarterly print brochure with all of our library programs, posters around the library for many programs, large monitors in the library showing coming programs, and we post programs on our Web site and Web site calendar."

Local businesses and institutions. Chad Robinson at Matheson Memorial Library in Wisconsin: "We use a wide variety of outreach efforts that includes a bimonthly newsletter, social media, mass e-mail campaigns, posters and signage both within the library and at multiple local businesses and institutions, and press releases to all of our local publications."

Print. *Athol Public Library in Massachusetts:* "We reach our 50+ adult population through fliers around town and in the library, a Friends newsletter mailed to members twice per year that highlights upcoming programs and other opportunities, information posted at the Senior Center, e-mail notifications to library card holders, and an eye-catching sign on the stairs in front of the library."

Social Media. *Meryle A. Leonard at Charlotte Mecklenburg Library in North Carolina:* "General advertising on social media, print, and e-mail."

Facebook. *Debra DeJonker-Berry at Eastham Public Library in Massachusetts:* "Our Web site, online weekly newsletter, Facebook . . . flyers, mostly inside the library, newspaper."

PAID ADVERTISING. *Ryan Johnson at O'Fallon Public Library in Illinois:* "Specifically, we do utilize paid advertising (or Boosts) on Facebook for certain events. You can set the age range of your target audience, among other factors. We typically leave the age range for those ads at 16 to 65+, simply again because of word of mouth. One person may see it and tell someone else about. Our Boosted events typically see good turnout. We typically spend $15 on an ad and run it for the three days leading up the event. These funds, again, come out of our programming budget. As for marketing, we rely heavily on our print and e-mail newsletter. We have also found that simple signage in the building catches a lot of people's attention. Social media is also huge for all of our events (especially Facebook). More and more older adults are on Facebook these days, but even if they aren't, friends and family may see the event posting and then pass it along via word of mouth."

Instagram. *Leslie DeLooze, community services librarian at Richmond Memorial Library in New York:* "We market in a variety of ways that include posters and flyers in the library, a monthly e-newsletter, community calendar items to local newspapers and Pennysavers, Facebook and Instagram posts, online calendar, direct e-mail for certain programs, and community posters. We send information to our local Office for the Aging, which is included in their newsletters."

Private social network. *Santa Barbara Public Library in California:* "In-house digital displays, e-newsletter, social media, flyers, posters, local newspaper (print and online), Neighborhood Nextdoor, and word of mouth." (Neighborhood Nextdoor is a private social network of different neighborhoods in Santa Barbara.)

Twitter. *Greenwood County Library System in South Carolina:* "The library advertises its programs on its Web site and through social media (Facebook and Twitter). Computer classes are advertised monthly in the local newspaper, and word of mouth has filled, even overfilled, the library's book clubs."

Television. *John J. Trause, director at Oradell Public Library in New Jersey:* "Our public relations announcements go out to the newspapers and online media outlets . . . on the public bulletin board and Oradell Public Television (OPTV), on the library Web site . . . the weekly library e-newsletter, flyers in-house and in public."

Quincy Public Library in Illinois: "Word of mouth, newspaper, television ads, radio spots, posters, e-newsletters, fliers, and Facebook."

United States Mail. *Brianne Columbo at Fairfield Free Public Library in New Jersey:* "The Fairfield Free Public Library sends press releases for upcoming events and services to the local newspapers and to our township TV station. In-library, we hang flyers and have our seasonal newsletters available. We send physical, seasonal newsletters three times a year to all the residents in the township by mail so that patrons who may not use a computer can still see our full season's offerings at home. We also strive to keep our Web site design clear, clean, and concise, which promotes easy access for all computer users. We keep up-to-date information on our library Web site and Facebook page."

Web sites

Community Web site. Lisa C. West at Homewood Public Library in Alabama: "We market all our programs basically the same. Advertising goes online at our Web site, Facebook, and Twitter. We have a Web site about 'goings-on' in our area . . . plus our local area newspaper. . . . We have in-house posters, display boards constantly running our program displays, and programming sheets that can be picked up. . . . We do market specifically to seniors in the *Senior Living* magazine in our area."

Library Web site. Jenneffer Sixkiller: "Word of mouth, library Web site, paper flyers, social media. . . . I use the same flyer background and branding logo for our library for consistency and familiarity."

Specific adult 50+ page. Marie Corbitt at Westerville Public Library in Ohio: "We have flyers, newsletters, e-newsletters. We do have a specific spot in our Adult Programming flyer that highlights the programs we have at the local senior centers. For our programs outside of the library, we largely rely on the activities directors to put the information in the facility's newsletters and calendars. We also have specific pages on our Web site devoted to this audience and the services we offer."

CHAPTER SUMMARY

This chapter discussed different marketing strategies we can use to get the word out about our programs and services for adults 50+ in our library communities. Using a variety of marketing methods will ensure that we reach a wider audience by creating multiple avenues to relay information to all types of individuals.

10

Where Has All the Money Gone? Funding Strategies

Creating a budget for programming and services is different for everyone and is usually dependent on various elements such as the library size, the location of the library, the community that is being served, and other factors (Lear, 2013). Some libraries have funding within their budget for adult programming, but very few have funds that are typically allocated for adult midlife and older programming. Many libraries have provided programming to their patrons on little or no budget. Ideas and suggestions from our peers and hearing how they are managing their own programs can help with our own budget concerns. Asking for money for programming and services from different sources can help supplement our funds so we can provide a variety of programs and services that might require more money than what we have in our budgets. Some of the sources that can help provide us with funding are specific grants from local, state, or national organizations; Friends of the Library groups; private donations; fundraisers; or even charging fees for certain programs can help with costs. Depending on the program or service that requires extra funding, make sure to have a clear plan of how to continue the program or service if the funding ends or becomes unavailable.

Finding funding takes time and careful planning. Plus, it is not a "one size fits all" when it comes to our own library's needs. What works for one library might not work for another. However, this chapter is created to give some ideas and suggestions as well as how some public libraries are allocating their budgetary funds. The Web sites that are suggested within the following text can be found with their corresponding links in Appendix B. It is a good idea to keep a record of funding opportunities as well as a record of organizations and individuals who donate funds and the service or program that was provided from the funds. Keeping careful documentation will help when information is needed for future funding endeavors.

GRANTS

Grant funding can be an excellent avenue to find financing for certain programs or services. Different types of grants are available from local, state, or national organizations and businesses. It is important to read the guidelines and specific requirements carefully for grants because they will vary. Some important aspects to keep in mind when writing for a grant are to follow all the directions given; provide clear, concise information; and include everything that is requested. The Purdue Online Writing Lab is a good resource for general grant guidelines, as well as providing links with some examples to help with the process. Other Web sites are also available that will help you with the grant writing process. Some typical components needed for a grant are a cover letter, an executive summary of the proposal, a statement of why the project is necessary, a project description, the budget for the project, the organization's information, and a summary of the proposal's main points. Try to keep it simple, but elaborate on key points that are beneficial to know why the funding is needed. Remember not to use acronyms because the reader might not be familiar with some of the terms used within the library field. Try to also have a way to measure the objectives for the program, such as a number of attendees. This will give a clear indication to the funding organization that the money was allocated effectively. In addition, have some form of an evaluation or feedback from attendees of the program or service provided by the grant. For example, get quotes from people who attended and appreciated the program (Miner & Miner, 2008). Depending on the funding source, there are sample successful grant applications and proposals available online that can be viewed as examples. These will give you a guide as to how much information is needed for your grant proposal.

Finding grant opportunities can be challenging. Looking for funding locally can be an excellent option, especially if there is a local affiliate of a larger organization. Keep in mind that local organizations can have specific community requirements or restrictions of affiliations, so read the information carefully. However, some local funding organizations have fewer requirements and have an easier application process. State and national grants also have excellent opportunities, especially if larger funding is needed, though the competition is greater for these types of grants and there can be more restrictions.

The following are some local, business, state, and national grants that might spark interest or ideas for future programming and services for adults 50+. The list is not exhaustive and was created to showcase the types of grants that are available when searching for funding sources. In addition, examples from contributors to this text are noted to show how funds were allocated for particular grants. However, other funding sources from the contributors are also listed because many libraries rely on different funding sources to finance their programs and services.

Business Examples

When looking for funding from business grants, look at associations that might allocate funds to nonprofit organizations and look at their requirements of how they will allocate the funding. Also, check to see if the business has local connections in the community. This will help answer some questions that can arise, such as if there is a city or county requirement to allocate funds.

Scholastic library grants. Different types of opportunities for youth to all ages are available from organizations that vary in terms of requirements. We can use this grant for a possible intergenerational opportunity between adults 50+ and youth in the community. For instance, a W. K. Kellogg Grant that engages youth in learning within the community can be beneficial for a program supporting transportation to an assisted learning facility where youth interview residents about their life in the Great Depression.

Bank of America. This corporation provides funding opportunities for organizations in certain areas across the country. Currently the organization is looking to fund programs on economic mobility. For instance, this type of funding might be beneficial for adult 50+ programs that encompass job preparedness training and skill building.

Walmart. This business has community grants that range in value and type depending on what area of funding is needed at the library. For instance, a library can apply for a Quality of Life grant to receive funding for arts and cultural experiences for low-income adults 50+.

State Examples

We need to check our state libraries for possible grants from national organizations and other funding sources. A simple Web search of a state library for grants will typically retrieve links and information of different grants available. Again, this will take time to search through the information, but if funding is needed, it might be worth taking a peek at what is being allocated for the year.

New Mexico general obligation bonds. Go Bonds are funds allocated to public and other libraries for furniture, equipment, and installation of broadband Internet statewide. This can be helpful for services to adults 50+ with economic disadvantages or can be used for assistive technological equipment such as large keyboards or adjustable computer desks for wheelchairs.

New York State adult literacy library services program. This program is currently promoting adult literacy and workforce development in New York State library systems. This can be a good funding source for digital literacy development for adults 50+, or possibly second career initiatives.

State public library fund. *Findlay-Hancock County Public Library in Ohio:* "As with other programs and services, it is part of the general library budget, with funding from the state Public Library Fund and a local levy."

Brianne Columbo at Fairfield Free Public Library in New Jersey: "New Jersey state law mandates that municipal public libraries allocate funding according to the one-third mill formula. . . . Within that allotted yearly amount for our library, a percentage is designated for our adult events and programs. Certainly, we strive to partner with local organizations, businesses, etc., to coordinate free informational lectures and events for our adult and senior programming, which helps to stretch our allotted programming budget."

Individual state library. *Yolo County Library Davis in California:* "Yolo Book Read has had prior grant funding from California State Library Books to Action and our local Davis Soroptimist International group (a global volunteer organization). Books by Mail is funded for the first year by a California State Library LTSA grant. Additional funding for large-print books for the Books by Mail service was funded by a Sacramento Region Community Foundation Whitney Pinkerton Fund."

National Examples

National grants, as stated earlier, can have larger funds to allocate and have a varying number of recipients to give funding to, which increases the chance of receiving an award depending on how much is needed and how the funds are allocated. It is extremely important to read ALL instructions carefully because national grants are quite competitive and if the directions are not followed exactly, the application will be disqualified. Most national organizations have someone to speak with about applying for the grants and are willing to help with any questions about the application process. It is good to remember to check deadlines and how long it will take to receive the allocated funds. Planning far in advance is key. So do not expect funding right away, especially if it is needed for a program or service that will be taking place in a couple months' time. It is a good idea to keep careful records of dates and timelines of the entire process as well as the name of the grant and any other pertinent information. Most national grants have a link to application status on their Web site. An excellent option when applying for a national grant is to collaborate with one or more organizations. This can help with the application process and it might increase the chances of receiving allocated funds.

Center for the book in the Library of Congress. Some state libraries are affiliated with the Center for the Book, which can provide funding to support programs such as literacy and cultural endeavors. Consider contacting them to collaborate on a program or to help support a statewide program.

Institute of Museum and Library Services. IMLS has funding grants for museums and libraries. Funding opportunities and forms are available 90 days before the deadline. The Web site has past funding grantees, which can help determine if a program or service might be eligible for funding. There are no current grants for funding of library services for adults 50+ as of November 2017. Check back for future funding endeavors.

Administration on Aging. This agency grants opportunities such as supportive services for individuals with Alzheimer's or engagement initiatives that support social networks for adults 50+. These are just a few that are on their Web site for 2017. The Administration on Aging usually has state and local affiliates, which could also have funding initiatives depending on the state.

EBSCO grants and funding sources for libraries. This company has a list of different types of funding grants from nongovernment, state, and federal sources.

FINRA Investor Education Foundation. This foundation collaborates with nonprofits and agencies to help provide resources and grants pertaining to financial literacy.

Anonymous: "Occasional grants, for example, a FINRA grant to provide financial education and NY Humanities grants for public scholars."

Foundation center. This online directory provides a database of resources and information for different grant makers. This is a subscription Web site that will store data, identify the best funding sources, and help with building skills in grant writing.

Library works. This online portal has links to grants and funding opportunities within the library field. For example, currently the portal has an ongoing grant called TechSoup for funding for technology services or the Wish You Well Foundation that supports new and existing literacy programs. These opportunities might be helpful for new tablets to support digital literacy initiatives for adults 50+ in your community.

ALA grants. The American Library Association is a great resource that has different types of grants in alphabetical order for easy reference. Some of these grants might not be active or are past their due date for applications. However, they are a good source for inspiration.

National Endowment for the Humanities. NEH provides funding to individuals and organizations that promote the humanities, lifelong learning, and our diverse heritage. State or local affiliates might also have different funding opportunities besides the ones displayed on the national Web site. Check your state humanities council for more information.

Meryle A. Leonard at Charlotte Mecklenburg Library in North Carolina: "For 32 weeks, a group of 50+ plus participants, many with mobility challenges, participated in a book club in their adult care facility. The People and Stories program was designed to offer a literacy experience, especially to people who had limited opportunity to read or be exposed to the humanities. The program was also designed to build conversations around various topics to engage participants in healthy discussion as they gained a deeper understanding of diversity through literature. The program was funded by the National Endowment for the Humanities. Each week participants raved about the program and how much they enjoyed the short stories. They shared what they learned about other cultures, traditions, and lifestyles and how much they enjoyed the fellowship and being heard. One participant stated they were lonely and the book club was so much more than an opportunity to read, listen, and talk."

Rebecca at Guthrie Public Library in Oklahoma: "The annual cost of LTAIO is $3,600 to $4,000. Half of the program is funded by a twice-annual grant through Oklahoma Humanities. It is a very straightforward process, and the consultant with Oklahoma Humanities is very easy to contact with any questions an applicant might have. Each grant requires the applicant to match funds for use." (LTAIO is Let's Talk About It Oklahoma).

Adrienne Doman Calkins at Sherwood Public Library in Oregon: "We are able to provide most of the programs on a minimal budget, only paying for some light refreshments in some cases. . . . Besides our regular budget, we also have support from our Friends of the Library, who pay for our writing workshop series and other programs for adults and all ages. We also have received sponsorship from Oregon Humanities for their Conversation Project programs."

Federal Examples

According to ALA Government Relations (2017), most library funding is distributed through the Institute of Museum and Library Services for each state through LTSA (see next).

LTSA (Library Services and Technology Act). Congress provides each state funding to administer to libraries. The funds can be used to assist diverse populations such as adults 50+ depending on the grant offered.

Administration for Community Living. ACL provides state and local governments, nonprofit organizations, educational institutions, and small businesses funding opportunities. The Web site has helpful tips for grant writing and managing your grant. Most grants on this site can also be found on Grants.gov.

Grants.gov. This is a federal grant center that showcases information on how to apply for grants and the different types of grants that are currently available. Typing in the search engine "library" or "older adults" retrieves different grants available with descriptions and deadlines. Remember to type in different words for midlife and older adults to retrieve more results.

Melanie Wehrle at Pikes Peak Library District in Colorado: "We have been successful offering a five-session Acrylic Painting Class for Beginners once or twice a year that is taught by a working painter who is in his early 80s. This class series began under the Creative Aging in America's Libraries program with grant funding from the Institute of Museum and Library Services in collaborations with Lifetime Arts, Inc., AARP Foundation, American Library Association, and Westchester Library System. As part of the grant we offered a series of eight painting classes for our 55+ patrons. A unique feature of this grant funding was that art supplies were required to be provided to the participants to keep. The goal was mastery of the art skills so participants could continue making art well past the end of the class series. Because the class size was limited to 12, we had long waiting lists. With the overwhelming positive feedback from the participants, we continue to offer an abbreviated five-week class series that includes painting supplies for the participants to take home. Many of the participants have told us that the cost of art classes in our community and the required purchase of supplies have made it too costly for them to try a new skill that they may not enjoy. They were happy to have a fun way to see if they like painting before they invested any of their limited funds in learning it. We use funds from the district senior programming budget combined with branch programming funds to pay for this class series."

FUNDING RESOURCES

Besides exploring grant opportunities, many public libraries have a budget where funds can be allocated to programming and services. Depending on the budget size, this will determine if there will be money for programming and if there will be monies allocated for adults 50+ services. Most of the contributors to this text indicated that within their library budget, there is a line for programming, but it was not specifically allocated to adults 50+. In addition, there are many libraries that have a "Friends of the Library" group and library foundations. These organizations contribute money and other helpful support, which can enhance the services and resources available at our libraries. Friends groups and foundations support their library by volunteering, through advocacy, and monetary gifts (Reed, 2012). They also help with fundraising and with promoting and marketing the library in the community. Friends groups and library foundations have different degrees of priorities depending on their mission and the current need of the library.

The following are examples from contributors to this text that highlight different funding sources for easy reference. However, information about other areas of funding are left in the examples to indicate other sources.

Adults 50+ budget. *Fife Lake Public Library in Michigan:* "Our budget does include a line item specific to senior programming. It is minimal, but with partnering, collaborating, and sponsorship, most of our programs and activities are free. . . . We also receive funding from the senior center to support funds for supplies, guest speakers, and entertainers. Our local credit union . . . is supportive with funding for special events. We also seek funding and donations from local businesses and institutions in Fife Lake. The seniors also donate items and funds to support their programs."

Melanie Wehrle at Pikes Peak Library District in Colorado: "We also have a small senior services budget that supports outreach costs to the older adult population such as tables at the annual senior expo, as well as branch programming targeting older adults. At times, we fund programming costs for expensive programming by using funds from multiple budgets."

Debbi Gallucci: "We do have a separate budget for programming and services for our 50+ population."

Adult programming budget. (some typical responses) *Santa Barbara Public Library in California:* "Grants, Friends groups, and regular programming budget. . . . We have a budget for programming for adults but not specifically for 50+."

Jenneffer Sixkiller: "We have a programming budget for my department. . . . We request our money to be approved by the town board (town municipal library) and our department head allocates how much each programming staff member can spend . . . not specifically for seniors; adult services has a separate budget from teen services and children's services to cover ages 18 and up."

Alexandra Annen: "Within the adult programming budget . . . not specific for seniors."

General programming budget. *Mariel Carter, adult service reference librarian at Marinette County Consolidated Public Library Services in Wisconsin:* "My library has a programming budget, but does not distinguish an amount to be used by a particular age demographic."

Ryan Johnson at O'Fallon Public Library in Illinois: "We have a programming budget line item in our overall budget. All supplies, marketing, presenter fees, etc., come out of the line item. That same line item covers adults, teens, and children . . . there is no specific budget for older adults."

New Durham Public Library in New Hampshire: "Not specifically, any programs would fall under programming."

General operating funds. *Chris Jackson special audiences strategist:* "Costs are minimal, we provide refreshments at some of the events, plus handouts and binders of information. Funds are from each of the partnering agencies' program budgets. . . . Most of our funding comes out of the library's general operating fund, and we also get significant programming support from our Friends group."

Anoka County Library in Minnesota: "There is no separate budget for adults 50+ programming. All programming funds come from the same budget."

Terry Soave at Ann Arbor District Library in Michigan: "Programming costs come from our operating budget."

Materials budget. *Anonymous:* "My library maintains a large-print collection that is about 18 percent of our materials budget."

Quincy Public Library in Illinois: "We do receive some grants and donations, but primarily fund through the library budget. The Friends of the Library generally pay for the movie license. . . . We have a budget for purchasing large-print books and a small collection of DVDs. Staffing, supplies, vehicles . . . are part of the general library budget."

Outreach programming budget. *Marie Corbitt at Westerville Public Library in Ohio:* "We do not have any special funding. Our Outreach Department has its own budget and that budget did increase when we added the position of Outreach and Program Librarian since we will be doing more programming. . . . That money is mostly used on programming for seniors, but also used for some children's programs. Our Adult Services Department also has a budget for adult programming, but not specifically for older adults . . . costs for our programming [are] minimal. Most of what we buy are craft-type materials for activities, but many of our needed materials are also found in-house."

No budget. *Tracy Trotter, library director at Adams Memorial Library in Pennsylvania:* "We have no budget for programming of any kind other than the annual Summer Reading Program (which we do also run for adults as well). If I really, really believe we need to offer a program and I can't find anyone to underwrite it, I will very occasionally pull money out of our book budget to pay for it."

Library foundations and board. *Heather Johnson at River Falls Public Library in Wisconsin:* "Funding for the programs come from an assortment of places, including, but are not limited to, The River Falls Library Foundation, The River Falls Library Board, The River Falls Public Library programming budget, and various grants and community organizations that provide funding for programs offered."

Friends of the library. *Mariel Carter, adult service reference librarian at Marinette County Consolidated Public Library Services in Wisconsin:* "We receive a donation to help with the cost of the Marinette County Reads Project; our Friends of the Library group purchases and provides coffee grounds, desserts, and tableware when requested for special events."

Leslie DeLooze, community services librarian at Richmond Memorial Library in New York: "We have a designated budget line for programs for adults, but we do not specifically budget for an age range. In addition, we have funding for supplemental or special programming expenses from the Friends of the Library."

Elizabeth Eisen, adult programming librarian at Appleton Public Library in Wisconsin: "Some of our speakers ask for an honorarium. These funds are provided through the Friends of Appleton Public Library. . . . Our Friends group is our main source for funding."

Lynn Harthorne: "Our current programs are no cost. We do have funding from our Friends of the Library."

Jaci Defelice at Cranberry Public Library in Pennsylvania: "This year, our Friends group gave us funding for adult programming, which will cover speakers for the year."

Debra DeJonker-Berry at Eastham Public Library in Massachusetts: "Our Friends group is very supportive both with volunteers (most are 50+) as well as financially supporting our programming (we have no programming budget outside the Friends)."

Webster Public Library in New York: "We have no special funding in the operating budget for programming, all of our offerings are either free or paid through the Friends of the Webster Library."

Fees, fines, and donations

Materials. Tracy Trotter, library director at Adams Memorial Library in Pennsylvania: "As much as possible we try to find programs that cost nothing to the library. We never charge for attending programs other than a materials fee for the crafts programs. That fee is based on our actual cost for materials."

Jaci at Cranberry Public Library in Pennsylvania: "Typically, we do not charge for programs. We are going to experiment with program[s] in which we will charge in August. The program is mandala painting and participants will have to pay $5.00 to cover the cost of materials. The presenter usually charges more, but she was willing to charge less for the patrons."

Programs. Lisa C. West at Homewood Public Library in Alabama: "Literary Libations . . . learn about the drinks that fueled famous works and were created in them with bartender and writer. . . . Cost to the library varies due to supplies required . . . the alcohol is donated by distributers, patrons pay $10 for tickets which includes two adult beverages . . . at least half our crowd falls into senior status. We usually make several $100 dollars on this programming series per show."

Fines. Greenwood County Library System in South Carolina: "Bookmobile program supplies are paid for out of fines and fees money."

Donations. New Durham Public Library in New Hampshire: "We do not charge for any library program; we do, however, ask for a five dollar donation to cover supplies at Paint Nights."

COLLABORATIONS

Developing partnerships and collaborating with other organizations and businesses will help with the budgeting of various programs. Collaborating with local organizations can also help a small budget and keep down costs. Some organizations will split the cost or pay for some of the fees for a program or service. For instance, some businesses or individuals will provide a service or present at the library for no charge, whereas others trade free advertising or they will provide materials or snacks. Consider collaborating with other public libraries in surrounding communities to share presenters, programs, or even technical equipment, which could help with expenses. Some organizations ask for a donation instead of charging a set fee for presenting at the library, which leaves the cost up to what the library wants to give for the service. However, keep in mind that the honorarium will affect future collaborations. The following are examples from contributors to this text of some of the collaborations that help with funding for their library.

Tracy Trotter, library director at Adams Memorial Library in Pennsylvania: "Sometimes we can negotiate better prices if we band together with other libraries, such as for group discounts or consortia pricing."

Simsbury Public Library in Connecticut: "The majority of funding for programs comes from the Friends of the Simsbury Public Library or grants, with a small amount of funding from the town of Simsbury. We stretch our dollars by collaborating with organizations, businesses, and community groups. . . . This has been especially successful with the senior center because they pay for half of all the programs we collaborate on. Some organizations, such as the Simsbury High School Culinary Arts Department, only required that we pay for materials."

John J. Trause, director at the Oradell Public Library in New Jersey: "Because of our excellent connections to local and community groups . . . many of those who appear to offer programs at the library do so for free."

Lisa C. West at Homewood Public Library in Alabama: "We partner with community partners who are anxious to get the word out on their services, and providing an informative program alerts our community to their existence. It's a 'win-win' situation for all of us (the program provider, our community, and the library)."

Matthew Riley at Friendswood Public Library in Texas: "Most funding for adult programming comes from our Friends of the Library group, which raises funds through book sales and other fundraising efforts. We also partner with many individuals and groups who freely share their expertise and time with the community."

Melanie Wilks at Pioneer Memorial Library in Kansas: "We have to make the money stretch so we have worked very hard at cultivating relationships with many groups and organizations to bring programing to our community together. This makes us all more effective and lowers the cost. It helps us with grants and funding because we are working with others."

Kristi Haman: "Our main source of funding is the library budget for programming and the Friends of the Library. Patrons and nonprofit organizations also offer their time and expertise for free. . . . We receive a grant each year. . . . We encourage everyone in the community to read the same book and come together to experience a full slate of events to enlighten, educate, and spark introspection and lively discussion. The grant is offered by the . . . Humanities Council, Friends of the . . . Libraries . . . and multiple libraries."

Beth Neunaber: "We have received grant funds from the Lions Club to expand our large-print selection, which is predominantly used by mature adults."

Christy Wagner at ELA Area Public Library in Illinois: "I have a book budget for my large-print collection and a programming budget for events, speakers, and programs. From time to time we receive memorial donations, we are also beginning to partner with ELA Township '55-Plus' to co-sponsor the development of Caregiver Kits. Some of the kits will be held at their facility, and the remaining will be available for check-out through the library."

Athol Public Library in Massachusetts: "The library receives funding for most of our programs from our very active Friends of the Athol Library group. Some funding for programs is provided by the Athol Cultural Council. A trust fund that was set up to provide funds for services to Athol senior citizens usually grants money annually for large-print books and magazines."

FUNDRAISING, DONATIONS, AND OTHER OPTIONS

Sometimes, we simply do not have the funding that we need due to budget constraints. Some programs can be offered at little or no cost just by making a few changes. For instance, consider talking with a local instructor to donate time and have attendees pay a small fee if materials are needed for a program. Furthermore, asking for donations of materials or services can help defray costs. There are also library patrons who might have talents or stories they would like to share. As adults age, their social relationships can diminish. Having an opportunity to socialize and share information can lead to better health and better life satisfaction (Chang, Wray, & Lin, 2014). Talking with adults 50+ in our communities can provide different programming ideas or possible contacts to viable presenters and performers. In addition, having fundraisers once or twice a year can bring in extra funding that can help with costs to future programs and services. Plus, depending on the program or service, patrons might not mind paying a small fee, especially if the cost is lower than what they would normally pay for the actual performance or service. Remember to talk with other libraries in surrounding communities at how they are finding funding for their programs. This can create a network of information providing ideas, assistance with issues that arise, or possible collaborations. The following are examples from contributors about other funding options they had at their libraries.

Fundraisers. *John J. Trause, director at Oradell Public Library in New Jersey:* "The Friends of the Library and the Oradell Public Library Foundation provide fundraising activities. We have partnered on fundraisers with local businesses."

Kelly Martin Laney at Birmingham Public Library in Alabama: "There is no charge for any of our programs, but we do fundraisers throughout the year for participants to make donations or help raise money to pay for adult program supplies. Since we have many excellent quilters in our group, they collaborated on a quilt, which was then raffled, with proceeds going to the adult programs. This has allowed us to offer better crafts. We also have many, many donations of materials and supplies. When someone in the community who had a lot of yarn, material, etc., passes away, the word has gotten around that the library can use piecemeal supplies. . . . The family of one of our patrons who died requested all memorial contributions be donated to the adult programs at Springville Road because their mother enjoyed the program so much."

Heather Johnson at River Falls Public Library in Wisconsin: "Funding for programming for adults ages 50+ is secured through several different sources. The primary source of funding is provided through the annual library budget. . . . Other sources of funding come from the River Falls Library Foundation, community grants, donations to the library designated specifically for programs, and from the two large fundraising events held at the library in the spring (Mini-Golf in the Library) and in the fall (Kirby Symes Memorial 5K)."

Debra DeJonker-Berry at Eastham Public Library in Massachusetts: "We have just opened a new library with lots of technology, including vision and hearing assistance. All this equipment was purchased through fundraising from our Eastham Building Fund, Inc."

Private donations. *Tracy Trotter, library director at Adams Memorial Library in Pennsylvania:* "We have no special funding as a regular thing. We go after grants when appropriate, and we have been lucky to have donors who have given specifically for programming for adults. The General Ulysses S. Grant program . . . will cost us $200, and that is being paid for by someone who donated in honor of friends celebrating a wedding anniversary."

Lucine Kauffman, SAGE coordinator in New York: "The SAGE (Services to the Aging in Genesee County) Program is privately funded through an annual grant to Richmond Memorial Library. The grant pays for two part-time SAGE employees' wages, purchases of multimedia library materials, office supplies, some travel expenses, and other miscellaneous expenses. The . . . fund was set up in 1998 through a generous bequest of a local resident. The Rochester Area Community Foundation provides administrative and fiduciary oversight for the fund and works closely with the Genesee County Office for the Aging."

Kate Skinner: "Program was costly to initiate but the funding was all sourced from two different donors who supported the notion of the library offering free yoga."

Memorial donations. *Anonymous:* "One of our patrons passed away a few years ago and left us a substantial amount of money earmarked for adult programming."

Free presenters. *Chad Robinson at Matheson Memorial Library in Wisconsin:* "I enjoy an operating budget specifically earmarked for hiring performers. However, I must add that we host a great many local speakers who perform for free. . . . Our adult operating budget is usually sufficient for most programs, but we sometimes apply for grants or ask our Friends group for funding of special programs and projects."

CHAPTER SUMMARY

This chapter looked at various funding sources and opportunities that can be investigated to bring additional monies for adult 50+ programs and services. Different grants are available at the local, state, national, and federal level. Collaborating with others can help with the application process and can improve chances of award success. Friends groups as well as donations, fundraisers, and other small fees can also help assist with programming when budgets are tight.

11

Going Down a Two-Way Street:
Engagement Strategies

Reaching out to adults midlife and older and attracting them to the library for programs and other services are an important part of our mission in engaging all our community patrons. Collaborating with local groups such as Meals on Wheels or nurse associations to bring library information with them when visiting an individual's home can showcase how the library can also deliver materials to homebound individuals. Creating traditional postal mailing lists as well as e-mail lists of organizations and agencies that serve adults 50+ can broaden the range of adults you reach. Engaging adults 50+ can take many forms such as reaching out to different locations in the community where they might frequently attend and offering library services and programs or encouraging adults 50+ to become actively involved in the library environment. Besides attracting adults midlife and older to the programs and services the library has to offer, we need to remember adults 50+ are also a valuable resource for the library (Ristau, 2010). We can engage adults 50+ in our libraries in a variety of ways. For instance, we can utilize library patrons to present or assist at programs, advocate for the library in our communities, and have adults 50+ on our advisory boards. We need to create opportunities for our adults 50+ to be involved because it can be beneficial for them and for the public library.

ENGAGEMENT OPPORTUNITIES: TIPS AND IDEAS

The following are a few typical responses on how the contributors to this text have engaged adults 50+ within their library.

Yolo County Library in California: "We offer services, outreach, and volunteer opportunities."

Tamar Kreke, adult and technical services coordinator at Green County Public Library in Ohio: "We speak at Rotary Clubs, Council on Aging, senior centers, and other community groups."

Debra DeJonker-Berry at Eastham Public Library in Massachusetts: "They are heavily engaged and are included . . . in the board of trustees, Friends, volunteers, and we have many committees . . . which are comprised heavily of 50+ (and older)."

Brianne Columbo at Fairfield Free Public Library in New Jersey: "The Fairfield Free Public Library aims to engage seniors 50+ most significantly by listening closely to this senior community's wants and needs. We provide many adult events with their interests in mind. Much of what we do and offer is shaped by the voices of our senior library patrons."

VOLUNTEERS

Library volunteers can be wonderful assets for our libraries. For instance, they can expand our library services that we cannot fund or if we did not have the staffing to run the program. They can assist in shelf reading, conduct programs outside of the library, prepare or be an extra hand in the craft program, or help other adults 50+ with computer skills. There are many volunteer opportunities that can be of assistance to our libraries and, depending on the library, will vary in what the volunteer will perform and how many volunteers will be needed for certain library services.

Volunteering can give a feeling of self-worth, which is important for adults 50+ who want to give back to their community (Williamson, Bannister, & Sullivan, 2010). We need to encourage volunteers to recruit their friends and others to volunteer to create a list for future endeavors and to increase our value within our communities. Plan a workshop for volunteers to review library policies and to take a tour of the library. During this time, the volunteers can meet any staff they will work with and also discuss the expectations for their volunteer work. Consider writing a volunteer job description to give to volunteers and to have on hand for library staff. In addition, volunteers can be great advocates for the library by promoting the value of our services and providing great PR in the community. A nice resource to recruit volunteers is the Retired Senior Volunteer Program (see Appendix C). This is a national program of individuals 55+ that serve communities in a variety of capacities. The following are some tips and ideas that contributors to this text mentioned about the volunteers in their library, how they are acquired, and the types of services they provide for their library.

Volunteer age range. *Marie Corbitt at Westerville Public Library in Ohio:* "We do have volunteers at our library who are 50+, but we do not really market for that age group directly. That age group just seems to be a large portion of the population that applies to volunteer here."

Beth Neunaber: "Many of our volunteers that assist throughout the year are over 50."

Volunteer collaborators

Civic organizations. Simsbury Public Library in Connecticut: "Volunteers from the Lions Club, most of whom are retirees, help us with our monthly Coffeehouse series."

State organizations. Muncie Public Library in Indiana: "Our volunteers come from a variety of age groups, but we do have volunteers who are age 50+. Some of these volunteers come from volunteer organizations such as RSVP, some are volunteering to earn benefits through a partnership with a funded program such as the Senior Employment Program at Bridges Community Services, and some volunteer independently." (RSVP is a volunteer match program in central Indiana.)

Volunteer incentives. *Athol Public Library in Massachusetts:* "Most of our volunteers are 50+. The town also has a program, senior tax abatement volunteers, who can earn a portion of their taxes each year in return for working, volunteering. The library is fortunate to have several of these individuals each year, many of whom work many more hours than the program reimburses them for."

Volunteer opportunities

Friends of the library book shop. Anonymous: "We also have many 50+ aged volunteers who work in the book shop run by our Friends of the Library group, and the profits from that shop provide support for library needs."

Fundraising. Heather Johnson at River Falls Public Library in Wisconsin: "Adults ages 50+ are provided with numerous opportunities to be engaged with the library. These opportunities include, but are not limited to, volunteering in the library . . . help[ing] out with the library's fundraising events . . . and help[ing] with the annual Holiday Open House and Volunteer Appreciation events."

Information assistance. Dan Hubbs at Saratoga Springs Public Library in New York: "We have senior volunteers helping in the Saratoga Room and at the Information Desk."

Outreach. Christy Wagner at ELA Area Public Library in Illinois: "Our department relies on the dedication of a dozen library volunteers to assist us in our work and help us extend what we do in the community. I absolutely could not offer the level or scope of outreach site visits without the help of my volunteers in Outreach."

Ocean County Library in New Jersey: "Another very rewarding volunteering opportunity is the Home Borrowers Service where volunteers bring library materials to the county's homebound citizens who live in their own private residences. Most of the volunteers with the Home Borrowers Service are 50+."

Program assistance. Kate Skinner: "We take on volunteers to help especially with reshelving library material and with programming. For example, to wield the glue gun at craft programs with younger children, where we want a responsible adult in charge of the glue gun, or to staff a craft table at a Family Night."

Program initiators. Quincy Public Library in Illinois: "We have volunteers and an active Friends of the Library, as well as the programs designed to accommodate their interests. Some of the discussion groups and book clubs were actually started by individual volunteers."

Program presenters. Fife Lake Public Library in Michigan: "Yoga . . . a volunteer leads the group by using a variety of videos that we purchase for them . . . Fitness Over 50 . . . a volunteer leads the group with low-impact exercises put to music. They have more fun at fitness than any of our other programs. There is always a lot of laughing during their workout."

Alexandra Annen: "We have one senior volunteer that runs bingo."

Kathleen Handy, computer instructor at Saratoga Springs Public Library in New York: "Many retirees help us through volunteering and help us broaden our class offerings by sharing their skills and talents. . . . We encourage volunteers, and sometimes people can be asked to help lead classes or programs [with] which they are experienced."

Kelly Martin Laney at Birmingham Public Library in Alabama: "Body Changers is open to all adults and is a weight management support program led by volunteers assisted by staff. Participants are required to have a food plan, which they may get from their doctor or they may choose themselves (resources are made available for checkout), but they are not given one in the program. Participants register, choose their goals, weigh in weekly, and are recognized for reaching milestones, completing assignments, and consistent attendance. Homework assignments include keeping a record of meals, using a specific healthy ingredient in a meal plan, exercising, and presenting information to the group on health tips and recipes."

Shelving. Mary at Wilbraham Public Library in Massachusetts: "We have a Senior Tax program in which seniors over 60 apply for a shelving job at the library. They can work a set number of hours . . . each year and apply it towards their property taxes. This is a really popular position that gets many applicants a year. We currently fill four positions."

Special services. Simsbury Public Library in Connecticut: "We utilize volunteers who help in Circulation and Technical Services and on special projects in Reference and Children's. Whenever we have work available, we also supervise people who need to do mandated community service through the courts. Some of these are in the 50+ age group (in fact, they are the age group that works out the best)."

Tutors. Findlay-Hancock County Public Library in Ohio: "Some of the volunteer tutors for our adult literacy program are also in this category [50+]."

ADVOCATES

Many adults midlife and older want to be involved in public concerns and are looking for opportunities to participate in their communities. Public libraries are a safe, neutral place to explore ideas and information on any topic. We can position ourselves as a place to facilitate civic engagement on complex issues within our communities where individuals will feel free to express their different points of view and opinions. Advocating on behalf of our libraries is important to show our value in our communities. Adults 50+ are excellent advocates who can express how the library has provided vital services and programs that have positively affected their lives (Manheimer & Kidahashi, 2010). These testimonials can provide evidence to important decision makers who control support for library services. Many adults 50+ want to make a difference and are looking for opportunities to engage in activities that have a purpose (Ristau, 2010). We need to consider encouraging adults midlife and older to join library boards and volunteer work within the library. The following are a few examples of how the contributors to this text have engaged the adults 50+ as advocates in their libraries.

Library and foundation board. *Meryle A. Leonard at Charlotte Mecklenburg Library in North Carolina:* "We also engage the 50+ community on our library and foundation board."

Mariel Carter, adult service reference librarian at Marinette County Consolidated Public Library Services in Wisconsin: "Most of the people on the library board and Friends of the Library are over 50."

Planning committee. *Simsbury Public Library in Connecticut:* "Simsbury Public Library's most recent planning committee had [a] diverse representation of people 50+ to help shape the vision and future of the library."

FORUMS

Listening to adults 50+ in our communities will help in determining the programs and services that they need. We can conduct formal or informal forums, which will have different types of discussions and responses. Formal forums can occur at a certain time and place and are usually monitored by someone who will ask questions and keep the discussion focused on the point at hand. Formal forums can be difficult for retrieving honest opinions if individuals are not able to voice their opinion. This can be due to others monopolizing the time to speak on a certain topic. Other attendees might feel they cannot voice their honest opinions about programs and services because library staff are hosting the meeting or they feel anxious speaking out in front of other individuals. However, formal forums can allow for information to be acquired that can be helpful in formulating programs and services around the needs of the library community (Roberts & Bauman, 2012). Having focused questions about a certain subject can improve certain services or questions that arise from the discussion and can prompt others to speak up, which can inspire and create new ideas. Informal forums can increase the number of individuals who are able to attend and voice their opinions due to the lack of a formal time that the discussion takes place.

Informal forums typically have a walk-in policy whereby the individuals can visit when it is convenient for their schedule. The library can have someone present to listen to comments and concerns as well as the types of programs and services the individuals would like to see implemented at their library. Informal discussions typically have fewer people who are attending at one time, which can be helpful for someone who might not voice their opinion in a room full of people. However, the discussion might be difficult to begin or it might prompt an individual to stay and not talk about the subjects at hand. Having potential topics to discuss or asking attendees their thoughts can help prompt discussions. Formal and informal discussion forums can also take place in an online environment. These online forums are a great place to have patrons share information on a certain topic or have a certain group share information about their wants and needs. Online forums are excellent for informal discussions because patrons can contribute at a time that is convenient for them (Tangient, 2017). In addition, live chat forums typically have a designated time for individuals to speak to members, such as library board members or reference librarians.

Library staff can manage forums. However, this can be an excellent opportunity for library volunteers. Having a volunteer in charge of the forum can possibly let attendees feel more comfortable voicing their honest opinion to their peers in the community and not someone employed by the library. Forums can also take a lot of time, which can take staff away from their normal duties at the library. Thus by utilizing a volunteer, it can free the library staff to do other duties.

Forums are typically intergenerational with everyone welcome to attend in the library community. This will give a broad range of ideas and opinions about the library. We need to consider having different kinds of forums to determine what is best for the community, such as having one forum for all library community members and another with only adults 50+. Having a forum with a focused age of attendees will give more specific information about the intended audience that might not have been voiced from a more generalized forum due to time constraints and other issues raised for other age groups in attendance. The following are examples of forums that contributors to this text have at their libraries.

Formal. *Chris Jackson, special audiences strategist:* "During our strategic planning cycles we do conduct formal community listening events where we try to ensure we're hearing from the 50+ community."

Informal. *Richard Conroy at Essex Library Association in Connecticut:* "We have a large number of volunteers (well over 100) who put in anywhere from a few hours a year to several per week. The vast majority of them are seniors, and we do pay close attention to their suggestions and what they have to say about our services. We do not utilize formal outreach methods such as forums or outreach groups. We have tried that method in the past, but found it difficult to recruit participants. They would much rather interact with us informally, and I suspect that may in part be due to the fact that we are a small community."

SURVEYS AND FOCUS GROUPS

Surveys and focus groups can help us gain a better understanding of our library communities. This is important when making decisions about adult 50+ programming and services because we can gain important feedback and insight on the thoughts and feelings of this age group. We need to ask questions about what types of programs and services they would like to have and their opinions on the current programs and services already being offered at the library (Higa-Moore, Bunnett, Mayo, & Olney, 2002). This information is necessary to determine if improvements or changes need to be made, such as the timing of a particular program, or if better modes of advertising of services need to be expanded. Additionally, informal focus groups, where someone can just walk in at any time of the day, might create more interest and receive more responses than a formal time for the focus group, which can limit the individuals who can attend because of other time commitments.

Surveys can be a quick way to achieve valuable information. When creating a survey, we need to try not to make the surveys too long or complicated to understand. In addition, consider creating the survey text in at least 14 point font for easier reading. One nice suggestion from a fellow librarian in this text is to consider having a short survey with a pencil on the chairs of a current program and ask attendees to fill it out before they leave. This will give instant feedback about the program or the types of future programs they would like to attend at the library.

Following is a sample survey that contains five short questions that can be created for attendees to answer. Under each question, lists of possible responses can be added for patrons to check off for easier reference. Make sure to allow ample space for attendees to write in responses as well. This will provide ideas that might not have been considered from the checklist of options.

Program: (Put name of program here)

1. How did you hear about the program?
2. What did you like about the program?
3. How can we improve the program?
4. What types of programs would you like to see in the future at the library?
5. Which times are best for scheduling future programs?

Another possible survey option is to create a suggestion box where library patrons can feel confident that their responses, if they choose, can be anonymous. Some individuals feel they can be more honest about a program if they can be anonymous, especially if they did not like the program. Additionally, ongoing surveys that can be dropped in a suggestion box can build program diversity and increase library patron attendance by giving the community what they suggest as possible future options. We can also consider creating an online survey on our Web site that can be quick and easy to fill out to reach patrons outside of the library environment. Asking patrons about programming and services can give a sense of ownership that their opinions matter in their community (Higa-Moore et al., 2002). We are a public institution creating a space for the community; therefore, we need to provide programs and services that meet our public needs. Asking for input from our community members will help us achieve that goal.

Moreover, focus groups are another option to gain important information from our library community. Choose what questions will be answered before starting the focus group. However, keep in mind that the group can get off topic due to responses or questions brought up during the conversation. This can also bring up interesting points and ideas not originally thought of by library staff. Try to let the flow of the conversation go naturally. However, try to keep to 5 to 10 minutes per question to keep the discussion moving along. It would be helpful to have a good age range of individuals aged 50+ to be able to attain a variety of responses. An important thing to remember is that there will be positive and negative feedback giving different perspectives on adults 50+ programming and services at the library. The following are some examples from contributors to this text on surveys and focus groups conducted in their libraries.

Comment or suggestion box. *Kristi Haman:* "Patrons often offer suggestions directly to the manager or the director. We also have a comment box at our library and patrons offer program suggestions."

Focus groups. *Meryle A. Leonard at Charlotte Mecklenburg Library in North Carolina:* "This demographic is also part of library surveys, focus groups, and forums."

Ocean County Library in New Jersey: "The library does numerous service-rating surveys and focus groups to determine how well we are meeting the needs of this age group and to identify those areas where the library might need to develop programs."

Informal discussions. *Ryan Johnson at O'Fallon Public Library in Illinois:* "We do not have any formal channels. We do request feedback when patrons register for events. Asking things like 'How did you hear about this event?' and 'What other types of events would you be interested attending?' This helps inform our decisions as we plan events and look for community partners."

Surveys. *Kate Skinner:* "Survey the community before deciding to do anything."

Melany Wilks at Pioneer Memorial Library in Kansas: "We keep close relationships with those attendees. Ask for ideas, and give surveys out for help."

Heather Johnson at River Falls Public Library in Wisconsin: "I have a survey at each of my programs where I give away small (donated) incentives in a drawing from the surveys. These surveys are instrumental and priceless in the information that they provide to me about the types of programs that people in the community want."

ADVISORY GROUPS

Advisory boards composed of adults 50+ can provide input for relevant library programming and services. These groups can assist the library in various ways. For instance, some advisory boards brainstorm ideas for new services, provide help in developing programs, determine resources that might be needed that the library does not have, and can help in library short- and long-range planning (Mates, 2003). Consider having a variety of individuals on the advisory board such as different occupations, genders, and a variety of age ranges over 50. A diverse advisory board will create a mixture of ideas and provide for all types of adults 50+ within the community. Advisory board members also make excellent advocates for the library. The following are examples of advisory groups and boards that contributors to this text have at their libraries.

Chad Robinson at Matheson Memorial Library in Wisconsin: "Our most valuable tool is our Adult Program Advisory Group that was founded a year ago. They have been invaluable not only in providing great ideas for future programs, but in helping us market said programs through their own community contacts."

Kate Skinner: "We have a volunteer Library Advisory Board."

Leslie DeLooze, community services librarian at Richmond Memorial Library in New York: "We have an advisory group for the Books Sandwiched In program . . . a committee of community members meets twice a year to select books and speakers. It is tremendously helpful for this particular program, because we have people who know many different people out in the community who might be good speakers for specific books."

Adrienne Doman Calkins at Sherwood Public Library in Oregon: "We have a Library Advisory Board with several members who are representative of adults 50+."

FRIENDS OF THE LIBRARY

Friends of the Library groups provide many types of benefits to help support our libraries. They help generate funds, run book sales of discarded or donated items, volunteer their time for programs, advocate for the library to receive additional funding from other resources, and promote to others the value of the library in the community (United for Libraries, 2017). Adults 50+ are typically involved with Friends of the Library groups. According to Reed (2012), Baby Boomers want to volunteer and become involved in their communities. Encouraging adults 50+ to join the Friends group at our libraries can provide potentially more adult 50+ volunteers for library programs, increasing library advocates and possibly providing new patrons to library programs and services. Friends of the Library groups typically provide funding for various programs and services, adding support to a library budget. It is important to acknowledge the help the Friends group provides, such as verbally thanking them at the given program, acknowledging their contribution with a written notice on marketing materials or thank you note, or a special event can be held for Friends members to show appreciation for all the help they provide during the year to the library. The following are examples from contributors to this text about the Friends groups at their libraries.

Membership. *Athol Public Library in Massachusetts:* "Our Friends of the Library board and organization is made up of many 50+ adults. The executive board of this organization has ten members, nine of which are 50+."

Findlay-Hancock County Public Library in Ohio: "The Friends of the Library run a used book store in our lower level with volunteers, many of whom are in this category [50+]."

John J. Trause, director at Oradell Public Library in New Jersey: "The Friends of the Library and the Oradell Public Library Foundation as well as most of the staff of the library, including me, the library director, are 50+."

Fundraising. *Simsbury Public Library in Connecticut:* "This is an all-volunteer organization, which does an annual book sale to raise funds for our programming. Many of the volunteers with the Friends and the people they enlist to help with the book sale sorting and sales are in the 50+ age range."

Program assistance. *Elizabeth Eisen, adult programming librarian at Appleton Public Library in Wisconsin:* "We do have a large number of volunteers. They plan, facilitate, and assist me with book discussions, movies, concerts, writing and coloring programs, and special events as needed. I host a quarterly program planning meeting, and two of our primary program volunteers attend this meeting of the programming staff."

Kristi Haman: "We have the Friends of the Library and adult volunteers. They often help us out by volunteering in the library and assisting with the yearly Book Sale."

Annual appreciation. *Webster Public Library in New York:* "Our Friends of the Webster Library is a very active group that tends to be made up of retired folks. We have an annual 'thank you' event each year to honor the important work they do for us."

CHAPTER SUMMARY

This chapter was about engaging adults 50+ in our communities. This can be by providing programs and services for them to attend, advocating for volunteers, creating surveys and forums to gain their opinions, or asking them to be on advisory boards or a Friends of the Library group. Providing different types of engagement opportunities will give important information to the library for the services and programs for their age group and provide advocates for the library in the community.

12

Future Outlook

This text was motivated by the need for more resources on the topic of adult 50+ library services and programming. With the large population of Baby Boomers getting older, it is essential to focus more attention on this underserved age group and provide different types of services and programs to meet their various wants and needs. When examining the newly revised ALA Guidelines for Adults 60+ and the 55 libraries that contributed information to this text, we can see that many of our libraries are providing some wonderful programs and services for our adults midlife and older in our library communities. However, this is only a small portion of public libraries that were explored throughout the United States. More still needs to be done for this growing age group.

Ageism is still present in today's society even though portrayals of adults 50+ are slowly changing. We need to continue to provide a neutral space and welcoming environment that avoids stereotypes. We can help by offering a variety of experiences for our adult population, which can be accomplished by knowing our adult 50+ library patrons. Consider having a dedicated library position or providing opportunities for library staff to attend training and webinar sessions on adults midlife and older. This can include meetings or workshops in other similar fields that serve adults 50+. The more we know and understand about the age group, the better we can serve our adult 50+ library community.

It has been noted that some adults 50+ have certain challenges and that they need assistive technologies to help in retrieving and accessing information effectively. Only some of the libraries in this text had assistive technologies available for their patrons. More needs to be done in offering a variety of assistive technologies at our libraries. Plus, more marketing strategies need to be considered so these services are noted as being available for their community members. In addition, providing a diverse selection of programs for our adults 50+ with a variety of times and days will provide ample opportunity for working and nonworking adults 50+ to attend the programs. Most public libraries examined in this text are providing different types of programs. However, some libraries are not focusing on their adult patrons. The needs of our library patrons will change over time. Periodically assessing our adult 50+ community members will determine what types of programs and services are needed at our libraries.

Technology is important in today's society. We need to provide opportunities for adults 50+ to learn the digital literacy skills necessary to use computerized systems to access and retrieve information. Most of our libraries are providing basic computer classes or one-on-one technology help to their adult 50+ library patrons. We need to keep offering different types of technology programs to help our patrons learn new systems, expand their digital literacy skills, and increase their comfort level in using new devices. We need to keep in mind that as adults age, they can experience a decline in physical and cognitive abilities. This can affect their confidence in using a technological device and limit their success in accessing information online. We need to provide more hands-on learning experiences with technology to build confidence regarding learning new functions and to provide digital literacy skill development to retrieve the information they need. Plus, some adults 50+ experience difficulty when exploring the Internet. We should consider having a dedicated page on our Web sites that can be simplified with less information and have larger font sizes for easier reading. We can also supply links to information that would be beneficial for the adult 50+ creating a valuable resource that can be accessed from one Web site location. Furthermore, overcoming barriers to accessing information for our patrons can be challenging, especially when we are faced with our own set of challenges for adequate funding for broadband. Providing a stable broadband connection needs to be a major priority. We need to continue to advocate for our libraries to have better access for our communities. This will help our patrons who rely on us for their Internet access.

Fostering lifelong learning pursuits is beneficial to people of all ages, especially adults 50+. Offering literacy programs or the resources to improve literacy skills in adults are important to be able to view and gather information effectively, especially from an online environment. Only some of the libraries examined in this text were offering literacy programs or resources that were gathered from their library Web sites. Providing formal and informal learning opportunities can have a positive impact on adults 50+. By collaborating and partnering with other organizations, we can help promote civic engagement and increase the potential of learning different experiences. These partnerships can be beneficial to the library and to the partner association. We can potentially reach more adults 50+ and broaden the types of programs we offer to our community members. Developing relationships with our community partners can be a win-win situation, but it takes time.

Open communication and leaving the door open for future endeavors is important. You never know when a partnership will be established.

Outreach services have always been an important service we provide for our community members who cannot come to our physical library environment. Providing different services, including programs and materials, will help all members of the community enjoy what the library has to offer. Marketing outreach services is key to ensure our target audience knows about the outreach services available to suit their needs. Only some of the libraries explored in this text had outreach services advertised on their Web site pages. We need to consider having different types of marketing outreach strategies to reach a variety of individuals who use different forms of media to gather their information. When examining marketing strategies, most of the libraries in this text promoted programs and services in a variety of venues. This is important to reach a wide variety of adults 50+ in your community. Besides printed marketing materials, we need to consider social networking sites and electronic communication strategies to increase our marketing audience.

Funding for programs and services is always a hot topic. As librarians, we are amazing at squeezing out programs on a shoestring budget. Finding valuable sources is a never-ending task that takes time and consideration. Collaborating with other libraries and organizations can help when applying for external funds, taking some of the workload and increasing the chances of success in winning a grant or award. Cultivating relationships with peers can provide a new partnership or showcase new funding sources that you can investigate. In addition, developing a rapport with patrons not only increases the value of the library with the community, but also increases the network potential that can have a range of possibilities such as increasing Friends of the Library members, increasing private donations, and establishing strong advocates to support our future endeavors. We are doing an excellent job of finding different funding resources if we examine the libraries in this text and what they have been doing for their libraries. The trick is finding the time to hunt for the right funding to suit our needs. Consider starting a list of potential resources that can be referred back to when funding is needed for future programming.

As the population of adults 50+ grows, we need to expand and create more formal and informal services and programs to meet the needs of our midlife and older adult community members. Listening to their opinions and having adults 50+ on our boards and foundations can give us valuable insight into creating the types of services and programs they want from our libraries. Some of the libraries in this text have staff who are age 50+, which can be helpful; having members of the community can provide more diverse opinions and different ways of looking at certain situations. We also need to consider having some form of communication with our adult 50+ community on a regular basis to keep up to date on their wants and needs. When reviewing the contributing libraries in this text, there was not a universal age or word that was used to describe adults midlife and older. Many used the terms adults 50+, seniors, elderly, or other ages over 50 to describe and talk about their services and programs they offered for this age group. This could be because of the diversity in characteristics that makes it hard to pinpoint what to call this age group.

When examining our nation's libraries in different rural, suburban, and urban settings, it is apparent that we are off to an excellent start in providing for our adult 50+ library patrons. What we have to offer and how we promote our services and programs greatly vary. We are in a position to provide primary access to information for adults 50+. By working together and sharing resources and best practices, we can increase awareness and open new pathways for our libraries and for our adult 50+ library patrons.

Appendix A

Randomly Selected U.S. Public Libraries

Alabama
Andalusia PL
Annie L. Awbrey PL
Carbon Hill City Library
Collinsville PL
Daphne PL
Emma Knox Kenan PL
Enterprise PL
Fayette County Memorial Library
Flomaton PL
Geraldine PL
Haleyville PL
Hayneville-Lowndes County PL
Helen Keller PL
Hightower Memorial Library
Homewood PL
Irondale PL
Jacksonville PL
Jane Boyd Holmes PL
Lincoln PL
McGregor-McKinney PL/Hartford PL
Oxford PL
Pelham PL
Slocomb PL
Tallassee Community Library
Thomas B Norton PL

Alaska
Cantwell Community School Library

Cordova Public Library
Dermott O'Toole Memorial Library
Dillingham PL
Haines Borough PL
Kettleson Memorial PL
Kuskokwim Consortium Library
Nenana PL
Valdez Consortium Library

Arizona
Apache Junction PL
Benson PL
Chandler PL
Cocopah Tribal Library
Kaibab Paiute PL
Oracle PL
Parker PL
Quartzsite PL
Salt River Tribal Library
San Carlos PL
Superior PL
Tonto Basin PL
Young PL

Arkansas
Baxter County Library-Donald W
    Reynolds Library
Boone County Library
Calhoun County Library

Columbia County Library
Fayetteville Public Library
Greene County Library
Hempstead County Library
Lewisville PL
Saline County Library
Trumann PL

California
Benicia PL
Berkeley PL
Beverly Hills PL
Chula Vista PL/Civic Center
Colton PL
Colusa County Free Library
Contra Costa County Library
Covina PL
Daly City PL-Serramonte Main Library
Del Norte County Library District
Downey City Library
El Centro PL
El Dorado County Library
Escondido PL
Inglewood PL
Lakeport Library
Marin County Free Library
Menlo Park PL
Ontario City Library-Ovitt Family
    Community Library
Orange County PL and History Center
Palo Alto City Library
Riverside PL
San Bernardino County Library
San Diego County Library
Santa Barbara PL
Yolo County Library

Colorado
Buena Vista PL
Burlington PL
Combined Community
    Library-Ordway
Cortez PL
Douglas County Libraries
Englewood PL
Flagler Community Library
Haxton PL
Jackson County PL

Lafayette PL
Lake County PL
Park County PL
Penrose Community Library
Pikes Peak Library District
Rangley Library District
South Routt Library District-Oak
    Creek
Woodruff Memorial Library-La Junta

Connecticut
Abington Social Library
Broad Brook PL
Cheshire PL
Chester PL
Clark Memorial Library
East Granby PL
Essex Library Association
Fairfield PL
Jonathan Trumbull Library
Kent Memorial Library
Levi E Coe Library
Meriden PL
Norfolk Library
Plymouth Library Association
Pomfret PL
Seymour PL
Simsbury PL
Slater Library
Thomaston PL
Trumbull Library
Union Free PL
Wallingford PL
West Hartford PL
West Haven PL
Westbrook PL
Wolcott PL
Woodbridge Town Library

Delaware
Dover PL
Rehoboth Beach PL
Selbyville PL
Wilmington PL

Florida
Altamonte Springs City Library
Bushnell PL

Brockway Memorial Library
Collier County PL
Delray Beach PL
Eustis Memorial Library
Flager County PL
Fort Myers Beach PL
Hialeah Public Libraries-John F
  Kennedy Library
Lake Worth PL
Largo PL
Leesburg PL
Mandel PL of West Palm Beach
North Miami PL
North Miami Beach PL
Orange County PL
Parkland Library
Sanibel PL District
Selby PL
Winterpark PL

Georgia
Live Oak PL
Oconee Regional Library
Roddenbery Memorial Library
Sara Hightower Regional Library
Smyma PL

Hawaii
Aiea Haina PL
Hilo PL
Kapolei PL
Mountain View Public and School
  Library
Pearl City PL
Thelma Parker Memorial Public and
  School Library
Waimanalo Public and School Library

Idaho
Ada Community Library-Victory
  Branch
American Falls District Library
Boundary County District Library
Coeur d'Alene PL
East Bonner County Free Library
  District
Emmett PL
Little Wood River District Library

Lost Rivers District Library
Mackay District Library
Nampa PL
North Bingham County District
  Library
Oakley Library District
Priest Lake PL
Stanley Community PL
Wallace PL

Illinois
Alsip-Merrionette Park PL District
Auburn PL
Barry PL
Berkeley PL
Bluffs PL
Broadview PL District
Brown County PL District
Cambridge PL District
Carnegie-Schuyler Library
Caseyville PL District
Catlin PL District
Centralia Regional Library District
Chadwick PL District
Chatsworth Township-Baltz Library
Cherry Valley PL District
Chillicothe PL District
Christopher PL
Coulterville PL
Danvers Township Library
Doyle PL District
Earlville Library District
East Alton PL District
El Paso PL
Ela Area PL District
Eldorado Memorial PL District
Elizabeth Titus Memorial Library
Elmhurst PL
Elwood Township Carnegie Library
Flagg-Rochelle PL District
Fox Lake Public District Library
Freeburg Area Library
Glen Carbon Centennial Library
Glen Ellyn PL
Grand Prairie of the West PL
Grande Prairie PL District
Greenfield PL
Gridley PL District

Hartford PL District
Homer Community Library
Homer Township PL District
Hudson Area PL District
Jacksonville PL
Kansas Community Memorial Library
Kitchell Memorial Library
Lake Forest Library
Madison PL
Maquon PL District
Marengo-Union Library District
Mattoon PL
McCook PL District
Neoga PL District
New Baden PL
Newman Regional Library District
Newton PL and Museum
Nippersink District Library
Norris City Memorial PL District
Northlake PL District
O'Fallon PL
Ohio PL District
Orland Park PL
Palatine PL District
Pankhurst Memorial Library
Paw Paw PL District
Petersburg PL
Plainfield PL District
Plano Community Library District
Potomac PL
Quincy PL
Rantoul PL
Robert R. Jones PL
Robert W. Rowe PL District
Roselle PL District
Rosiclare Memorial PL
Royalton PL District
Shawneetown PL
Shelbyville Free PL
Six Mile Regional Library District
Spoon River PL District
Stickney-Forest View PL District
Sugar Grove PL District
Sycamore PL
Town and Country PL District
Western District Library
Westville PL District
Williamsville PL

Willow Branch Township Library
Windsor Storm Memorial PL District
Woodridge PL
Zion-Benton PL District

Indiana
Andrews Dallas Township PL
Aurora PL District
Bartholomew County PL
Benton County PL
Delphi PL
Fayette County PL
Francesville-Salem Township PL
Franklin County PL District
Hammond PL
Johnson County PL
Kewanna PL
Linden-Carnegie PL
Linton PL
Michigan City PL
Monroe County PL
Muncie PL-Maring-Hunt Library
Noble County PL
Owen County PL
Owensville Carnegie PL
Oxford PL
Pendleton Community Library
Peru PL
Poseyville Carnegie PL
Shelby County PL
Vermillion County PL
Vigo County PL
Wabash Carnegie PL
Wakarusa-Olive and Harrison
     Township PL
Washington Carnegie PL
Westchester PL
Westfield Washington PL
Whiting PL
Winchester Community Library

Iowa
Algona PL
Bode PL
Buffalo Center PL
Burt Public Library
Bussey Community PL
Cambridge Memorial Library

Carnegie-Stout PL
Chelsea PL
Clare PL
Coulter PL
Cresco PL
Crew PL
Davenport PL
Dayton PL
Dike PL
Dolores Tillinghast Memorial Library
Dows Community Library
Drake PL
Dubuque County Library/Asbury
    Branch
Duncombe PL
Elk Horn PL
Elkader PL
Everly PL
Fort Dodge PL
Gilmore City PL
Gowrie PL
Harcourt Community Library
Hawkeye PL
Hedrick PL
Humboldt PL
Humeston PL
Huxley PL
Ida Grove PL
Jamaica PL
Kendall Young Library
Kirchner-French Memorial Library
Kling Memorial Library
Lawler PL
Le Mars PL
LeClaire PL
Lewis PL
Lied PL/Essex Lied PL
M-C Community Library
Manchester PL
Marengo PL
Martelle PL
Melvin PL
Menlo PL
New Sharon PL
Norma Anders PL
Olin PL
Palmer PL
Panora PL

Postville PL
Richland PL
Roland PL
Rolfe PL
Ross and Elizabeth Baty Monticello PL
Rowan PL
Royal PL
Sac City PL
Sloan PL
South English PL
Spencer PL
Spillville PL
Springmier Community Library
Stockport PL
Upham Memorial Library
Victor PL
Wall Lake PL
Walnut PL
Washta PL
Webb PL
West Point PL
Winthrop PL
Woodbury County Library

Kansas
Andale District Library
Arma City Library
Ashland City Library
Axtell PL
Barnard Library
Belleville PL
Bern Community Library
Bird City PL
Buhler PL
Copeland PL
Corning City Library
Emporia PL
Finney County PL
Florence PL
Goddard PL
Graham County PL
Graves Memorial PL
Greeley County Library
Hardtner PL
Harper PL
Havsville Community Library
Ida Long Goodman Memorial
    Library

Iola PL
Kearny County Library
Kensington Community-School
    Library
Kingman Carnegie Library
Kinsley PL
Kismet PL
Leon PL
Lillian Tear Library
Linwood Community
    Library
Macksville City Library
Manhattan PL
Mankato City Library
Minneapolis PL
Moline PL
Pioneer Memorial Library
Potwin PL
Pratt PL
Pretty Prairie PL
Randall PL
Sedan PL
Sheridan County PL
Spearville Township Library
Sunshine City Library-Prairie
    View City Library
Vermillion PL
Viola Township Library

Kentucky
Breckinridge County PL
Clark County PL
Cynthiana-Harrison County PL
Estill County PL
Henderson County PL
John L Street Library
Johnson County PL
Kenton County PL
Lexington PL
Metcalfe County PL
Mount Sterling Montgomery
    County Library
Pike County PL District
Rockcastle County PL
Rowan County PL
Shelby County PL
Spencer County PL
Warren County PL

Louisiana
Bienville Parish Library
Concordia Parish Library
Lafayette PL
Natchitoches Parish Library
Red River Parish Library
Richland Parish Library
Saint John the Baptist Parish
    Library
West Carroll Parish Library
Winn Parish Library

Maine
Ashland Community Library
Auburn PL
Brown Memorial Library
Brownville Free PL
Buck Memorial Library
Caribou PL
Casco PL
Chase Emerson Memorial Library
Cherryfield Free PL
Friendship PL
Jackman PL
Julia Adams Morse Memorial Library
Lawrence PL
Liberty Library-Ivan O Davis Library
McArthur PL
Mildred Stevens Williams Memorial
    Library
Northeast Harbor Library
Ogunquit Memorial Library
Old Town PL
Rangeley PL
Somesville Library Association
South China PL
Stonington PL
Stratton PL
Sturdivant PL
Vassalboro PL
Vinalhaven PL
Vose Library
Waldoboro PL
Warren Free PL
Waterford Library Association
Webster Free Library
Weld Free PL
West Buxton PL

West Paris PL
Whitman Memorial Library

Maryland
Carroll County PL
Dorchester County PL
Talbot County Free Library

Massachusetts
Agawam PL
Aquinnah PL
Athol PL
Bancroft Memorial Library
Beals Memorial Library
Beaman Memorial PL
Berkshire Athenaeum-Pittsfield's PL
Bolton PL
Charlton PL
Chase Library
Chelsea PL
Cheshire PL
Clapp Memorial Library
Cotuit Library
East Brookfield PL
Eastham PL
Goshen Free PL
Grace Hall Memorial Library
Griswold Memorial Library
Hamilton Memorial Library
Harvard PL
Hinsdale PL
Hyannis PL Association
Jones Library, Inc
Lakeville PL
Lenox Library Association
Lilly Library
Meekins Library
Melrose PL
Merrick PL
Millicent Library
New Salem PL
Peru Library, Inc.
Petersham Memorial Library
PL of Arlington/Robbins Library
Richard Salter Storrs Library
Richard Sugden Library
Russell Memorial Library
Sandisfield Free PL

Scituate Town Library
Springfield City Library
Stevens Memorial Library
Walpole PL
Warwick Free PL
Watertown Free PL
Wayland Free PL
West Bridgewater PL
West Tisbury Free PL
Whelden Memorial Library
Whitman PL
Wilbraham PL
Woods Hole PL

Michigan
Aitkin Memorial District Library
Ann Arbor District Library
Armada Free PL
Auburn Hills PL
Baldwin PL
Benton Harbor PL
Burlington Township Library
Burr Oak Township Library
Cadillac-Wexford PL
Cedar Springs PL
Central Lake District Library
Crystal Falls District Community
   Library
Deckerville PL
Detroit PL
Dowagiac District Library
Elk Rapids District Library
Fife Lake PL
Gary Byker Memorial Library
George W Spindler Memorial Library
Glen Lake Community Library
Harper Woods PL
Hesperia Community Library
Highland Township PL
Hopkins PL
Howe Memorial Library
Huntington Woods PL
Indian River Area Library
Lawrence Memorial PL
Lawton PL
Leighton Township Library
Leroy Community Library
Lincoln Township PL

Luther Area PL
Manchester District Library
Mendon Township Library
Merrill District Library
Monroe County Library System/
  Mary K. Daume Library Service
  Center
Morton Township PL
North Branch Township Library
Osceola Township Public and School
  Library
Paw Paw District Library
Plymouth District Library
Portage Lake District Library
Portland District Library
Rauchholz Memorial Library
Rawson Memorial District Library
Ruth Hughes Memorial District
  Library
Salem-South Lyon District Library
Salem Township Library
Shelby Township Library
Surrey Township PL
Wayne PL
Willard Library

Minnesota
Anoka County Library
Aurora PL
Bovey PL
Browns Valley PL
Chisholm PL
Coleraine PL
Dodge Center PL
Grand Marais PL
Hennepin County Library
La Crescent PL
Lake Benton PL
Le Roy PL
Mabel PL
Marble PL
Martin County Library
McKinley PL
Morgan PL
New Ulm PL
New York Mills PL
North Mankato Taylor Library
Pelican Rapids PL

Virginia PL
West Concord PL
Windom PL

Mississippi
Covington County Library System-RE
  Blackwell Memorial Library
Lee County Library
Marks-Quitman County Library
Meridan-Lauderdale County PL
Neshoba County PL
Union County Library-Jenny Stephens
  Smith Library

Missouri
Bonne Terre Memorial Library
James Memorial Library
Little Dixie Regional Libraries
Lockwood PL
Louisiana PL
Marshall PL
Mississippi County Library District-
  Clara Drinkwater Newman Library
Moniteau County Library @ Wood
  Place
Monroe City Public Library
Mountain View Public Library
Neosho/Newton County Library
Norborne PL
Oregon County Library District/Alton
  PL
Ozark Regional Library
Reynolds County Library
  District-Centerville
Robertson Memorial Library
Rock Hill PL
Sikeston PL
University City PL

Montana
Conrad PL
Denton PL
Dutton/Teton PL
Hearst Free Library
Henry A. Malley Memorial Library
Laurel PL
Liberty County Library
Manhattan Community Library

Sheridan County Library
Sheridan PL
Stillwater County Library
Toole County Library

Nebraska
Ainsworth PL
Bennington PL
Broken Bow PL
Bruning PL
Bruun Memorial PL
Butler Memorial PL
Clay Center PL
Dorchester PL
Emerson PL
Faith Memorial
Fullerton PL
Gilbert PL
Grant County Library
Hayes Center PL
Jenson Memorial Library
John G. Smith Memorial PL
Kimball PL
Lied Battle Creek PL
The Lied Randolph PL
Lincoln City Libraries
Meadow Grove PL
Millington PL
Oshkosh PL
Rising City Community Library
Rushville PL
Saint Paul Library
Sargent Township Library
Seward Memorial Library
Shelton Township Library
Springbank Township Library
Stanton PL
Stuart Township Library
Tekamah PL
Thomas County PL
Tobias PL
Valentine PL
Weeping Water PL

Nevada
Carson City Library
Mineral PL
Washoe County Library System

New Hampshire
Abbie Greenleaf Library
Boscawen PL
Bridgewater Town Library/River Road
Brookline PL
Bryon G. Merrill Library
Chesley Memorial Library
Chesterfield PL
Chichester Town Library
Dover PL
Elkins PL
Frost Free Library
Griffin Free PL
Hebron Library
James A. Tuttle Library
Kensington Social and PL
Kingston Community Library
Laconia PL/Lakeport
Lincoln PL
Mason PL
Meriden PL
Nesmith Library
New Durham PL
North Conway PL
North Hampton PL
Orford Free Library
Patten-North Havehill Library
Piermont PL
Shedd-Porter Memorial Library
Sutton Free Library
Taylor Library
Webster Memorial Library
Westmoreland PL
Wilmot PL

New Jersey
Bloomfield PL
Bradley Beach PL
Bridgeton Free PL
Cranbury PL
Cranford Free PL
Delanco PL
Demarest PL
Denville Free PL
Dover Free PL
Dunellen PL
East Orange PL
Emerson PL

Fairfield PL
Fairview Free PL
Free PL of Monroe Township
Gill Memorial Library
Haddonfield PL
James H. Johnson Memorial Library-
    Deptford Free PL
John F. Kennedy Memorial Library
Kearny PL
Kinnelon PL
Little Ferry Free PL
Manasquan PL
Matawan-Aberdeen PL
Mercer County Library System
Milford PL
Millburn Free PL
Morris Plains Library
Oakland PL
Ocean City Free PL
Ocean County Library
Oradell Free PL
Orange PL
Red Bank PL
Ringwood PL
River Vale Free PL
Riverdale PL
Rochelle Park Library
Upper Saddle River PL
Vineland PL
Warren County PL
Westfield Memorial Library

New Mexico
Aztec PL
Clayton PL
Clovis-Carver PL
Edgewood Community Library
Eleanor Daggett PL
Espanola PL
Lordsburg-Hildago Library
Magdalena PL
Portales PL
Pueblo of Pojoaque PL
Zuni PL

New York
Adams Center Free Library
Alexander Findley Community Library

Amherst PL/Audubon
Amityville PL
Argyle Free Library
Ballston Spa PL
Bay Shore-Brightwaters PL
Bell Memorial Library
Bellmore Memorial Library
Bristol Library
Caldwell-Lake George Library
Champlain Memorial Library
Cheney Library
Chester PL
Clarence PL
Cold Spring Harbor Library
Comsewogue PL
Dexter Free Library
East Fishkill PL District
East Hampton Library
East Meadow PL
Eden Library
Ellenville PL and Museum
Essential Club Free Library
Falconer PL
Fishers Island Library
Frothington Free Library
George P. and Susan Platt Cady
    Library
Gowanda Free Library
Grafton Community Library
Grand Island Memorial Library
Great Neck Library
Greenville PL
Greenwich Free Library
Hampton Bays PL
Harrison PL
Hempstead PL
Henrietta PL
Hepburn Library of Norfolk
Hillview Free Library
Holland Patent Free Library
Honeoye PL
Hurley Library District
Interlaken PL
Jasper Free Library
Lakewood Memorial Library
Lamont Memorial Free Library
Levittown PL
Lewisboro Library

Lewiston PL
Liberty PL
Long Lake PL
Macedon PL
Manlius Library
Marlboro Free Library
Massena PL
Mastics-Moriches-Shirley Community
    Library
Middleburgh Library Association
Monroe Free Library
Mooers Free Library
Morristown PL
Nanuet PL
Newfane Free Library
Newman Riga Library
Nineveh PL of Colesville Township
North Shore PL
Northern Onondaga PL-Cicero
Northport-East Northport PL
Norwood Library
Oyster Bay-East Norwich PL
Paine Memorial Free Library
Patterson Library
Pawling Free Library
Penfield PL
Peru Free Library
Philmont PL
Phoenix PL
Poestenkill PL
RCS Community Library
Red Creek Free Library
Richmond Memorial Library
Rose Memorial Library
Saratoga Spring PL
Sherburne PL
Sherman Free Library
Sinclarville Free Library
Solvay PL
Stamford Village Library
Stewart B Lang Memorial Library
Syosset PL
Tappan-Spaulding Memorial Library
Theresa Free Library
Thousand Island Park Library
Town of Chester PL
Town of Johnsburg Library
Town of North Collins PL

Trot PL
Valatie Free Library
Vestal PL
Walworth-Seely PL
Wantagh PL
Wead Library
Webster PL
Westhampton Free Library
Whitesville PL
William H. Bush Memorial Library
The William K. Sanford Town
    Library-Colonie
Yonkers PL

North Carolina
Bladen County PL
Braswell Memorial PL
Charlotte Mecklenburg Library
Farmville PL
George H. and Laura E. Brown
    Library
Granville County Library System-
    Richard H. Thornton Library
Hickory PL
Jackson County PL
Mauney Memorial Library
McDowell County PL
Mooresville PL
Nashville PL-Harold D Cooley
    Library
New Hanover County Library
Onslow County PL
PL of Johnston County
Sheppard Memorial Library
Southern Pines PL
Wilson County PL

North Dakota
Bottineau County PL
Drake PL
Hatton School and PL
Kindred PL
Lake Region PL
Lidgerwood City Library
Linton PL
Mohall PL
Rolla PL
Satre Memorial Library

Ohio
Alexandria PL
Amherst PL
Arcanum PL
Barnesville Hutton Memorial Library
Bellevue PL
Belmont County District Library/
    Martins Ferry
Bettsville PL
Bexley PL
Birchard PL of Sandusky County
Chillcothe and Ross County PL
Cleveland PL
Crestline PL
Delta PL
Dorcas Carey PL
Evergreen Community Library
Findlay-Hancock County District PL
Fort Recovery PL
Garnet A. Wilson PL of Pike County
Greene County PL
Marion PL
Marvin Memorial Library
Mary L. Cook PL
Massillon PL
Mechanicsburg PL
Milan-Berlin Township PL
Minerva PL
Montpelier PL
Morley Library
Pickaway County District PL
Rossford PL
Shaker Heights PL
Southwest Public Libraries
Tiffin-Seneca PL
Upper Sandusky Community Library
Wauseon PL
Wickliffe PL

Oklahoma
Altus PL
Alva PL
Anadarko Community Library
Cherokee-City County PL
Coweta PL
El Reno Carnegie Library
Elk City Carnegie Library
Fairview City Library

Frederick PL
Guthrie PL
Haynie PL
Kaw City PL
Kellyville PL
Kingfisher Memorial Library
Margaret Carder PL
Medford PL
Okmulgee PL
Tonkawa PL
Walters PL
Woodward PL

Oregon
Clackamas County Library-Oak
    Lodge
Dora PL
Enterprise PL
Estacada PL
Fossill PL
Gilliam County PL
Harrisburg PL
Lake County Library District
Ledding Library of Milwaukie
McMinnville PL
Monmouth PL
Mount Angel PL
Myrtle Point Library
Oakridge PL
Sherwood PL
Tualatin PL
Wagner Community Library
Warrenton Community Library
West Linn PL

Pennsylvania
Adams Memorial Library
Altoona Area PL
Annie Halenbake Ross Library
Avon Grove Library
Baldwin Borough PL
Bellwood-Antis PL
Bosler Memorial Library
Boyertown Community Library
Carnegie Free Library
Carrolltown PL
Centre County Library and Historical
    Museum

Chartiers-Houston Community
Library
Claysburg Area PL
Community Library of Castle Shannon
Community Library of Shenango
Valley
Cranberry PL
Darby Free Library
Elizabethtown PL
Factoryville PL
Forest County Library-Marienville
Area PL
Foxburg Free Library
Free Library of Northampton
Township
Free Library of Springfield Township
Friends Memorial PL
Gallizin PL
Genesee Area Library
Glatfelter Memorial Library
Glenolden Library
Green Tree PL
Highland Community Library
Horsham Township Library
Hyndman Londonderry PL
J. Lewis Crozer Library
Joseph and Elizabeth Shaw PL
Juniata County Library
Kutztown Community Library
Laceyville PL
Mahanoy City PL
Manor PL
Marple PL
Matthews PL
McCord Memorial Library
Memorial Library of Nazareth and
Vicinity
Mengle Memorial Library
Mercer Area Library
Montgomery Area PL
Newport PL
North Versailles PL
Pittston Memorial Library
Pleasant Hills PL
Prospect Park Free Library
Richland Community Library
Ridley Park PL
Ridley Township PL

Saint Mary's PL
Samuel W. Smith Memorial PL
Sarah Stewart Bovard Memorial
Library
Saxton Community Library
Sayre PL
Schlow Centre Region Library
Spring City Free PL
Sykesville PL
Tidioute PL
Tinicum Memorial PL
Towanda PL
Village Library of Wrightstown
Western Allegheny Community
Library
Windber PL
Wissahickon Valley PL
Youngsville PL
Zelienople Area PL

Rhode Island
Barrington PL
Coventry PL
George Hail Free Library
Hope Library
Jesse M Smith Memorial Library
North Providence Union Free
Library
West Warwick PL

South Carolina
Chester County Library
Chesterfield County Library System
Colleton County Memorial Library
Dillon County Library
Greenwood County Library

South Dakota
Bennett County PL
Britton PL
Carnegie PL
Huron PL
Hyde County Library
Leola PL
Parker PL
Siouxland Libraries
Wessington PL
Woonsocket Community Library

Tennessee
Benton County PL
Bolivar-Hardeman County Library
Burritt Memorial Library
Cannon County Library System
Charles Ralph Holland Memorial
    Library
Clarksville-Montgomery County PL
Clay County PL
Decatur County Library
Fayetteville-Lincoln County PL
HB Stamps Memorial Library
Hamilton Parks PL
Johnson County PL
Lebanon-Wilson County Library
Lucius E. and Elsie C. Burch Library/
    Collierville Burch Library
Macon County PL
Millington PL
Morristown-Hamblen Library
Mount Juliet-Wilson County PL
Nashville PL
Niota PL
Oak Ridge PL
Ridgely PL
Signal Mountain PL
Vonore PL
WG Rhea PL
The W. H. and Edgar Magness
    Community House and Library

Texas
Andrews County Library
Arthur Temple Sr. Memorial Library
Atlanta PL
Aubrey Area Library
Austin Memorial Library
Bell-Whittington PL
Betty Foster PL
Bremond PL and Visitors Center
Butt-Holdsworth Memorial Library
Calhoun County Library
Caprock PL
Celina PL
Charles J. Rike Memorial Library
The Colony PL
Crockett County PL
Crystal City Memorial Library

Dallam-Hartley County Library
Decatur PL
Dr. Eugene Clark Library
Dustin Michael Sekula Memorial
    Library
El Paso PL
Florence PL/Eula Hunt Beck PL
Forest Hill PL
Friench Simpson Memorial Library
Friendswood PL
Frisco PL
Gibbs Memorial Library
Grapeland PL
Hale Center PL
Hall-Voyer Foundation/Bertha Voyer
    Memorial Library
Haskell County Library
Helen Hall Library
Hondo PL
Howe Community Library
Hurst PL
Imperial PL
Karnes City PL
Keller PL
Kent County Library
Lago Vista PL
Laguna Vista PL
Lampass PL
Lancaster Veterans Memorial Library
Laredo PL
Liberty Hill PL
Library of Graham
Lindale Library
Little Elm PL
Lucy Hill Patterson Memorial Library
Madison County Library
Martin County Library
McAllen Memorial Library
Mickey Reily PL
Mitchell County PL
Mount Pleasant PL
New Braunfels PL
New Waverly PL
Newton County PL
Nixon PL
Nueces County Keach Family Library
Pasadena PL
Pearsall PL

Post PL
Rowlett PL
Santa Ana Library
Sergeant Fernando de la Rosa Memorial Library
Seagoville PL
Seguin-Guadalupe County PL
Shiner PL
Silsbee PL
Southlake PL
Stamford Carnegie Library
Sulphur Springs PL
Sweetwater County-City Library
Tawakoni Area PL
Tye Preston Memorial Library
Tyler PL
Wimberley Village Library
Winkler County Library
Yorktown PL
Zula Bryant Wylie PL

Utah
Brigham City Library
Delta City Library
Gunnison Civic Library
Logan Library
Orem PL
Salina PL
Summit County Library
Wasatch County Library

Vermont
Bent Northrop Memorial Library
Brandon Free PL
Charles B. Danforth PL
Charlotte Library
Fair Haven Free Library
Fletcher Free Library
Greensboro Free Library
Hartland Public Libraries
Ilsley PL
Island Pond PL
Isle La Motte Library
Lincoln Library
Martha Canfield Memorial Free Library
Mount Holly Town Library
Pierson Library

Platt Memorial Library
Quechee PL
Readsboro Community Library
Saint Albas Free Library
Sheldon PL
Springfield Town Library
Starksboro PL
Weathersfield Proctor Library
Wells Village Library
West Hartford Library
Woodbury Community Library

Virginia
Blue Ridge Regional Library
Central Virginia Regional Library/
    Farmville Prince Edward Library
Chesapeake PL
Essex PL
Fairfax County PL
J. Robert Jamerson Memorial Library
James L. Hamner PL
Mathews Memorial Library
Poquoson PL
Richmond PL
Samuels PL
Wythe-Grayson Regional Library

Washington
Anacortes PL
Castle Rock PL
Cathlamet PL
Denby Ashby Memorial Library-Pomeroy PL
Ellensburg PL
Enumclaw PL
Port Townsend PL
Roy City Library

West Virginia
Alderson Library
Belington PL
Bridgeport PL
Cabell County PL
Greenbrier County PL
Keyser-Mineral County PL
Logan Area PL
New Martinsville PL

Roane County PL
Shepherdstown PL
Upshur County PL
Valley Head PL
Vienna PL

Wisconsin
Abbotsford PL
Allen Diezman Library-Livingston PL
Appleton PL
Barrett Memorial Library
Black Earth PL
Blair-Preston PL
Brownsville PL
Campbellsport PL
Deer Park PL
Delafield PL
Durand PL
Dwight Foster PL
Dwight T. Parker PL
Edith Evans Community Library
Fairchild PL
Frederic PL
Hales Corners Library
Hammond Community Library
Hildebrand Memorial Library-
    Boscobel PL
Independence PL
John Turgeson PL-Belmont PL
LD Fargo PL
La Crosse PL
Lena PL
Lomira QuadGraphics Community
    Library
Manitowoc PL

Marinette County Library System-
    Stephenson PL
Marion PL
Matheson Memorial Library
Mead PL
Mercer PL
Milton PL
Monroe PL
New Berlin PL
North Freedom PL
Oak Creek PL
Oostburg PL
Oregon PL
Plainfield PL
Portage PL
Prescott PL
River Falls PL
Slinger Community Library
Soldiers Grove PL
Strum PL
Taylor Memorial Library
Theresa PL
Tomah PL
Turtle Lake PL
Walworth Memorial Library
Washburn PL
West Bend Community Memorial
    Library
Westfield PL
Winter PL

Wyoming
Carbon County Library System
Johnson County Library
Laramie County Library System

Appendix B

Resource Links

AARP: http://www.aarp.org (information, resources, stats, resources, stats)

Administration for Community Living: Grants: https://www.acl.gov/grants

Administration on Aging: https://aoa.acl.gov (government services)

Alliance for Aging Research: http://www.agingresearch.org (information, aging research)

Alzheimer's Association: http://www.alz.org (Alzheimer's disease information)

American Foundation for the Blind: http://www.afb.org/ProdBrowseCatResults.asp?CatID=53

American Library Association: http://www.ala.org/tools/atoz/older-adults (resource section on 50+ adults)

American Library Association: ALA Grants: http://www.ala.org/awardsgrants/awards/browse/grnt?showfilter=no

American Library Association: Association of Specialized and Cooperative Library Agencies (ASCLA): http://www.ala.org/ascla/resources/tipsheets

American Library Association: Office for Diversity, Literacy, and Outreach Services: http://www.ala.org/aboutala/offices/diversity

American Library Association: Outreach Resources for Services to Older Adults: http://www.ala.org/advocacy/diversity/outreachtounderservedpopulations/servicesolder

American Library Association Traveling Exhibits: http://www.ala.org/programming/exhibitions.

American Library Association: 21 Ideas for the 21st Century: http://www.ala.org/rusa/sections/rss/rsssection/rsscomm/libraryservage/ideas21stcentury

American Society on Aging: http://www.asaging.org (resources, information)

Americans with Disabilities Act, ADA Standards for Accessible Design: https://www.ada.gov

ASCLA (The Association of Specialized and Cooperative Library Agencies) Library Accessibility: http://www.ala.org/ascla/resources/tipsheets (disability accommodations, tips on library accessibility)

Bank of America: https://about.bankofamerica.com/en-us/what-guides-us/find-grants
-sponsorships.html#fbid=zjiggbTPHUW

Catholic Golden Age: http://www.catholicgoldenage.org (information and concerns
for Catholics age 50+)

Centers for Medicare & Medicaid Services: https://www.cms.gov/Outreach-and
-Education/Outreach/Partnerships/LibraryToolkit.html

Chemo Caps: http://www.crochetforcancer.org/donate/cap-donation-guidelines/

Corporation for National Community Services (Senior Corps, Veterans and Military
Families): https://www.nationalservice.gov (volunteer organizations and resources)

Crash Course in Library Services to People with Disabilities, ABC-CLIO: http://www
.abc-clio.com/ABC-CLIOCorporate/product.aspx?pc=F2185P

EBSCO Grants & Funding Sources for Libraries: https://help.ebsco.com/inter
faces/EBSCO_Guides/Resources_for_Librarians/Grants_Funding_Sources_for
_Libraries

ElderSong (publications and activities): http://www.eldersong.com

Experience Works: http://www.experienceworks.org/site/PageServer (job training and
assistance)

FINRA Investor Education Foundation: http://www.finrafoundation.org/grants/

FirstGov (U.S. government Web portal): http://www.firstgov.gov (federal information, agencies with speakers)

Foundation Center: http://foundationcenter.org

Gilder Lehrman Institute of American History: http://www.gilderlehrman.org
/programs-exhibitions/traveling-exhibitions

Grants.gov: https://www.grants.gov

Institute of Museum & Library Services Grants: https://www.imls.gov/grants/apply
-grant/available-grants

Institute of Museum & Library Services Self-Assessment Tool: https://www.imls.gov
/issues/national-initiatives/museums-libraries-and-21st-century-skills/getting
-started

JASA (Jewish Association Serving the Aging): http://www.jasa.org (programs and
information for individuals age 50+ of the Jewish faith)

Justice in Aging (formally: National Senior Citizens Law Center): http://www.justicei
naging.org (advocacy, senior poverty, and the law)

Keys to Engaging Older Adults @ your library: http://www.ala.org/offices/olos/tool
kits/olderadults (tips, tools, advice on programming)

Libraries and Aging with Creativity: http://creativeagingtoolkit.org (free resource for
librarians)

Library of Congress Center for the Book: http://www.read.gov/cfb/state-affiliates.php

Library of Congress Exhibits: https://www.loc.gov/exhibits/loan/

Library Services and Technology Act: https://www.imls.gov/grants/grants-states

Library Works: https://www.libraryworks.com/grants--funding

Libraries Unlimited Makerspaces: https://www.abc-clio.com/ABC-CLIOCorporate
/SearchResults.aspx?type=a

Lifetime Arts: http://www.lifetimearts.org

Lunar and Planetary Institute: http://www.lpi.usra.edu/exploration/education/exhibits/

Make It @ Your Library: http://makeitatyourlibrary.org

Meals on Wheels America: http://www.mealsonwheelsamerica.org (meals, companionship, safety checks)

NASA Speakers Bureau: https://www.nasa.gov/about/exhibits/index.html (NASA speaker information)

National Aging Pacific Center on Aging: http://napca.org (advocacy, resources, information)

National Association of Area Agencies on Aging: http://www.n4a.org (advocacy, resources, services)

National Association of Nutrition and Aging Services Programs: http://www.nanasp.org (nutrition and healthy aging)

National Caucus and Center for the Black Aging: http://www.ncba-aged.org (advocacy, resources, information)

National Council on Aging: https://www.ncoa.org (advocacy, resources, information, healthy aging)

National Endowment for the Humanities: https://www.neh.gov/grants

National Hispanic Council on Aging: http://www.nhcoa.org (advocacy, resources, information)

National Indian Council on Aging: http://nicoa.org (advocacy, resources, information)

National Institute on Aging Senior Web Site Checklist: https://www.nlm.nih.gov/pubs/checklist.pdf

National Library Service for the Blind and Physically Handicapped: https://www.loc.gov/nls/ (free Braille and talking book library service)

New York State Adult Literacy Library Services Program: http://www.nysl.nysed.gov/libdev/literacy

Palm of the Hand: http://www.foothillspublishing.com/poh/index.htm

Public Libraries Online Makerspaces: http://publiclibrariesonline.org/tag/makerspaces/

Project Linus: https://www.projectlinus.org

Purdue Online Writing Lab: Introduction to Grant Writing: https://owl.english.purdue.edu/owl/resource/981/1/

Quilts of Valor: https://www.qovf.org

RUSA: Reference and User Services: Library Services to an Aging Population (Senior Sites on the Web): http://www.ala.org/rusa/library-services-aging-population

Scholastic Library Grants: http://www.scholastic.com/librarians/programs/grants.htm

Senior Community Service Employment Program: https://www.ncoa.org/economic-security/matureworkers/scsep/ (job training program)

Smithsonian Institution Traveling Exhibition Service: http://www.sites.si.edu

Traveling Exhibits: http://www.travelingexhibits.org

21st Century Skills: Institute of Museum & Library Services: https://www.imls.gov/assets/1/workflow_staging/AssetManager/293.PDF

Veterans Affairs (Geriatrics and Extended Care): https://www.va.gov/geriatrics/ (information, resources for military families)

Veterans History Project: www.loc.gov/folklife/vets/kit.html

Walmart Foundation: http://giving.walmart.com/apply-for-grants/local-giving-guidelines

Appendix C
Patron Links for Library's 50+ Web Site Page

AAA (American Automobile Association) Senior Drivers: https://www.aaafoundation .org/senior-drivers (information for drivers 65+)

AgeVenture: http://www.demko.com (active aging, news, information)

Alzheimer's: https://alzheimers.acl.gov (for people helping individuals with Alzheimer's)

American Senior Association: https://americanseniors.org (benefits, information)

APlaceforMom: http://www.aplaceformom.com (assisted living information)

Baby Boomers: http://www.babyboomers.com (news, information)

Baby Boomer Headquarters: http://www.bbhq.com (news, information)

Benefits Checkup: https://www.benefitscheckup.org/#/ (free online tool on benefits)

Center for the Book in the Library of Congress: http://www.read.gov (booklists, webcasts)

Corporation for National Community Services Senior Corps: https://www.national service.gov/programs/senior-corps (volunteer organization links)

Corporation for National Community Services Veterans and Military Families: https://www.nationalservice.gov/focus-areas/veterans-and-military-families (Services and Support to Military Families)

Elder One Stop: http://www.elder-one-stop.com (resource for ideas and links)

Eldercare Locator: http://www.eldercare.gov/Eldercare.NET/Public/Index.aspx (local and state information, resources)

Elderweb: http://www.elderweb.com (information, resources on long-term care, senior housing)

Elder Rights: http://www.inpea.net (The International Network for the Prevention of Elder Abuse)

Experience Works: http://www.experienceworks.org/site/PageServer (job training and assistance)

Family Caregiver Alliance: https://www.caregiver.org

Fifty-Plus Fitness Association: https://agingblueprint.org/orgs/fpfa.cfm (promotes active lifestyle)

Generations United: http://www.gu.org (intergenerational program information)

Genealogy: Cyndi's List of Genealogy Sites: http://www.cyndislist.com/us/ (genealogy information)

Grandparents Raising Grandchildren: https://www.usa.gov/child-care (issues and programs for grandparents raising grandchildren)

Long-Term Care Planning: http://longtermcare.gov (services, information)

Medical site: http://www.webmd.com (medical information, drug information)

Medicare: https://www.medicare.gov (plans, information)

National Center for Assisted Living: https://www.ahcancal.org/ncal/Pages/index.aspx (information on assisted living and long-term care)

NIHSeniorHealth: https://nihseniorhealth.gov (health, wellness, information)

Retired Senior Volunteer Program: http://www.nationalservice.gov/programs/senior-corps/rsvp

Road Scholar: https://www.roadscholar.org (learning travel adventures for adults 50+)

SAGE USA: http://www.sageusa.org (services, advocacy for lesbian, gay, bisexual, and transgender [LGBT] older adults)

Senior Citizen Bureau: http://www.seniorcitizensbureau.com (caregiver information and support)

Senior Net: http://www.seniornet.org (computer and Internet education)

Senior Service America: http://www.seniorserviceamerica.org/our-programs/the-senior-community-service-employment-program/ (employment and training opportunities)

60 plus Association: http://60plus.org (issues, advocacy)

Social Security Association: https://www.ssa.gov (information, services)

TechBoomers: https://techboomers.com (educational Web site on computers and Internet usage)

Third Age: http://thirdage.com (information, resources for 50+ women)

Travel: https://travel.state.gov/content/passports/en/go/older-traveler.html (U.S. passports and international travel)

Universal Classes: https://www.universalclass.com

Worldwide Programs Providing a Better Way to Deal with Aging: http://www.programsforelderly.com/social-cyber-seniors-nursing-homes-canada.php (programs, documentaries, information)

Appendix D

Contributing Public Libraries

Adams Memorial Library
1112 Ligonier St.
Latrobe, PA 15650

Ann Arbor District Public Library
343 South Fifth Ave.
Ann Arbor, MI 48104

Anoka County Library
707 County Rd. 10 NE
Blaine, MN 55434

Appleton Public Library
225 N. Oneida St.
Appleton, WI 54911

Athol Public Library
568 Main St.
Athol, MA 01331

Birmingham Public Library
1224 Old Springville Rd.
Birmingham, AL 35215

Carroll County (MD) Public Library
1100 Green Valley Rd.
New Windsor, MD 21776

Charlotte Mecklenburg Library
310 North Tryon St.
Charlotte, NC 78202

Cranberry Public Library
2525 Rochester Rd, Suite 300
Cranberry Twp., PA 16066

Eastham Public Library
190 Samoset Rd.
Eastham, MA 02642

ELA Area Public Library
275 Mohawk Trl.
Lake Zurich, IL 60047

Essex Library Association
33 West Ave.
Essex, CT 06426

Fairfield Free Public Library
261 Hollywood Ave.
Fairfield, NJ 07004

Fife Lake Public Library
77 Lakecrest Lane,
Fife Lake, MI 49633

Findlay-Hancock County Public
Library
206 Broadway
Findlay, OH 45840

Friendswood Public Library
416 S. Friendswood Dr.
Friendswood, TX 77546

Greene County Public
Library
76 E. Market St.
Xenia, OH 45385

Greenwood County Library
System
600 S. Main St.
Greenwood, SC 29646

Guthrie Public Library
201 N. Division St.
Guthrie, OK 73044

Homewood Public Library
1721 Oxmoor Rd.
Birmingham, AL 35209

Marinette County Consolidated
Library System
1700 Hall Ave.
Marinette, WI 54143

Matheson Memorial Library
101 N. Wisconsin St.
Elkhorn, WI 53121

Muncie Public Library
2005 S. High St.
Muncie, IN 47302

Nashville Public Library
615 Church St.
Nashville TN 37219

New Durham Public Library
2 Old Bay Rd.
New Durham, NH 03855

Ocean County Library
101 Washington St.
Toms River, NJ 08759

O'Fallon Public Library
120 Civic Plaza
O'Fallon, IL 62269

Oradell Public Library
375 Kinderkamack Rd.
Oradell, NJ 07075

Pikes Peak Library District
20 N. Cascade Ave.
Colorado Springs, CO 80903

Pioneer Memorial Library
375 W. 4th St.
Colby, KS 67701

Quincy Public Library
526 Jersey St.
Quincy, IL 62301

Richmond Memorial Library
19 Ross St.
Batavia, NY 14020

River Falls Public Library
W10314 860th Ave.
River Falls, WI 54022

Santa Barbara Public Library
40 E. Anapamu St.
Santa Barbara, CA 93101

Saratoga Springs Public Library
49 Henry St.
Saratoga Springs, NY 12866

Sherwood Public Library
22560 SW Pine St.
Sherwood, OR 97140

Simsbury Public Library
725 Hopmeadow St.
Simsbury, CT 06070

Wallingford Public Library
200 N Main St.
Wallingford, CT 06492

Webster Public Library
980 Ridge Rd.
Webster, NY 14580

Westerville Public Library
126 S. State St.
Westerville, OH 43081

Wilbraham Public Library
25 Crane Park Dr.
Wilbraham, MA 01095

Wimberley Village Library
400 RR 12
Wimberley, TX 78676

Yolo County Library
315 E. 14th St.
Davis, CA 95616

References

Abram, S. (2010). Old Dogs, New Tricks: The Myths and the Realities. In P. Rothstein & D. Schull (Eds.), *Boomers and Beyond: Reconsidering the Role of Libraries* (pp. 107–126). Chicago: American Library Association.

ADA Standards for Accessible Design. (2010). *Information and Technical Assistance on the Americans with Disabilities ACT.* Retrieved from https://www.ada.gov/2010ADAstandards_index.htm

Administration on Aging Administration for Community Living. (2016). A Profile of Older Americans: 2016. *U.S. Department of Health and Human Services.* Retrieved from https://www.giaging.org/documents/A_Profile_of_Older_Americans__2016.pdf

Ahlvers, A. (2006). Older Adults and Readers' Advisory. *Reference and User Services Quarterly, 45*(4), 305–312.

ALA Digital Literacy Task Force. (2011). *ALA Office for Information Technology Policy Digital Literacy Definition.* Retrieved from http://connect.ala.org/files/94226/what%20is%20digilit%20%282%29.pdf

ALA Government Relations: Appropriations. (2017). Retrieved from http://www.ala.org/advocacy/advleg/federallegislation/libraryfunding

Alzheimer's Association. (2017). Stay Mentally Active. Retrieved from http://www.alz.org/we_can_help_stay_mentally_active.asp

American Federation for the Blind. (2017). CCTV's/Video Magnifiers. Retrieved from http://www.afb.org/prodBrowseCatResults.aspx?CatID=53

American Library Association. (2017). Number of Libraries in the United States: ALA Library Fact Sheet 1. Retrieved from http://www.ala.org/tools/libfactsheets/alalibraryfactsheet01

American Library Association. (2017). Public Library Use. Retrieved from http://www.ala.org/tools/libfactsheets/alalibraryfactsheet06

American Psychological Association. (2017). Fact Sheet: Age and Socioeconomic Status. Retrieved from http://www.apa.org/pi/ses/resources/publications/age.aspx

American Psychological Association. (2017). Older Adults: Health and Age-Related Changes. Retrieved from http://www.apa.org/pi/aging/resources/guides/older.aspx

Anderson, M., & Perrin, A. (2017). Tech Adoption Climbs among Older Adults: Technology Use among Seniors. *Pew Research Center Internet & Technology.* Retrieved from http://www.pewinternet.org/2017/05/17/technology-use-among -seniors/

Association of Specialized and Cooperative Library Agencies. (2010). Assistive Technology: What You Need to Know Library Accessibility Tip Sheet 11. Retrieved from http://www.ala.org/ascla/sites/ala.org.ascla/files/content/asclaprotools/acc essibilitytipsheets/tipsheets/11-Assistive_Technol.pdf

Balazs, A. (2014). Forever Young: The New Aging Consumer in the Marketplace. In C. Harrington, D. Bielby, & A. Bardo (Eds.). *Aging, Media, and Culture* (pp. 25–36). Lanham, MD: Lexington Books.

Bandura, A. (1994). Self-Efficacy. In V. S. Ramachaudran (Ed.), *Encyclopedia of Human Behavior* (Vol. 4, pp. 71–81). New York: Academic Press. (Reprinted in H. Friedman [Ed.], *Encyclopedia of Mental Health*. San Diego: Academic Press, 1998). http://www.uky.edu/~eushe2/Bandura/BanEncy.html

Bateson, M. C. (2010). In Search of Active Wisdom: Libraries and Consciousness-Raising for Adulthood II. In P. Rothstein & D. Schull (Eds.), *Boomers and Beyond: Reconsidering the Role of Libraries* (pp. 49–56). Chicago: American Library Association.

Bennett-Kapusniak, R. (2013). Older Adults and the Public Library: The Impact of the Boomer Generation. *Public Library Quarterly*, 32(3), 204–222.

Bennett-Kapusniak, R. (2015). Baby Boomers and Technology: Factors and Challenges in Utilizing Mobile Devices. *Dissertations & Theses @ University of Wisconsin Milwaukee; ProQuest Dissertations & Theses Global*. Retrieved from https://dc.uwm.edu/cgi/viewcontent.cgi?article=2045&amp=&context =etd&amp=&sei-redir=1&referer=https%253A%252F%252Fscholar.google.c om%252Fscholar%253Fhl%253Den%2526as_sdt%253D0%25252C33%25 26q%253Dbennett-kapusniak%2526btnG%253D#search=%22bennett -kapusniak%22

Bernard Osher Foundation. (2005). Retrieved from https://www.osherfoundation .org/index.php?index

Borgman, C. (1986). Why Are Online Catalogs Hard to Use? Lessons Learned from Information-Retrieval Studies. *Journal of the American Society for Information Science*, 37(6), 387–400.

Butcher, W., & Street, P. (2009). Lifelong Learning with Older Adults. *Australasian Public Libraries and Information Services*, 22(2), 64–70.

Butler, R. (2005). Ageism: Looking Back over My Shoulder. *Generations*, 29(3), 84–86.

Centers for Disease Control and Prevention. (2016). *National Center for Health Statistics*. Retrieved from https://www.cdc.gov/nchs/fastats/life-expectancy.htm

Chang, P-J., Wray, L., & Lin. Y. (2014). Social Relationships, Leisure Activity, and Health in Older Adults. *Health Psychology*, 33(6), 516–523.

Cohen, G. (2009). Research and Creativity and Aging: The Positive Impact of the Arts on Health and Illness. *Generations*, 30(1), 7–15.

Cooke, N. (2016). Reference Services for Diverse Populations. In L. Smith & M. Wong (Eds.), *Reference and Information Services: An Introduction* (5th ed.) (pp. 338–366). Santa Barbara, CA: Libraries Unlimited.

Cornwell, E., & Waite, L. (2009). Measuring Social Isolation among Older Adults Using Multiple Indicators. *The Journals of Gerontology: Series B*, 64B(1), 38–46. doi: 10.1093/geronb/gbp037

Czaja, S., Charness, N., Fisk, A., Hertzog, C, Nair, S., Rogers, W., & Sharit, J. (2006). Factors Predicting the Use of Technology: Findings from the Center for Research and Education on Aging and Technology Enhancement (CREATE). *Psychology and Aging*, 21(2), 333–352.

Decker, E. (2010). Baby Boomers and the United States Public Library System. *Library HiTech* 28(4), 605–616. doi: 10.1108/07378831011096268

Edwards, J., Rauseo, M., & Unger, K. (2013). Community Centered: 23 Reasons Why Your Library Is the Most Important Place in Town. *Public Libraries Online*. Retrieved from http://publiclibrariesonline.org/2013/04/community-centered-23-reasons-why-your-library-is-the-most-important-place-in-town/#_ftn1

Federal Interagency Forum on Aging-Related Statistics. (2016). Older Americans 2016: Key Indicators of Well-Being. Retrieved from https://agingstats.gov/docs/LatestReport/Older-Americans-2016-Key-Indicators-of-WellBeing.pdf

Fisk, A., Rogers, W., Charness, N., Czaja, S., & Sharit, J. (2009). *Designing for Older Adults: Principles and Creative Human Factors Approaches* (2nd ed.). Boca Raton, FL: CRC Press.

Geiger, A. (2017). Most Americans—Especially Millennials—Say Libraries Can Help Them Find Reliable, Trustworthy Information. *Pew Research Center: Internet & Technology*. Retrieved from http://www.pewresearch.org/fact-tank/2017/08/30/most-americans-especially-millennials-say-libraries-can-help-them-find-reliable-trustworthy-information/

Hales-Mabry, C. (1993). *The World of the Aging: Information Needs and Choices*. Chicago: American Library Association.

Harper, S., Yesilada, Y., & Chen, T. (2011). Mobile Device Impairment . . . Similar Problems, Similar Solutions? *Behaviour & Information Technology*, 30(5), 673–690. doi: 10.1080/01449291003801943

Hart, T., Chaparro, B., & Halcomb, C. (2008). Evaluating Websites for Older Adults: Adherence to "Senior-Friendly" Guidelines and End-User Performance. *Behaviour & Information Technology*, 27(3), 191–199.

Higa-Moore, M. L., Bunnett, B., Mayo, H., & Olney, C. (2002). Use of Focus Groups in a Library's Strategic Planning Process. *Journal of the Medical Library Association*, 90(1), 86–92.

Honnold, R., & Mesaros, S. (2004). *Serving Seniors: A How-To-Do-It Manual for Librarians*. Chicago: American Library Association.

Horrigan, J. (2016). Libraries. *Pew Research Center Internet & Technology*. Retrieved from http://www.pewinternet.org/2016/09/09/libraries-2016/

Howarth, L., & Hendry, E. (2013). Memory Cues, Recall Strategies, and Alzheimer's Disease. *iConference 2013 Proceedings* (pp. 519–523). doi: 10.9776/13267

Hutchison, D., Eastman, C., & Tirrito, T. (1997). Designing User Interfaces for Older Adults. *Educational Gerontology*, 23, 497–513. doi: 10.1080/03601 27970230601

Information Today's American Library Directory Online. (2016). Retrieved from http://www.americanlibrarydirectory.com/default.asp

Institute of Museum & Library Services. (2014). Talking Points: Adults Gain Skills at the Library. Retrieved from https://www.imls.gov/sites/default/files/publications/documents/adultliteracy.pdf

Institute of Museum & Library Services. (2017). Museums, Libraries, and 21st Century Skills: Getting Started in Your Institution. Retrieved from https://www.imls.gov/issues/national-initiatives/museums-libraries-and-21st-century-skills/getting-started

Irvall, B., & Nielsen, G. S. (2005). Access to Libraries for Persons with Disabilities—Checklist. *International Federation of Library Associations and Institutions IFLA Professional Reports, No. 89.* The Hague, Netherlands: IFLA. http://www.ifla.org/files/assets/hq/publications/professional-report/89.pdf

Jaeger, P., Bertot, J., McClure, C., & Rodriguez, M. (2007). Public Libraries and Internet Access Across the United States: A Comparison by State 2004–2006. *Information Technology and Libraries,* 26(2), 4–14.

Joseph, M. (2009). Public Library Strategies for the over 50s: Everything Old Is New Again—Or Is It? *Australasian Public Libraries and Information Services* 22(3), 115–119.

Koppen, J., & Anderson, G. (2008). *Retired Spouses: A National Survey of Adults 55–75.* Washington, D.C.: AARP.

Kuhlthau, C. (2005). Kuhlthau's Information Seeking Process. In K. Fisher, S. Erdelez, & L. McKechnie (Eds.), *Theories of Information Behavior* (pp. 230–234). Medford, NJ: Information Today.

Kulpinski, D. (2009). Partnership for a Nation of Learners: Joining Forces, Creating Value (IMLS-2009-RES-03). Washington, D.C.: *Institute of Museum and Library Services.* Retrieved from http://www.imls.gov/assets/1/AssetManager/PNLReport.pdf

Kurti, S., Kurti, D., & Fleming, L. (2014). Educational Makerspaces: The Philosophy of Educational Makerspaces: Part 1 of Making an Educational Makerspace. *Teacher Librarian.* Retrieved from http://teacherlibrarian.com/2014/06/18/educational-makerspaces/

Lear, B. (2013). *Adult Programs in the Library* (2nd ed.). Chicago: American Library Association.

Library of Congress National Library Service for the Blind and Physically Handicapped. (2017). NLS at the Library of Congress. Retrieved from https://www.loc.gov/nls/

Lifetime Arts. (2017). Retrieved from http://www.lifetimearts.org

Lu, K. (2017). Pew Research Center: Growth in Mobile News Use Driven by Older Adults. Retrieved from http://www.pewresearch.org/fact-tank/2017/06/12/growth-in-mobile-news-use-driven-by-older-adults/

Madden, M. (2010). Older Adults and Social Media. *Pew Research Center Internet & Technology.* Retrieved from http://www.pewinternet.org/2010/08/27/older-adults-and-social-media/

Manheimer, R., & Kidahashi, M. (2010). Information-Questing Moments: Retirement-Age Americans at the Library Door. In P. Rothstein & D. Schull (Eds.), *Boomers and Beyond: Reconsidering the Role of Libraries* (pp. 57–61). Chicago: American Library Association.

Martyn, H., & Gallant, L. (2012). Over 50 and Wired: Web-Based Stakeholder Communication. *First Monday,* 17(6), 1–12. Retrieved from http://firstmonday.org/htbin/cgiwrap/bin/ojs/index.php/fm/article/view/3449/3262

Mates, B. (2003). *5-Star Programming and Services for Your 55+ Library Customers.* Chicago: American Library Association.

McFadden, S., & Basting, A. (2010). Healthy Aging Persons and Their Brains: Promoting Resilience through Creative Engagement. *Clinics in Geriatric Medicine,* 26(1), 149.

Miner, J., & Miner, L. (2008). *Proposal Planning and Writing* (4th ed.). Westport, CT: Greenwood Publishing Group. Retrieved from http://213.55.83.214:8181 /Project%20Management/Proposal%20Planning%20&%20Wri ting.pdf

Moyer, J. (2007). Learning from Leisure Reading. *Reference & User Services Quarterly,* 46(4), 66–79.

National Endowment for the Humanities. (2017). State Humanities Councils. Retrieved from https://www.neh.gov/about/state-humanities-councils

National Institute on Aging. (2013). At the Intersection of Arts and Aging. Retrieved from https://www.nia.nih.gov/newsroom/features/intersection-arts-and-aging

National Institute on Aging. (2017). Research Suggests a Positive Correlation between Social Interaction and Health. Retrieved from https://www.nia.nih.gov/about /living-long-well-21st-century-strategic-directions-research-aging/research-suggests-positive

Ng, C.-H. (2007). Motivation among Older Adults in Learning Computing Technologies: A Grounded Model. *Educational Gerontology,* 34(1), 1–14.

Nycyk, M., & Redsell, M. (2010). Making Computer Learning Easier for Older Adults: A Community Study of Tuition Practices. In N. Reynolds & M. Turcsányi-Szabó (Eds.), *Key Competencies in the Knowledge Society* (Vol. 324, pp. 292–300). Boston: Springer.

Older People. (2015). Library of Congress Subject Headings. Retrieved from http://id .loc.gov/authorities/demographicTerms/dg2015060014.html

Perrin, A. (2016). Book Reading 2016. *Pew Research Center Internet & Technology.* Retrieved from http://www.pewinternet.org/2016/09/01/book-reading -2016/

Perrin, A., & Duggan, A. (2015). Americans' Internet Access: 2000–2015 as Internet Use Nears Saturation for Some Groups, A Look at Patterns of Adoption. *Pew Research Center Internet & Technology.* Retrieved from http://www.pewinternet .org/2015/06/26/americans-internet-access-2000-2015/

Pew Research Center Internet & Technology. (2017). Social Media Fact Sheet. Retrieved from http://www.pewinternet.org/fact-sheet/social-media/

Pew Research Internet Project. (2009). Generational Differences in Online Activities. Retrieved from http://pewinternet.org/Reports/2009/Generations-Online-in-2009 /Generational-Differences-in-Online-Activities.aspx

Piper, D., Palmer. S., & Xie, B. (2009). Services to Older Adults: Preliminary Findings from Three Maryland Public Libraries. *Journal of Education for Library and Information Science,* 50(2), 107–118. Retrieved from https://www.webjunction .org/content/dam/WebJunction/Documents/webjunction/Service Study.pdf

Population Reference Bureau. (2013). Elderly Immigrants in the United States. Retrieved from http://www.prb.org/Publications/Reports/2013/us-elderly-immig rants.aspx

Population Reference Bureau. (2017). Fact Sheet: Aging in the United States. Retrieved from http://www.prb.org/Publications/Media-Guides/2016/aging-unitedstates -fact-sheet.aspx

Public Libraries Association. (2011). PLA Mission and Goals. Retrieved from http://www.ala.org/pla/about/documents/mission

Public Libraries Online. (2017). Posts Tagged Makerspaces. Retrieved from http://publiclibrariesonline.org/tag/makerspaces/

Rainie, L. (2012). Baby Boomers and Technology. *Pew Research Internet Project*. Retrieved from http://www.pewinternet.org/2012/03/28/baby-boomers-and-technology/

Reed, S. (2012). *Libraries Need Friends: A Toolkit to Create Friends Groups or to Revitalize the One You Have*. Philadelphia: United for Libraries.

Reference and User Services Association. (2017). Guidelines for Library Services with 60+ Audience: Best Practices. Retrieved from http://www.ala.org/rusa/sites/ala.org.rusa/files/content/resources/guidelines/60plusGuidelines2017.pdf

Reitz, J. (2017). Online Dictionary for Library and Information Science. *ABC-CLIO*. Retrieved from http://www.abc-clio.com/ODLIS/odlis_b.aspx

Ristau, S. (2010). Work and Purpose after 50. In P. Rothstein & D. Schull (Eds.), *Boomers and Beyond: Reconsidering the Role of Libraries* (pp. 39–48). Chicago: American Library Association.

Roberts, A., & Bauman, S. (2012). *Crash Course in Library Services for Seniors*. Santa Barbara, CA: Libraries Unlimited.

Saad, L. (2016). Three in 10 U.S. Workers Foresee Working Past Retirement Age. Retrieved from http://www.gallup.com/poll/191477/three-workers-foresee-working-past-retirement-age.aspx

Salkowitz, R. (2008). *Generation Blend: Managing across the Technology Age Gap*. Microsoft Executive Leadership Series. Hoboken, NJ: John Wiley & Sons.

Saunders, J., McClure, C., & Mandel, L. (2012). Broadband Applications: Categories, Requirements, and Future Frameworks. *First Monday*, 17(11). Retrieved from https://firstmonday.org/ojs/index.php/fm/article/view/4066/3355

Schull, D. (2013). *50+ Library Services: Innovation in Action*. Chicago: ALA Editions.

Schull, D., & Thomas, S. (2010). Reconsidering Age: The Emerging Role of Cultural Institutions. In P. Rothstein & D. Schull (Eds.), *Boomers and Beyond: Reconsidering the Role of Libraries* (pp. 63–70). Chicago: ALA Editions.

Singer, D., & Agosto, D. (2013). Reaching Senior Patrons in the Digitized Library. *Public Libraries*, 52(6), 38–42.

Slegers, K., & van Boxtel, M. (2013). Actual Use of Computers and the Internet by Older Adults: Potential Benefits and Risks. In R. Zhang, R. Hill, & M. Gardner (Eds.), *Engaging Older Adults with Modern Technology: Internet Use and Information Access Needs* (pp. 161–190). Hershey, PA: IGI Global.

Smith, A. (2014). Older Adults and Technology Use. *Pew Research Center Internet & Technology*. Retrieved from http://www.pewinternet.org/2014/04/03/older-adults-and-technology-use/

Speros, C. (2009). More Than Words: Promoting Health Literacy in Older Adults. *The Online Journal of Issues in Nursing*, 14(3). Retrieved from http://www.nursingworld.org/MainMenuCategories/ANAMarketplace/ANAPeriodicals/OJIN/TableofContents/Vol142009/No3Sept09/Health-Literacy-in-Older-Adults.html%23FIFARS

Tangient, LLC. (2017). Discussion Forums. Retrieved from http://www.kstoolkit.org/Discussion+Forums

TechBoomers. (2017). Library Partners. Retrieved from https://techboomers.com/library-partners

Thiele, J. (2016). Information Access in Rural Areas of the United States: The Public Library's Role in the Digital Divide and the Implications of Differing State Funding Models. *Dissertations & Theses @ University of Wisconsin Milwaukee; ProQuest Dissertations & Theses Global.* Retrieved from https://dc.uwm.edu/cgi/viewcontent.cgi?referer=https://scholar.google.com/scholar?hl=en&as_sdt=0%2C33&q=Information+Access+in+Rural+Areas+of+the+United+States%3A+The+Public+Library's+Role+in+the+Digital+Divide+and+the+Implications+of+Differing+State+Funding+Models.+&btnG=&httpsredir=1&article=2217&context=etd

United for Libraries. (2017). Friend Your Library. Retrieved from http://www.ala.org/united/Friends

Wapner, C. (2014). FCC Workshop Highlights Need for Higher Capacity Broadband in Rural Libraries (Web log comment). *District Dispatch.* Retrieved from http://www.districtdispatch.org/2014/03/fcc-workshop-highlights-need-higher-capacity-broadband-rural-libraries/

Williamson, K., Bannister, M., & Sullivan, J. (2010). The Crossover Generation: Baby Boomers and the Role of the Public Library. *Journal of Librarianship and Information Science,* 42(3), 179–190.

Wisconsin Department of Public Instruction. (2017). Wisconsin Talking Book and Braille Library (WTBBL). Retrieved from https://dpi.wi.gov/talkingbooks

Wolfram, D., & Zhang, J. (2001). The Impact of Term-Indexing Characteristics on a Document Space. *Canadian Journal of Information & Library Sciences,* 26(4), 21.

Wright, J. (2014). Two Billion for E-rate Provides "2-for-1" Benefits." *District Dispatch.* Retrieved from http://www.districtdispatch.org/2014/04/two-billion-e-rate-provides-2-1-benefits/

Xie, I. (2012). Information Searching and Search Models. In M. Bates (Ed.), *Understanding Information Retrieval Systems: Management, Types, and Standards* (pp. 31–46). Boca Raton, FL: CRC Press.

Zheng, R. (2013). Effective Online Learning for Older People: A Heuristic Design Approach. In R. Zhang, R. Hill, & M. Gardner (Eds.), *Engaging Older Adults with Modern Technology: Internet Use and Information Access Needs* (pp. 142–159). Hershey, PA: IGI Global.

Zickuhr, K. (2010). Generations: Online Activities. *Pew Research and Internet Project.* Retrieved from http://www.pewinternet.org/2010/12/16/generations-2010/

Zickuhr, K., & Madden, M. (2012). Older Adults and Internet Use. *Pew Research Center: Internet & Technology.* Retrieved from http://www.sainetz.at/dokumente/Older_adults_and_internet_use_2012.pdf

Zickuhr, K., Rainie, L., & Purcell, K. (2013). Library Services in the Digital Age. *Pew Internet & American Life Project.* Retrieved from http://libraries.pewinternet.org/2013/01/22/library-services/

Zickuhr, K., Rainie, L., Purcell, K., & Duggan, M. (2013). How Americans Value Public Libraries in Their Communities. *Pew Internet & American Life Project.* Retrieved from http://libraries.pewinternet.org/2013/12/11/libraries-in-communities/

Index

About the Author

RENEÉ K. BENNETT-KAPUSNIAK, PhD, is currently a librarian at the Saratoga Springs Public Library in Saratoga Springs, New York. She earned her doctoral degree in information studies with an emphasis on 50+ adults' access and retrieval of information from the University of Wisconsin Milwaukee. She is the author of multiple publications in peer-reviewed journals, including the *Journal of the Association for Information Science and Technology* and *Public Library Quarterly*. She has been a recipient of several grants, including a fellowship sponsored by the Institute of Museum and Library Services Laura Bush 21st Century Library Program. She is a member of the American Library Association Library Service to the Aging Population Committee and assisted with the development of the new ALA guidelines for the 50+ population.